Mike Venturin

SHOOTING IRON

Thumb Bustin' Musings From The Duke

A complete collection of Mike "Duke" Venturino's Shooting Iron column
originally published in *American Handgunner* Magazine
from 2005 through 2024.

Published By
FMG Publications
A Division Of
Publishers' Development Corporation
© All Rights 2024

ISBN: 979-8-9873814-5-8

INTRODUCTION

By Roy Huntington, FMG Publications

If I told you Mike Venturino wanted to be a "gun'riter" as he called it, since his college days, would you believe that? Not just any gun writer, but a full-time writer – something that didn't exist then. Most had primary jobs or retirements or just dabbled in it. But Mike set his course. Along the way, he was a High School history teacher for a bit, drove a dump truck in Yellowstone Park (and wrangled some horses too), even owning his own movie theatre for six years. But when he was 23, about 1973 or so, he sold his first real "gun" article.

By the time he was 32 he was a full-time "gun'riter" working for name brand gun magazines. He even wrote an article for Guns Magazine back in those days! As he told me, "Who'd a thought? And my parents wanted me to be a lawyer. I fooled them, didn't I?"

I got to know Mike, or "Duke" as he was fondly called by most, in the late 1990s when we attended a class teaching how to "fight" with old school cowboy guns. Duke already knew his way around Colt Single Actions, Sharps rifles and all the rest (and later wrote books on all of them), but a week there showed us all another side to those marvelous guns. Duke and I became fast friends from then on, and being a part-time "gun'riter" myself during my police career, we got along splendidly. Duke mentored me, encouraged me and taught me all about those great old West guns.

By a supreme quirk of fate, I ended up as editor of *American Handgunner* Magazine in 2001. One of the first things I did was pick up the phone and try to get Duke to jump ship and come over to us, but he said he was doing okay for the time. Around 2004, Duke finally gave in, I think do to my incessant pleadings, and came over to ride for our brand.

Duke brought legions of loyal followers with him and was one of the strong backbones of our family of writers. His home-town, friendly style won the hearts of tens of thousands, and he always had a kind word or short note for everyone who reached out to him. In life, Duke was the same as he was in print — honest, capable, a friend to all, decent, quick to shake a hand — and even faster to grin at you. You always felt better after being with Mike.

And let's clear up one thing here. While Mike was wrangling those horses, his favorite horse was named Duke. He was Mike's constant companion and after a while, Mike started to be called "Little Duke" after Big Duke. After leaving Yellowstone, the name stuck and he was always just Duke to most of us.

Duke told me, just before he passed, "Roy, the smartest thing I ever did, next to marrying Yvonne, that is, was coming to work for you guys. You always treated me fairly, encouraged me to write about what I wanted to, and never, not even once, did I have to write an article about something I wasn't interested in. I can't thank you enough for that."

And Duke, we can't thank you enough for the friendship, knowledge, passion and honesty you brought to us all. We miss you a great deal.

Please, enjoy this book and think about the kind man who wrote it all.

Mike "Duke" Venturino and Roy Huntington

SHOOTING IRON
Table Of Contents

SHOOTING IRON
Table Of Contents (cont.)

Who Needs An Auto, Anyway?

I can already hear some readers saying, "Roy, did you bring this yokel aboard so he can feed us that same old revolver versus autoloader crap?" Well — yes and no.

I'm not here to repeat the same old arguments, but since I've attended classes at Thunder Ranch dedicated to all three types of handguns, I'd like to share a bit of insight I gained from the experiences.

My opinion is this: A single action revolver gives up exactly *nothing* to an autoloading pistol for the first *five* rounds. And that's both when the sights are used, or the thing is just stuck out in front of you and the trigger pulled. Are you thinking "rubbish" — or some less printable word?

Let me tell you this. At one class Clint asked me to use a Colt SAA .45 for a while so the rest of the group would be exposed to something different. A little into the course he asked me, and a class member using a 1911, to step forward. With the targets only feet away and with our handguns pointed out in front in both hands, he asked us to fire two shots as fast as possible on his command. He also told the rest of the class to judge who fired fastest.

Top, those are .45 Colt bullets. Who needs more?

Left, Thad Rybka, Bill Black and Ray Coffman might argue with you about the need for an auto.

Deadly Duke

I thought, "Great, Clint put me on the hot seat!" I'd never done such a thing before and had no idea how it would go. To the surprise of the entire class — including me — they couldn't tell which of us fired fastest. Clint had us do it again, and with the same results.

Last summer two young Marine friends just back from combat in Iraq stopped to visit me after seeing the movie *Open Range*. Inspired, they asked to shoot some SA revolvers and lever action rifles. We did the "Clint Drill" several times, and those young fellows were just as surprised that "old cowboy guns" could be fired as fast as "modern" combat handguns.

What about double action revolvers? In the spring of 2004 I attended a Thunder Ranch class dedicated to them. (Incidentally it was the one where the new Smith & Wesson Model 21-4 was unveiled.) And here's what I think. The double action revolver, when fired only DA, is the hardest of all handguns to shoot well. I could never keep the bullet holes on the targets as close with the guns I brought (N-frame S&W .38s and .44s) as I can do with either single actions or 1911s. In fact, my target often looked like someone had hit it with OO buck from a ways back.

Here's one important proviso. The autoloader and the DA revolver can easily be fired one-handed, as when the other hand is occupied — say in holding up your pants or some equally important task. To equal their speed of shooting, the single action must be manipulated with two hands. One to hold the revolver, aim it and press the trigger, and the other to cock the hammer. Be sure, I'm not talking about movie high jinks like fanning, but about aimed fire.

Shootin' Yer Foot Off

In the beginning, the phrase "first five rounds" was used. Aren't we talking about "sixguns" here? Absolutely, but if I thought that extra round was needed it most certainly would be in there. But for packing a traditionally styled single action about the only safe way is with the hammer down on the empty sixth chamber. Don't doubt it. I personally have known two people who died because they doubted it.

The kicker is the reload. Autoloaders are a breeze, as long as the spare magazines are there. So are DA revolvers, as long as the speed loaders are there. Single action revolvers require numerous small movements to bring them back up to speed. Here in Montana, I have a CCW and when exercising my right to carry usually have either a Les Baer Thunder Ranch Special or a Kimber Pro Carry .40 S&W.

However, when going about my everyday life, I almost always have a single action revolver within reach. If accosted would I run off screaming into the night because that's all the gun I possessed? I certainly hope not. Autoloaders are easy. Single actions are almost as easy for the first five shots. Double action revolvers? Now, that's a handgun for the experts. And that's my opinion on the matter.

SHOOTINGIRON™

Mike "Duke" Venturino

Tough ...

Not so tough.

Wonderful Contraptions

I don't have much use for adjustable sights on a handgun. Now that's not the same as saying adjustable handgun sights don't have much use. They do. Adjustable handgun sights are wonderful little contraptions that add much to precision shooting. They are especially useful on things like target pistols, and big game hunting revolvers.

For handguns that live in the world of hard knocks, they're considerably less wonderful. That said, let's make sure I'm clear about one thing. I'm not talking about law enforcement work. I know absolutely nothing about such things, as I've never been one. But, back in my younger days I traveled the mountains and backcountry of Montana and Wyoming many hundreds, perhaps even thousands of miles on horseback. Much of that time I wore one or another type of revolver, because my haunts contained most of the lower 48's grizzly population.

Short of sustained combat use, I doubt if there's anything that will beat up a handgun more than that. Weather is the most passive factor. Then there are things like branches snagging the sights, or being dumped by a horse and landing on it, or even the horse falling and rolling over you and the gun. I've had all that happen. Got the arthritis to prove it.

Before going on, though, let's draw a line. Target sights are almost always referred to as adjustable sights, but there is a difference. In my opinion all handgun sights are adjustable. I've never met a set I couldn't adjust, albeit at times some effort is required. Target sights are meant to be screwdriver-adjustable, and almost always for both windage and elevation. And they also usually set up high and prominent. That's how they should be for they are intended for precision shooting.

Un-Sighted-In

I strive to have my "using" handguns well sighted in, and did so back in my younger days too. Often on checking them after returning from a trip — they weren't. Sometimes, I had to remove debris from the sight blade just to shoot, but admittedly that's more a problem with holster design than the sights. Still, all those sharp edges collected crud. Sometimes I would throw a stirrup over a saddle to tighten the cinch and it would flop back and whack my handgun — right on the rear sight.

By the late 1970s I began to smarten-up and carry fixed-sight handguns. And, I never did have one come "un-sighted-in" on me. Since these were Colt SAAs they usually didn't start that way. I read in an old magazine article by Charles Askins, he used to sight in Border Patrol issue revolvers by bending the front sight, so I started to do the same to my Colt's. If you don't believe me just ask Clint Smith. He has a Colt .45 with pliers' tracks on the front sight. I gave it to him as a present on our mutual birthday a few years back. And I'll bet he'll tell you it still hits right to point of aim too.

Speaking of Clint, in a year's time he sees more handguns fired there at the school than anyone I know. Here's what he says about the matter, "True adjustable sights, like older Bomars and S&W revolver sights are somewhat fragile and often a 'box of razor blades' to handle. Hard, drift-able sights are best and it's a simple equation — the more parts on the gun the more stuff falls off while being worked hard in training or fighting. Adjustable cranks on them and moveable sights are for people who shoot different loads or tinker with ammo. Fixed-sights are truly best on fighting handguns and the more they are fixed, the better they are."

Duke likes to collect twigs in the field.

LOAD TINKERERS

Here's the main difference. If you're a reloader, then adjustable is right for you. If you are a dedicated fixed-sight shooter, then you'll have settled on a darn good load before ever worrying about the sights. Then you'll sight that gun in and never change the load. Perhaps our High Editorship Himself will allow me a future column on sighting-in techniques for fixed-sight handguns. Heaven knows I've got enough of them around here.

SHOOTINGIRON™

Mike "Duke" Venturino

THE DUKE

Now this is a dangerous man!

THE DANIEL BOONE & DANGEROUS MAN SYNDROMES

My first experience with the Daniel Boone syndrome came via my own grandfather. He was an eastern Kentucky coal miner, and in fact lived in the same coal camp that Loretta Lynn grew up in. He always kept handguns, mostly S&W .32s, .38s and .44s. As a young boy, when we visited from West Virginia one of my favorite things was for him to bring them out and let me look them over. Then he would regale me with stories of his marksmanship. His favorite was how he could sit on the back porch and shoot clothes pins off his wife's clothes line.

It wasn't until I was a bit older that realization dawned on me that never in my young life had I ever seen him fire a gun of any sort. No one else in the family had either. He was a prime example of what I've come to call the *Daniel Boone Syndrome*.

The DBS often afflicts American males, and the symptoms consist of them thinking of themselves as gifted marksman. Never mind they don't shoot often, may not at all, or may not have shot *ever*. The fact remains many American males consider themselves good shots.

And, not surprisingly, the DBS is not limited to specific regions either. It's just as alive in places like Montana or Wyoming. After moving to Montana, I expected to live in an area of fine marksmen. After all wasn't this where Elmer Keith grew up? Sadly, I often heard the following remark, usually from someone sitting on a bar stool. "Why, I can't hit paper, but you put hair on the target and I can hit it every time." As I witnessed, sometimes that was true, but unfortunately the hit was often in the animal's butt or foot or jaw. The DBS was alive and prospering.

DANGEROUS IS AS DANGEROUS DOES

Then there's the *Dangerous Man Syndrome*. That's when someone thinks just because they have a CCW, it makes them a man not to be trifled with. Here's a for-instance. A fellow showed up at my place one day while I was practicing with a 1911 at torso targets from about 15 feet. He snickered and said, "That's a bit close isn't it?" Yes it was, but I'm not likely to get mugged by someone 25 yards away.

He showed me his concealed S&W Chief's Special .38, so I suggested he have a go at the target. He whipped it out with blinding speed and let fly all five rounds. Lead never touched paper. I suggested he slow down and try again, but he didn't have any more .38s on him. So I went in the house and got a handful of factory rounds. What happened next was interesting. His Chief's Special would only fire once in a while. He admitted he'd had a pistolsmith "lighten it up" but hadn't bothered to shoot it afterwards.

My advice was that perhaps he should

consider a self defense training class. Haughtily he replied, "I don't need that. I can take care of myself!" Let's see; couldn't hit paper, didn't have a reload on him, and his gun wouldn't shoot. Now that's a dangerous man.

No one is a born marksman, although some are born with a special spark. I've seen some of the best competition and exhibition marksman of today in action. Such would be Rob Leatham, Bob Munden and Bill Oglesby. But no great marksman, or even a basically proficient one, just *happens*. The people mentioned all put many, many thousands of rounds downrange in developing their abilities. By the same token I've put an astounding number of rounds downrange to become merely an adequate shot with a handgun, and a little better with a rifle. No matter how many guns you own or how much firearms enthusiasm is in your soul, you can't achieve Daniel Boone status without shooting — a lot. Even then, you may never be better than medicore. But I'll bet you'll have fun!

Lovers Not Fighters

What about becoming a Dangerous Man? That requires training, mind set and real-world experience. Personally, I'll settle for just never being considered dangerous to those around me when I'm handling guns. Besides, if I had my druthers, I'd rather be remembered as a lover. And if I can't be a stunning marksman, then I'll have to settle for just knowing a lot about guns. And even that remains to be seen!

SHOOTINGIRON™

Mike "Duke" Venturino

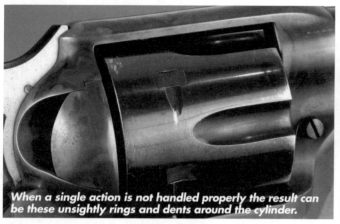

When a single action is not handled properly the result can be these unsightly rings and dents around the cylinder.

Checking to see if it's loaded? Don't spin the cylinder with the palm of the hand as they do in movies.

SINGLE ACTION-Action

At SHOT Show 2005 while at the United States Firearms Company's booth looking over their exquisite single action revolvers, I happened to notice none had their locking bolts installed. SHOT Show rules prohibit manufacturers from having firing pins in any guns on display, but otherwise guns there usually function normally. Curious, I asked USFA's President Doug Donnelly about this, and his answer satisfied me that he is a true single action guy.

He said, "If we don't take the locking bolts out then these guns will be virtually ruined by show's end. People who know nothing about how to handle single actions properly will see to it."

Hallelujah brothers! Nothing pains me more than watching well intentioned but unknowing people pick up a fine single action revolver to check it. Usually they go one of two routes. They will either hold the hammer back with a thumb and turn the cylinder slowly, or they hold the hammer back with a thumb and spin that

cylinder with the palm of their hand so fast it sounds like a windmill during a typhoon. If someone hasn't stopped them by this time, they will next lower the hammer back to its resting position.

At this point the cylinder will likely have a deep ring around it, and the lockwork will be well on its way to being un-timed. There's a proper way to handle a single action revolver with traditional lockwork. If the hammer is pulled back to its half-cock notch, the locking bolt will be lowered completely in its slot, and it won't leave any sort of ring around the cylinder. If someone pulls the hammer back part way *without* letting it come to rest in its half-cock notch, the result is far different. Then the locking bolt will disengage from its locking notch so the cylinder can turn freely, but not be lowered completely into its slot. When the cylinder is turned, the bolt rubs against it. If the cylinder is given a healthy spin like in the movies, then the locking bolt can actually rub a groove around it. That's an ugly thing to do to a fine revolver.

MORE SECRETS

Also it's evidently a little known fact with a traditionally-styled single action, that once the hammer starts back from its fully down position, it should go all the way back before starting down again. Let's assume someone is loading the revolver properly with the hammer at its half-cock position. The hammer should then be brought back to full cock and lowered all the way. If it's lowered directly from half-cock, the bolt begins to rise and is forced by spring pressure against the cylinder. Not only does that make a mark on the cylinder, but stress is put on the fragile bolt because it's now in a bind. Much of this and the timing will get out of whack or the bolt will break.

Also there is a specific way to get those five cartridges into a traditional single. Carrying a traditional single action revolver with six rounds loaded and the hammer resting on a primer is a fool's errand. The slightest blow on the hammer can fire that round. I've personally known several people who have shot themselves that way — sometimes with fatal results.

THE RIGHT WAY

Bring the hammer back to half cock so the cylinder rotates freely, and open the loading gate. Put one cartridge into a chamber and skip one chamber. Next load four cartridges. Close the loading gate and full cock the hammer. Now lower the hammer all the way, and if the revolver's lockwork hasn't been messed up by some nitwit's mishandling, it will be resting on the empty chamber. **Don't turn the revolver toward yourself and look in the front of the cylinder to see if all is well. If it isn't, you may find out in a disagreeable manner!** To see if things are as they should be, just look at the cartridge case rims at the rear of the cylinder. There shouldn't be one visible directly under the hammer. It's all pretty simple.

This is the way to keep the unknowing from ruining your single actions. Don't let people you don't know handle them! Being naturally a rather inoffensive creature myself, in the past I've had damage done to my single actions when I just handed them off to strangers to examine. Nowadays I don't do that. Unless the person is someone I know well, I'm the one who half-cocks the

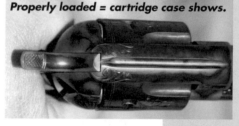

Properly loaded = cartridge case shows.

revolver and checks the cylinder for loads. Then I hand it to someone to admire with the admonishment; **"Don't function the action — please."** This way the revolvers stay in good condition and I don't get cranky.

SHOOTINGIRON™

Mike "Duke" Venturino

Photos: Yvonne Venturino

GUN'RITER 101

You'd be amazed at how many times I've been asked: "What's it take to be a gunwriter?" Many magazine readers think it must be the most wonderful life imaginable — getting up every morning with the only problem to consider being what gun you would like to shoot that day.

Brothers and sisters, it ain't the way it is. In many respects it's a job much like any other job. There are deadlines and responsibilities and never doubt it can get boring. Shooting is fun, but shooting some gun you don't care about, wouldn't own if someone gave it to you and wrapping up the shooting, writing and photography by someone else's deadline is a different matter.

But, you say, "Your byline is on newsstands nationwide so you become famous. You get paid big bucks, and you travel all over the world on free hunts, and what about all the free guns and ammo you get."

Famous? Sure I've been recognized in airports, restaurants, rest stops and even at gas stations. It's nice, and I always try to take a moment to visit and let them know I appreciate their kind comments. Yet, never once has the person recognizing and complimenting me been a beautiful young woman. There are no groupies in the true sense of the word in this business.

BIG BUCKS?

And I don't mean deer. The way to make a million dollars in this business is to start with two million. Gunwriting doesn't pay big bucks. It doesn't even pay middle-sized bucks. Many of the fellows doing it full-time have side incomes such as military or law enforcement retirements. One writer, now retired, told me it definitely helps to have a rich wife.

Travel all over the world? There's some truth to that. I've been fortunate in the 25 years I've been doing it full time to have been invited on trips to Europe. I did get to go to Canada once for whitetail deer. But to go on some of the exotic trips to the three "A's" — Africa, Aus-

tralia or Alaska — you have to be really good at schmoozing the big company's public relations people. I never was. Most of them have never heard of me.

As for other travel, consider this: How many ammunition and gunmaking factories can you tour before they all look alike? Here's what I think of travel. My agreement with my esteemed boss Mr. Huntington included the proviso I'm not asked to travel, except to the SHOT Show. I have what I consider the perfect home here in Montana and I don't like leaving it. (*Okay Duke, I won't ask you to go on that all-expense paid hunt to Africa next year since you don't like to travel! Editor.*)

Free Guns?

Yeah, right. I'll admit there've been a few free ones in the past 25 years. Very few. More often you get nagging letters and phone calls from the gun companies because you are overdue on the 90- or 120-day consignment period. Once, someone called and asked for a gun back before it had even arrived. Always nicely, but they do ask you to pay up or send back a loaner gun. I always have. By the way, that return shipping is almost always at your own expense.

Free ammo? Yes, and I've always tried to not overdo my requests — usually they are only for two boxes of any type at one time. But, get this, a couple of years ago, after 25 years of dealing with Remington, they turned me down. Some young MBA-type there told me if I wanted to do articles on the cartridges THEY wanted publicized, like their Ultra-Mags, they would send something, but otherwise take a hike. I don't shoot much Remington ammo anymore since I don't shoot those fancy magnums.

Back to the real question: What does it take to be a gunwriter? It helps to know guns. I mean really KNOW them, which means a lifetime of studying them in detail. A fantastic memory is a great boon. Through high school and college I studied guns, not exactly what those palaces of learning thought I should study. Perhaps that's the reason I've had some success at writing but graduated from college with a 2.11 grade point average.

However, really KNOWING guns isn't always the requirement it should be. So many of today's writers have proven what you really need to know is only a little more than the editor you're writing for. (Luckily at these digs the editors DO know guns and it keeps me hopping!) It also helps to own a great big cowboy hat, regardless of what part of the country you live in. (*Duke doesn't wear a cowboy hat 'cause he can't find one to fit that inflated head he has! John Taffin.*)

Being able to write is a benefit, but it isn't absolutely necessary. Few people know less about punctuation and grammar than Clint Smith does, yet I consider him the best natural writer I've ever read. I majored in journalism in college so editors don't have to work too hard on my material. I think that's why it started to get accepted in the first place — lazy editors.

Good Shot?

Some would say being able to shoot well would be a great benefit. A few friends have chided me saying, "If you could shoot those teeny-tiny groups some other gunwriters always do, you would go farther in your career." Maybe they're right. I've been sent the exact same handguns as many other writers and yet they wouldn't shoot as good for me even when mounted in my machine rest. I guess its one of my failings.

Having a desire to shoot does seem to help, even if you're not real good at it. I've been to "gunwriter get-togethers" at seminars and such, and its amazing how many of them will pass up all that free ammo. You would almost think they don't like to shoot in front of one another. I'm not so inhibited. At one seminar an ammo company put some H&K MP-5 sub-guns out with cases of 9mm shells. I stepped forward and said to one of our hosts, "Show me how to run one of these things." And brother did I have a ball then! But, all by myself.

Thickish Skin

Being a gunwriter takes patience and sometimes a thick skin. I've written over 1,200 articles concerning almost every type of firearm, from .17 HMRs to .58 caliber Civil War rifle-muskets in long guns, and .22 rimfires to .454 Casulls in handguns, yet I've had editors tell me I must be more versatile so their advertisers will like me better. Funny how those same editors never worried much about what the readers liked. Luckily our editors here realize no one ever bought a gun magazine to see what Mike Venturino had to say about some sort of Super Short Magnum, or the .500 S&W for that matter.

Thick skin? You bet. Occasionally readers will write telling you how stupid you are because their favorite load will shoot better than what you listed. Once in a great while there will be death threats because you said something derogatory about someone's favorite gun or cartridge. No one's made good on that yet.

So why do I do it? When in New Zealand a few years back I was asked that by one of their Ministers of Parliament. I told him it was because I was too lazy to work, and too dumb to steal. After he laughed politely, I told him the real reason — I failed as a bikini designer, although I do claim credit for inventing those thong types. But nobody knows that and I swear I don't get the credit I deserve for it either.

In grade school my goal was to become a Mexican bandit, but my West Virginia accent didn't fit there. In junior high I wanted to be a P-51 Mustang fighter pilot but literally grew too big to fit in their cockpits, and learned they weren't in use anymore anyway. In high school I decided to be a cowboy and later actually went west and tried that for a bit. It's really HARD work and dangerous too.

In college I finally decided to become a gunwriter. My parents thought that was absolutely ridiculous because they knew I was obviously lawyer material. There's no telling what Yvonne's parents thought when we began making marriage plans and she told them my dream was to become a "gunwriter."

And that's what I've been most of my adult like. My first article was printed when I was 23, and by age 32 I was doing it full time. Along the way I also briefly taught history in high school, drove a dump truck on a Park Service road maintenance crew in Yellowstone National Park and even owned my own movie theatre for six years.

Sage Advice

Would I advise anyone else to become a gunwriter? In this day and age, I'd say no. Besides I don't need the competition. Do I wish I'd gone down some other road? At times this road has been a hard one with many bumps, but it seems to have been the right one for me. And let's just say, I've met some "colorful" characters along the way.

My Favorite Handgun

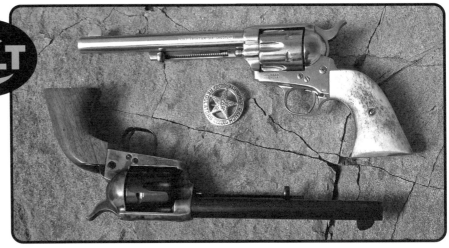

Okay, that's enough! First our esteemed editor asked John Taffin to detail his favorite handgun, and then it was Dave Anderson's turn. Now I want my 15 minutes of fame!

Picking my favorite handgun out of the many I have in the vault isn't the same as saying it's what I would choose if limited to one. Picking my favorite means settling on the one I take out when shooting just for myself for fun. And that's easy, because I like it so much I bought another just like it.

It might surprise you to know even though I consider myself a "hard-core" shooter, my favorite handgun is a commemorative. Yep, it's the 1873-1973 Peacemaker Centennial Commemorative; specifically the nickel-plated version in .44 WCF (.44-40). Why shoot a commemorative? It is the nearest thing I've ever found to a genuine 1870s Colt Frontier Six Shooter, yet is made of modern steels and uses closely-matching barrel/cylinder specs.

Interestingly, the Centennials didn't come out in 1973. Colt finally got them on dealer's shelves in 1975. And, there were two versions. One was finished in blue with color case hardened frame and hammer. It was in .45 Colt with 7½" barrel, and was a perfect rendition of the Colt SAA as bought by the U.S. Government for cavalry service starting in 1873.

The other half of the Centennials were those .44-40s I'm so fond of. Likewise they had 7½" barrels, the so-called blackpowder frame with its base pin securing screw angling in from the front and bullseye ejector rod button. The markings were even perfect for a 1870s vintage Colt, with three line patent dates on the frame and a tiny ".44CF" stamp on the left side of the trigger guard. The best marking, however, is the COLT FRONTIER SIX SHOOTER logo in a panel on the barrel's left side.

The sights are also the very fine types consisting of a groove down the frame's topstrap and a very thin blade front. When I say thin — it's sharp enough to cut you. Most shooters don't like those tiny sights because they indeed are hard to see. I had a special set of shooting glasses made to correct my tired, old eyes so I do like them.

PARTICULARS

The .44-40 version came with two different heights of front sight. The lower ones cause point of impact to be considerably above point of aim. The higher ones hit right to point of aim at about 25 yards. I discovered this when a friend brought his 1873-1973 Frontier Six Shooter over for some friendly competition. His gun's front sight was lower so it shot much higher. Subsequent examination of other Centennials confirmed it.

The best part is the .44-40s have .427" barrels and .428" chamber mouths. Consequently they're capable of tiny groups when fed good ammunition. Five shot groups of 1½" at 25 yards are common. They're just plain darn good shooting handguns.

What I didn't like were the grips. Colt put the hard rubber types on them and they were too thick for my hand. A friend made a set of custom grips for me cut from the thigh bones of bison bulls, which appear as elegant as ivory but much tougher. (My grip maker friend is now retired so I won't give his name or he'd hunt me down.) They made my favorite sixgun just about perfect.

A PERFECT PAIR

In fact, the Centennial was so perfect I searched out another, making sure it had the high front sight, and then had it fitted with bison bone grips too. So now I have a brace of favorites, and wear them for cowboy competition in a pair of matched holsters from Wolf Ear's Equipment *(702 S. Pine, Laramie, WY 32070)*. In cowboy matches I like to shoot blackpowder loads for the boom and smoke and true to their frontier heritage, these Centennials will function all day without binding up.

For my own fun, I use 6.8 grains of Hodgdon's HP38 (But am working with the new IMR Trail Boss powder, which may be the perfect propellant for black powder-type pistol cartridges) with just about any .428", 200-grain bullet I can find. Thousands of rounds have now been fired through each of them and the only problem has been a broken trigger/bolt spring on one. Colt produced only 2,002 each of the .45 and .44 Peacemaker Centennials. I've got the two, so there's another 2,000 out there floating around for you guys!

SHOOTINGIRON™

Mike "Duke" Venturino   Photos: Yvonne Venturino

THUMB BUSTIN'
MUSINGS FROM
THE DUKE

THE U.S. CAVALRY'S OTHER HANDGUNS

My feature for this issue is on the Colt SAA revolver as used by the U.S. Cavalry and my life-long search for the same. However, that model only served officially between 1873 and 1892, which begs the question of what other handguns served American horse soldiers before and after those years?

Mostly they were made by Colt and mostly revolvers. Although during the Civil War the federal government armed their horse soldiers with just about any revolver that could be purchased in quantity its "standard issue" was Colt's Model 1860 Army. That was a cap and ball revolver of .44 caliber, and it was on active duty until a metallic cartridge-firing revolver was adopted circa 1870.

That first U.S. revolver taking fixed ammunition happened to be S&W's Model No. 3, chambered for the cartridge eventually named .44 American. Its tenure was short, as was the Colt Richard's conversion in .44 Colt caliber, the adoption of which shortly followed the S&W. Actually the government only bought 1,000 of the Smith & Wessons and 1,200 of the Colts during that time.

1911 Horse Soldiers

In 1909 the army decided to return to a .45 caliber revolver, knowing full well it was a stopgap measure because they already were set on soon adopting an autoloader. The Model 1909 was simply the Colt New Service revolver chambered for .45 Colt again. However, to make sure extraction was positive the government-loaded .45s had a wider rim by about .025" than civilian issue .45 Colts.

When the U.S. Cavalry adopted the Colt Model 1911 they had the sidearm that stayed with them until horses were retired from active duty during World War II. That's probably a fact somewhat hard for most Model 1911 lovers to accept — it was actually designed with horse soldiers in mind.

Here's something interesting. Except for the .38 Colt, all of the U.S. Cavalry's handgun cartridges were similar in power. Mostly they fired 225-to 250-grain bullets at 725 to 750 fps. There's a fable the big .45 Colt used a 250-grain bullet over 40 grains of black powder for 900 fps. Not in government service, it didn't. Loads for the U.S. Army contained only 30 grains of powder with those 250-grain bullets, and would have been lucky to hit 750 fps.

A box of Model 1909 military .45 Colt loads I own says velocity with 250-grain bullets was 725 fps with a plus/minus factor of 25 fps. Nominal ballistics for the .45 ACP called for a 230-grain bullet at 830 fps, but the military surplus ammo I've personally fired chronographed more in the 750 to 770 fps range. So there you go.

Tough Moros

It's a little known fact the U.S. Cavalry also toyed with a single shot, cartridge-firing handgun in the early 1870s. This was the .50 caliber Remington Model 1871 using their rolling block form of action. It seems extremely odd the army issued such a handgun when revolvers had been common for decades, but then again governments have been known to do stranger things.

The Colt SAA was adopted in 1873, but S&W didn't give up easily. They were actually able to get a remodeled No. 3 adopted as "substitute standard" by the army in the mid-1870s. In fact their shorter .45 caliber cartridge was adopted as standard issue for both Colt and S&W revolvers as early as August 1874. Since an army officer named Schofield had redesigned this S&W Model No. 3, that informal moniker has stuck. By 1880, the army tired of having two types of sixgun in service and sold the S&Ws as surplus. The S&W "Schofield" had a 7"-barrel and walnut grips.

For a dozen years the Colt SAA reigned supreme, but in 1892 the army adopted its first standard-issue DA with swing out cylinder. The Colt DA .38 in its basic form with 6"-barrel and walnut grips was standard issue for nearly as long as the big Colt .45. Its puny .38 Colt cartridge used a 150-grain bullet moving at barely 750 fps, and this revolver was official issue during the Spanish-American War and the Philippine Insurrection. As such, it no doubt saw more action than the famous Colt SAA .45 did during the Indian Wars.

After all it was the .38 Colt DA, which spawned all the stories of U.S. troopers being killed after emptying their revolvers into attacking Moro warriors during the Philippine Insurrection. That led the U.S. military into going back to a large bore handgun; at least until the mid-1980s.

Remington's big single shot.

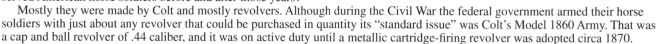

12

SHOOTINGIRON™

Mike "Duke" Venturino

Photos: Yvonne Venturino

**THUMB BUSTIN'
MUSINGS FROM
THE DUKE**

Accuracy Opinions

Photos: Yvonne Venturino

Sometimes I have to wonder about the people we get letters from. Recently one came to me critical because the handgun groups I had published with an article had been fired at the extreme distance of 25 yards. The writer said that since defensive handguns were seldom used at ranges past 10 yards it made no sense to test-fire them at such long range.

Am I missing something here? If a handgun delivers fine accuracy at 25 yards, won't it print even smaller groups at 10 yards, or seven yards, or whatever? Is a handgun going to spray bullets all over the place at 10 yards, but then be extremely accurate at 25 yards? Should I have a bulldozer come in and wipe away my 25-yard backstop and build a new one at 10 yards? Actually, that's not a bad idea since walking out to change targets at only 10 yards would be more convenient and faster too.

And oh, those poor ignorant U.S. Army Ordnance Board officers who tested the Colt SAA in 1873 before it was adopted for government service. Why they fired the test guns at 50 yards and sometimes even at 100 yards! What foolishness.

Sandbag Silliness

And then there was the fellow who complained because I often test handguns mounted in a Ransom Pistol Machine Rest. He said no one carries a machine rest around in their hip pocket so what did testing them in one prove? Duh? It proves how closely a given handgun will cluster bullets of a specific load to one another.

Conversely what does it prove when a human being fires a handgun over sandbags? It proves how well that individual can line up the sights and press the trigger. If groups are very tight then it has been proven the gun is accurate and the shooter can actually shoot well. If the groups are large what's been proven? Is the gun inaccurate or is the shooter mashing the trigger? Or both? If you're reading about it in a magazine and the author's groups are always phenomenally small then you probably have a good idea already what's going on.

The purpose of testing in a machine rest is to remove — or at least minimize — the human factor, so something might be learned about a handgun's inherent accuracy or the quality of the ammunition it's being fed. Here's my take on the matter. I can sit down at a bench rest and fire a few groups from a sandbag rest with confidence, especially if I wear my special glasses that focus on the handgun sights!

That's a few groups with standard velocity loads such as a .38 Special or .45 ACP. Put a magnum in my hands and you reduce the group count to one or two before I'll be mashing the trigger like an old-time telegraph operator. A machine rest allows the firing of hundreds of rounds in a day without shooter fatigue and eye strain becoming a factor. I love my Ransom Rest.

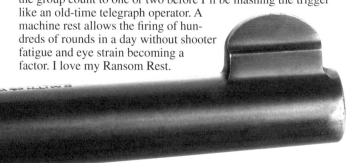

Duke loves his Ransom Rest for accuracy testing with handguns. Note the stately pose.

Get 'Yer Hands On It

Then there was the fellow who took me to task because I said a handgun can't be sighted-in from a machine rest — that it will print to a different point of aim when held in someone's *hands*. He said he had extensive experience with machine rests and you could sight handguns in perfectly with one. Maybe that's true on the planet he came from but not on this one.

When that handgun is bolted into the rest its recoil is dampened. No handgun held that way is going to recoil as it does in your own hands. Take a look at a handgun's sights, especially one with a long barrel chambered for a cartridge with heavy bullets. It will have a tall front sight, and if you look closely you'll see the barrel actually points slightly downward when sights are leveled. Huh?

Yup. Handguns begin to recoil the instant a bullet starts forward so the barrel will *rise* some before it exits. That's why heavier bullets impact higher on-target than lighter ones, with other factors being equal. That's also something the manufacturers take into account when determining how tall a front sight to put on a given model. That's also why when you hook an apparatus like a machine rest to a handgun it shoots to a different point than when held in your hands.

And we haven't even gotten to talking about what is suitable accuracy for a given handgun. We'll do that sometime, I promise.

SHOOTINGIRON™

Mike "Duke" Venturino

I KNOW BETTER

Let's play the, "I know better" game. We're talking about handgun cartridges here, and there are several about which I obviously know better in regards to what they should have been. In fact looking back at them you can't help but think some of the cartridge designers working for the various ammunition companies would have been better suited as government bureaucrats.

Let's start with the .38 Special. There certainly should have been a .38 Special. It just shouldn't have been what it was: a 158-grain .357 bullet fitted in a 1.16" case. What it should have been was precisely what the .41 Long Colt already was. In the black-powder era of the 1870s the .41 Colt started out as a "short" version. It had a .93" case and heel-type, outside-lubed

bullet. Handguns made for it had barrel groove diameters running from about .401" to .408". In the 1890s bullet diameter for .41 Colt was reduced to .386" and it was given a deep hollowbase so it would swell up on firing and grip the rifling of those oversize barrels. Case length was increased to 1.13", and thus was born the .41 Long Colt.

When S&W wanted to develop a .38 Special in the late 1890s, IF I HAD BEEN THERE, I would have designed the K-frame Military & Police revolver to have had a .386" groove diameter barrel, and chambered the cylinder for .41 Long Colt cartridges. It would have really been SPECIAL then and actually a .38 to boot.

L-R: .38 L Colt, .38 S&W Special and a .41 L Colt.

L-R: .45 ACP 230-gr. FMJ, .45 AR 230-gr. Lead, 225-gr. Cast and a 225-gr. WC.

L-R: .44 S&W Russian, .44 S&W Special and a BH 250-gr. .44 Special.

Photos by Yvonne Venturino

StilL DuMb

Smith & Wesson's cartridge designers didn't get any smarter by 1908, when they introduced the .44 Special. Like the .38 Special it used a 1.16" case, but exactly like the .44 Russian it was loaded with a 246-grain roundnose, .429" bullet. Now, the .44 Russian used a case only .97" long, but both Russian and Special .44s fired their bullets at identical velocities. That ended up being a nominal 755 fps by the time the Russian version was discontinued in the 1960s. Why have a short and long .44 with the exact same ballistics?

If they had had the benefit of my brain power in 1908 the new .44 Special would have been precisely what Black Hills Ammunition made it in 2004. That was with a BIG, SQUARE-nosed, 250-grain bullet at about 800+ fps. Certainly the guns would have taken it — the "triple-lock" (Hand Ejector, 1st Model) could take even more, and BIG, SQUARE-nosed bullets were already known. Heck, you could get 800 fps from a .44 Special and 250-grain bullets with BLACK POWDER. I know. I've done it.

The Sad Auto-Rim

Speaking of BIG, SQUARE-nosed bullets, one would have helped the poor .45 Auto-Rim too. Peters Cartridge Company came out with that one around 1921. It was just the .45 ACP case with a rim for revolver use. In the beginning it was loaded with 230-grain FMJ bullets just like its .45 ACP brother. But eventually what became standard was a lead 230-grain RN bullet identical in profile to those FMJ bullets. Then to add insult to injury, they made the .45 Auto-Rim cartridge MILDER than the .45 ACP. Why? The S&W and Colt Model 1917 revolvers it was meant for were perfectly safe with .45 ACP ammunition.

The only reason I can see was to go easy on those soft lead bullets, which were a stupid thing to load in the .45 Auto-Rim anyway. Those

Colt and S&W revolver barrels were cut with shallow rifling better suited to FMJ .45 ACP bullets. Mostly they shot the lead bullet factory loads horribly. The cartridge designers turned what should have been an exemplary .45 caliber revolver cartridge into a "red-headed stepchild."

Then think about the .41 Magnum, which shouldn't have been a magnum anyway. Why — when there was already the .44 Magnum? Why come out with a slightly inferior cartridge to what we already had? Being a "magnum" killed it for police use, which was what it was supposed to be anyway. But consider this: if the .38 Special had actually been the .41 Long Colt, instead of a .357 Magnum there could have been a .41 Magnum in the 1930s, and the whole three magnum thing could have been avoided. Then again, if the .44 Special had been what it should have been the whole idea of a .41 caliber police cartridge would have been moot. Oh, if they had only had me back then! And that's some cartridge history according to Professor Duke.

SHOOTINGIRON™

Mike "Duke" Venturino

Photo: Yvonne Venturino

Brennan and Duke. Brennan's the handsome one on the left.

COMPLACENCY

Are you complacent about your safety? I am. I often go about with my head up in the clouds, assured nothing bad is going to happen to me simply because nothing bad has ever happened to me. It can though, and it almost did, and was almost a disaster for myself, my wife and our assortment of feline and canine companions.

In brief, here's what happened. Recently I was walking the 100 yards or so from the house to our horses' water trough to see if it needed filling. At my side trotted our huge, majestic tri-color collie, Brennan. I was in la-la land, without a care in the world,

thinking how wonderful life was and enjoying the crisp Montana air. When I got to the trough I noticed Brennan was no longer at my side. Looking back I saw him in battle with a large skunk near one of our outbuildings.

Although I live on rural property in Montana where it would be perfectly legal for me to have a gun on my person, I was completely unarmed. Why? Because I was *only* going to the water trough and *nothing* untoward had

ever happened *just* going to the water trough. All I could do was scream at the dog to get back to the house. He obeyed with alacrity, with the skunk snapping at his heels every step of the way. It went right to the porch with him. For a bit I couldn't even get to the dog because the skunk was between us.

RABIES?

A skunk in broad daylight acting aggressive — what does that equal? RABIES! My heart was in my throat as I stood there helpless. Finally, I was able to get to my .222 coyote rifle I kept by the door. It was worthless. The skunk was too close for its 10X scope. I couldn't see it well enough to shoot and could only watch while it made its way back under the outbuilding. A shotgun was what I needed, but the Winchester Model 1897 was locked in the vault. I ran to grab it only to find that *all 12-gauge shells were in another outbuilding*. I know, I know.

While I kept the hole under the shed covered, my wife called animal control, and he arrived in a hurry. To condense two hours into a few words, we had to chain-saw-up part of the shed floor until the animal control guy could get a clear shot at the skunk, making sure not to damage the head. Only then did it turn loose of its horrible effluvia.

Everyone involved: the animal control guy, my wife, a friend who had incidentally dropped by, and myself, were convinced the skunk was rabid. Then to our horror we discovered that Brennan's vaccinations might not have been up to date because we had only adopted him a couple months previously. Nor were several of our other pets' shots. We were complacent.

The Wait

The 27 hours that elapsed between delivery of the skunk's head to the lab, and the report it definitely was not rabid were the worst hours of my life. We were not only facing putting down many of our beloved critters, but Yvonne and I both would have had to take the rabies treatment. Why had the skunk acted that way? Most probably Brennan had met it head-on coming around the outbuilding's corner, and the fight was on immediately. When I called off the dog, the skunk probably thought he was winning and gave chase.

What does all this have to do with *American Handgunner*? Complacency! I have had a CCW permit for 10 years, but haven't carried on my person in eight years. Why? It's uncomfortable, and the only places I go in day-to-day activities are the usual places I've gone to for 20 years. Places just like the water trough. My attitude has been: nothing bad has ever happened, ergo nothing bad will happen today.

What my recent experience taught me is that trouble doesn't wait for you to be prepared. Certainly, when the dog/skunk fight happened I couldn't have shot immediately even if I had had a handgun in my pocket. But I could have nailed it *before* it got under the outbuilding. That's not the point. The sharp end of this is my head was up in the clouds or in another place we won't mention here. Just the same as it is when going to the grocery store, or the ATM machine, or filling up at a convenience store. I've been living my life in condition white. I am complacent.

I had better change or the next curve ball thrown might smack me right in the kisser. It's something to think about.

15

THE QUEST

S&W "Victory Model" Military
& Police .38 S&W (sold to Britain)

Webley Mark
VI .455

Enfield No. 2
Mark I .38.

Remington-
Rand Model
1911A1
.45 ACP

Photos:
Yvonne
Venturino

World War I vintage
S&W Hand Ejector,
2nd Model .455.

A friend once said, "You're the luckiest fellow I know in finding good used handguns. I'd like to follow you around and just get a chance at your leavings." Examples of the guns he was talking about were things like my 1931 vintage S&W Heavy Duty .38-44, or my Enfield No. 2 Mark 1 .38 with RAF markings, or even my really clean Remington Rand Model 1911A1 .45 ACP with original World War II holster and belt.

The key to finding good used guns is "The Quest." You're likely to grow old and gray waiting for good used guns to come to you. You have to quest for them. You have to go where used guns are likely to be, such as in older, hole-in-the-wall type gun stores, or gun shows, or even "for sale" ads in newspapers. In my opinion the Internet's help with "The Quest" could be its only saving grace.

And, you have to talk about "The Quest" to everyone who will listen. Being the strong silent type might help with getting girls, but it won't with "The Quest." If people know that you quest, often they'll help. Unless they quest for the same guns themselves, that is. Personally, I'm not smart enough to quest for many different types of guns at the same time. My quests have to focus for something specific or at least a specific genre of guns.

Here's what I mean. Back when I was 18 years old my quest was for a Colt Single Action Army .45, but in 1968 in the coal fields of southern West Virginia Peacemakers weren't all that common. In fact I had never seen one. Still that was "The Quest" then and being vocal about things I had blathered to all my friends about how I sure would like to own one. That summer of 1968 my job was hustling freight on loading docks. One day a co-worker called me over saying, "Hey Mike, this truck driver here says he owns one of those cowboy guns you're always talking about." Sure enough, he did and within a month I had pestered him so much he sold it to me. That was the first time I experienced the power of "The Quest."

Eyes Of Superman

To truly be good at "The Quest" you have to develop a keen eye for detail. For instance, the day I found the S&W Heavy Duty .38-44, I was scanning the handgun cases at Capitol Sports in Helena, Montana. At that time "The Quest" was for any sort of blued N-frame Smith & Wesson revolver. Therefore my eye was trained to *not* see stainless steel ones or anything sporting rubber grips. That was almost a mistake for initially I passed by a rubber-gripped S&W — until my brain registered it also had the old half-moon shaped front sight. I did a double-take and sure enough someone had fitted modern rubber grips to that 1931-made sixgun. Questing on the Internet did help me land the proper vintage wood grips for that Heavy Duty.

A couple weeks before this writing, the reverse happened. At a little gunstore in Billings, Montana, my eye scanned the front sights of a case full of revolvers without seeing anything of interest. Then my mind registered one of those guns was fitted with old S&W Magna grips with diamond design around the screw escutcheon. It was a S&W Model 1950 Target .44 Special on which someone had fitted a red insert ramp front sight. That's why my eyes missed it at first.

Quest Detestors

Sometimes when you're very lucky the results of "The Quest" can be almost overwhelming. A few years back I went to a tiny Montana gun show questing only for military issue World War II handguns. At the end of the day, I walked out with my gun money wallet considerably lighter but with four new handguns. The earlier mentioned RAF marked Enfield .38 and Remington Rand Model 1911A1 .45 among them. I also earlier said good guns won't come to you but when word is out on "The Quest" that can actually happen. Recently a fellow dropped by the house saying, "Are you still looking for World War II handguns?" And I relieved him of a Nazi marked FN Browning Model 1922 .32 ACP.

Many wives detest "The Quest." They are misguided souls. Mine doesn't; perhaps because she knows that questing for good used handguns is one of the safer endeavors married men can engage in.

Lately I've been having a strange urge to try either a .30 Luger or a Broomhandle Mauser. I think "The Quest" is kicking in again.

SOCK DRAWER GUNS

Pray-tell what on earth are sock drawer guns? They're the handguns I've kept by my side of the bed my entire adult life. Coincidentally by that side of the bed is also where the drawer is in which my socks are kept. So it's handy to slip whatever serves as my current home defense handgun there too. That varies between autoloaders and DA revolvers, but one factor that never varies is that it is a trusted handgun. That means the sock drawer guns get shot more than most of my handguns.

Have I always been so smart? Nope. Over the decades my bedside sock drawer has held many different handguns; but recently a Kimber Model 1911 Pro Compact. 40 S&W has been there. After using it while writing an article a couple of years ago I bought it because it was darn accurate and reliable. At least I thought it was reliable. When putting it in my sock drawer I loaded its magazine with one company's "magic bullet" factory load. Then I had occasion to take it out fun shooting only to discover that particular load wouldn't function worth a hoot in my Kimber.

Photos:
Yvonne
Venturino

Left to right:
S&W Mod. 27
.357 Mag.,
Colt SAA .45,
S&W Mod.
21-4 .44
Special, S&W
Mod. 19 .357
Mag., and
S&W Mod. 10
.38 Special.
Top: Rem-
ington-Rand
Mod.1911A1
.45 ACP.

Empty Chambers!?!

And speaking of loaded magazines, the only death threat I've ever had was long ago in my unmarried years. The phone rang in the middle of the night and when I picked it up some yahoo was screaming how he was coming after me with a 12 gauge. I finally figured out he was upset about what turned out to be a mutual girlfriend. Finally I got a word in and asked where he was. His answer was "Weatherford, Texas." Since I was in Montana at the time I said, "Go to hell! You can't get here tonight." And then went back to bed. But I did pause to check my S&W Model 39. Its magazine was loaded but sure enough the chamber was empty. That's my only hang-up with autoloaders. Like many people I don't hesitate to keep one with full a magazine but sometimes balk about keeping the chamber loaded. On the other hand I don't give a thought to having a double action revolver fully stoked up.

Once when I referred to my home defense guns as sock drawer guns another fellow said, "That indicates to me you're not going to shoot that handgun much." He's wrong there. It's not often anymore I have time to just spend an hour or so just pleasure shooting for myself, but when I do it's often with one of my potential sock-drawer guns.

The very first time Clint Smith and I shot DA handguns together he started fussing at me. In his gentle way he said: "WHAT ARE YOU COCKING THE HAMMER FOR, YOU NIMROD? IT'S A DOUBLE ACTION!" So I've been working on learning DA shooting — and still not very good at it.

Duke's Heroic Vision

For the past year one of my sock drawer gun has often been the new S&W Model 21-4 .44 Special Thunder Ranch Revolver. With its 4" barrel and 250 grain Black Hills factory load, it's a dandy for such service. That's my opinion anyway. My new S&W Model 22-4 .45 ACP Thunder Ranch Revolver may even be better, what with the possibility of full-moon and half-moon clips. Other revolvers that can and have served are my pre-Model 10 M&P .38 Special, a S&W Model 27 .357 Magnum, a variety of S&W Model 19s and even a few single actions — mostly Colt .45s. Admittedly the wisdom of the latter choice can be debated, which might make a good column someday. To be honest there have been times in my life when the only suitable "sock drawer guns" I owned were single actions.

We all like to have heroic visions of ourselves if fate puts us in a bad situation. I can assure you stumbling around in the dark in my underwear with my eyes half glued together with sleep is not that. But at least my "sock drawer guns" will be ones I'm familiar with and have confidence in.

SHOOTINGIRON™

Mike "Duke" Venturino

THUMB BUSTIN' MUSINGS FROM THE DUKE

THE .38 WCF

.40 S&W   .38 WCF   .44 WCF

THE SAME ONLY DIFFERENT

Everything changes, but everything has a way of staying the same too — take .40 caliber handguns. That's precisely what the old .38 Winchester Centerfire (WCF) was. Despite the moniker, it fired a bullet of .400" diameter. As introduced in handguns its black powder loads gave a velocity of perhaps 850 to 1,000 fps depending on barrel length. Those are roughly the ballistics of today's .40 S&W pistols.

Why did I say "As introduced in handguns ... ?" The .38 WCF was introduced by Winchester in 1879 as a rifle cartridge for their Model 1873. It was a puny one, pumping out that 180-gr. lead bullet to only about 1,250 fps. It didn't take Colt long to realize such a cartridge would fit well in their revolvers. By 1884 they were chambering both the Single Action Army and their Model 1878DA for it.

The .38 WCF was a poor excuse for a deer cartridge in rifles, but it quickly gained acceptance as a fighting round in revolvers. This seems to have been especially true among Southwest lawmen. The following is my personal opinion. It seems the .38 WCF became more popular as the smokeless powder era dawned around the turn of the century. I base this on Colt serial numbers. It seems you see more Colt SAAs chambered for the .38 WCF dating from the early 1900s than you do from the late 1800s.

So far, I've referred to this cartridge only as .38 WCF while almost everyone today calls it .38-40. Winchester only stamped their long guns .38 WCF as did Colt their handguns; at least until recent years in the latter case. In fact it was Marlin who coined the .38-40 moniker. Marlin's name stuck, and today almost everyone knows it as the .38-40.

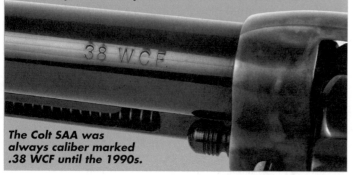

The Colt SAA was always caliber marked .38 WCF until the 1990s.

REBORN

Whatever you want to call it, the cartridge just darn near died out completely after Colt dropped the SAA in 1941. Winchester had already quit making lever guns for it some years before. Also it's worthy of note that Colt's large frame New Service double action was offered as .38 WCF for its 45 years of production.

Regardless, by the early 1990s only Winchester offered a single factory loading and nobody made .38-40 guns of any sort. Then the cowboy action sport really took off and that gave the cartridge new life. In 1993 Colt reintroduced it in the SAA in .38-40 and around that time Starline started making bulk packaged .38-40 brass. Black Hills Ammunition likewise brought out a factory load with 180 gr. lead bullet at about 850 fps from revolver barrels.

That Starline brass was especially welcome because until then the only way to get .38-40 brass was to shoot up Winchester's factory loads, which were priced at about $30 for 50. Also it was common to encounter Winchester factory loads with crimped — in primers. That has been the only commercially produced ammunition I've ever seen with crimped in primers and the crimp certainly had to be cut or swaged out before the case was reloaded.

Many guns have been chambered for the .38 WCF.

EASY-RELOADING

And speaking of reloading, right now I'm feeding two newly-made Colt SAA .38-40s (5½" & 7½" barrels) and a 1908 vintage New Service with 5½" barrel; plus a mess of Colt, Marlin and Winchester long guns. If casting my own bullets I use RCBS mold #40-180CM, for a 180 gr. RN/FP bullet. If shooting commercially cast bullets the 175 to 180 gr. RN/FP bullets from any custom caster using the Magma Engineering's .38-40 mold (that's most of them) work well. Both of these lead alloy bullets have the crimping groove located in the right spot for correct overall length. For those who load the .40 S&W, those bullets are great for use in guns rated for lead.

I've reloaded .38-40s with just about every smokeless powder, from Bullseye to 2400 in burning rate. But, since the new IMR Trail Boss powder made it debut, I've used nothing else. IMR's data list a max load of that new fluffy stuff as 5.5 gr. with the above bullets. That gives 800 to 850 fps from my revolvers. The great thing about this new powder is if you double charge it the case will overflow.

In the years leading up to 1990, companies and law enforcement agencies spent millions testing for a new law enforcement cartridge. The result was the .40 S&W. They should have just looked up some old Southwest lawmen who had packed Colt .38-40s. They would have probably saved some money.

Mike "Duke" Venturino

Handgun Tests Are Silly

Does it really matter if a handgun shoots groups like this ...

... or like this?

Gun tests are silly. I know, because I've done many of them in my career; often not because I wanted to, but because an editor made me. What do they prove? Nothing! The accuracy with a "test gun" is simply what an individual gun delivers on that specific day in the hands of that particular shooter and with that single batch of ammo. In regards to functioning, again it's just a single sample so the results, good or bad, are meaningless. In every run of any product there will be a best one and a worst one. That is a law of statistics. The key is if the manufacturer does their job well, the differences between top and bottom samples won't be noticeable in the real world.

A question often asked by gun magazine readers is "Why do you gun'riters always give good marks to every gun tested?" That's a very good question and it has many answers. The answer most seen on Internet forums is that all gun'riters are dirty, rotten liars who tell outrageous falsehoods because they are given all those free guns. Even if that were true I don't see the logic in it. Why would we want all those free guns if they were so bad you had to lie about them?

Regardless, and sadly, there is some truth to the charge. I know for a fact some of the gun tests I've seen printed in magazines are lies. That's why you need to grow to trust a magazine and writer before you believe everything you see in print.

I once had the opportunity to shoot the same gun used by another writer, and got nowhere near the accuracy from it he did. I mounted the gun in a Ransom Rest, and it still delivered groups two to three times as large as reported by the other guy. Furthermore its trigger pull was so light as to be dangerous; the gun would actually fire just from being jarred. I never read that in his article.

Gun tests should place an emphasis on the handgun's functionality and reliability. Duke is testing this S&W Thunder Ranch Model 22 during reloading drills.

DOG POO

There are at least two other reasons gun tests are always positive. One is that in cases where the gun sent to a writer was a piece of crap, it was just sent back. For instance, while on contract to another gun magazine many years ago, the editor sent me a brand new Colt P2000 9mm and said to do a gun test.

I put that thing in my machine rest and put up two paper targets side by side at 25 yards. Adjusting the Ransom Rest at the target on the left the first round was fired. The bullet landed on the right hand target. I thought I had just misremembered where I had aimed the first shot and so fired another. It went through the left target. The two bullet holes were about two feet apart. I then proceeded to shoot several more rounds and if any of them were within a foot of each other, I don't remember it. Thinking my machine rest might be faulty, that 9mm was then shot from sandbags with the same results. I packed it up and sent it back to the editor and told him I wouldn't write it up. That's why some writers never lavish praise on some guns. They don't want their name connected to them.

At *Handgunner* if you *don't* see an article about a gun, there's a good reason for it. Something to keep in mind.

The other reason gun tests are so positive is many editors (our esteemed one here excluded) won't print even a single negative word about a potential advertiser's products. Once I wrote three paragraphs describing the problems with a gun sent to me by a large manufacturer. Again this was years ago and for another magazine. That editor cut out all the negative comments and then printed a positive sounding article with my byline on it about what was at best a mediocre gun. Small wonder I quit that outfit.

For a test to be anywhere near valid, about a dozen samples of a specific model should be obtained, preferably with each one being from a different production run. Then they should be fired several thousand times, again preferably using a variety of ammo brands. When all that data was tabulated some insight might be gained about that model. Mind you, I said "insight" and not concrete knowledge.

Reviews Not Tests

Of course there is no chance of the above happening with each and every new gun introduced. Once a magazine had me do a project where 5,000 rounds of .45 Colt were fired through two single actions, a Colt Peacemaker and a Ruger Bisley. At the end all I had proven was that 5,000 rounds had been fired with nary a hitch. Both guns were still going strong, but I and my friends were sick and tired of shooting them.

What we should do with new introductions is "review" them looking at finish, fit, function and reporting flaws in such. Extreme emphasis should be placed on reliability and/or functioning. Shooting them for accuracy need not be more than cursory because it means little anyway.

REVISITING A REBORE
IS THIS THE PERFECT REVOLVER?
WRITTEN BY ROY HUNTINGTON

EXPERTS | INSIDER | HANDGUNS | REVOLVERS | WHEELGUN WEDNESDAY |
2022

With lines sure to have a positive impact on your heart rate, Roy's Bowen conversion of a classic 38/44 Heavy Duty to .45 Colt is notable for its singularity — and ability to whisper to whoever sees it.

S&W'S .38 SPECIAL VICTORY REVOLVERS
WRITTEN BY ROY HUNTINGTON

EXPERTS | INSIDER | HANDGUNS | REVOLVERS
2022

This 15-yard off-hand group with the war-weary Victory shows what they could do — and still can! Without the flyer, that's a solid 1" group using Black Hills 148-grain target wadcutter ammo. Roy didn't have enough original military ammo to shoot any groups.

Photos: Yvonne Venturino

COMMANDING PRESENCE

Colt Commander

1911A1 (Colt)

Kimber Pro Compact

Model 1911s have been made in a bewildering array of styles. Colt alone has made 1911s, 1911A1s, Gold Cups, Officer's ACPs, Delta Elites, Double Eagles and many more. That's not to mention all the 1911 clones out there, whose models duplicate Colts' and some go much further. Of all those 1911 variations, one is dearer to my heart than all others — the Commander. It's lighter, shorter, only marginally harder to shoot than full-size 1911s and more than accurate enough for its intended purpose as a carry pistol.

When I got a CCW here in Montana, for the first six months I carried religiously every day, trying a bunch of different handguns. They ranged from a Walther PP to N-frame S&Ws, with even a Colt SAA or two thrown in. The little Walther was discarded because it was a .32, and my jeans have enough stuffed in them besides adding the extra width of an N-frame or Colt SAA cylinder inside my belt. I used inside-the-pants holsters for all this.

No handgun suited me better than a Colt Commander .45 ACP. It's thin, powerful and the standard Colt Commander .45 ACP weighs 27.5 ounces. Standard Government Models are rated at 39 ounces. That extra three quarters of a pound doesn't sound like much, but anchor it to your belt all day long and you can feel the difference.

This is Duke's Kimber Pro Compact .40 S&W, which is Kimber's version of a Commander.

BIRTHDAYS

Colt introduced the Commander in 1949, the year I was born, and I bought my first one in 1970 on turning 21. It was the first 1911 I bought for myself. My father had given me an old military 1911A1 a couple years previously. Standard for a Colt Commander was a 4.25" barrel and aluminum alloy frame. Magazine capacity and sights were the same as for standard Government Models. Calibers were .45 ACP, .38 Super and 9mm. I've read that for export purposes only, some Commanders were made in 7.65 Luger. Note I said all that in past tense? Colt doesn't make Commanders anymore. Hells bells — do they actually make anything these days?

Somewhere along the line Colt introduced a Combat Commander. The difference was it was all steel and weighed 32 ounces. Its rationale for existing was the alloy frame Commanders tended to develop cracks after considerable firing. The Combat Commander was for shooting, while the standard Commander was for carrying. At one point I had both and that's precisely how they were used.

From left: .45 ACP, .38 Super, 9mm Luger, 7.65 Luger (Colt Comm. for export only). At far right is .40 S&W, which has been chambered by most companies making clones.

Duke's Mistake

Then I got a Les Baer Thunder Ranch Special 1911, and it was so exquisite a handgun I got rid of all my Colt-made 1911s, Commanders and all. But the true test of how you feel about something is to get rid of it, and then see if you actually miss it — just don't try that with wives. I missed my Commanders, especially the alloy frame one.

Sometime back Kimber sent me a Pro-Compact 1911 .40 S&W to use in an article. The Pro-Compact is Kimber's alloy frame version of a Commander, 4.25" barrel and all. It does wear better sights, though. When I saw just how well that little Pro-Compact shot, I sent Kimber a check for it, and was in practical effect back in the Commander business again.

Then a couple of years back I was visiting behind a friend's gun show table, and noticed on his neighbor's table a Colt Commander .45. It had been fitted with night sights, a Swenson ambidextrous safety and extended grip safety. I kept an eye on that Commander through the weekend and it was still there at closing time the last day. I made a ridiculously low offer for it and to my surprise the guy took it. Even more to my surprise after shooting it I determined it had no "bugs." My thoughts were that surely something had to be wrong with it for me to get it so reasonably. I get lucky sometimes, and I'm happy with it.

For several years there's been a Colt Commander 9mm floating around our Montana gun shows. It looks good, but no one seems to want it. If it's at the big winter show next month, who knows? I've done dumber things.

Photos: Yvonne Venturino

What Was I Thinking?

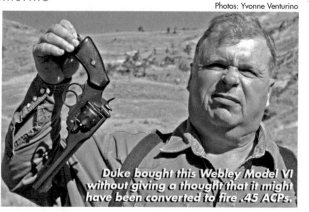

Duke bought this Webley Model VI without giving a thought that it might have been converted to fire .45 ACPs.

It's commonly known in the gun'riting business when a columnist wakes up some morning near deadline time without a clue as to what to write about, he'll do a "Guns I wish I'd never sold" piece. How about I switch that around and tell you about the handguns I wish I'd never bought in the first place?

First off let me say I'm impetuous; often leaping before I look. So my first "oops" back in 1972 could have been easily avoided. It was the first S&W Military & Police .32-20 revolver I had ever seen, and the price, at $75, seemed more than reasonable. FOR A REVOLVER WITH A BIG RING IN THE BARREL though, it wasn't that great a deal. If I had bothered to look down its barrel before grabbing my wallet I would have easily seen it. Sometimes a gun like that will still shoot quite well. This one didn't, keyholing bullets all over

the place. I sold it for $50 but at least told the new buyer about the ring.

For some reason it seems like many of my early faux pas came with autopistols. Back in the 1970s I traded into two identical Llama 1911 .38 Supers. Within 24 hours I looked at them and realized I didn't even want one .38 Super not to mention a 1911 with a silly looking ventilated rib. At this late date I can't even remember to whom and for what I traded them, but undoubtedly I lost money on the deal.

Another autoloader I regretted was a post-war Walther P38. They aren't bad guns, and in fact the one I bought shot pretty tight groups. Its problem was with its extractor, which kept departing the rest of the gun. The first time this happened I was shooting in about 6" of fresh snow and, wonder-of-wonders, I actually found it. The next time it flew off was on bare dirt and I never did find it that time. As soon as a new one was located, that P38 was peddled.

Still Stupid

Before ... **After**

Duke turned this ugly ducking of a "parts" Colt SAA .45 to a showpiece by having it restored, engraved and fitted with ivory grips.

Of all the hundreds of handguns I've owned in my 40-plus years of buying them, the single type of which I've owned the most has been Colt SAAs. Generally they're pretty good guns regardless of exact caliber or generation. However, there can be problems. It's not uncommon for 1st Generation Peacemakers to have mismatched barrel and cylinder chamber mouth dimensions. I learned this the hard way by owning two that wouldn't group on a good-sized cowboy hat at 25 yards. One was a .44-40 and the other a .32-20. The barrel on the former slugged out at .427" but the cylinder wouldn't accept loads with bullets sized larger than .425". The .32-20 had a .314" barrel groove diameter but the cylinder's chamber mouths were only .310" . At least I didn't lose any money on those Colts; selling them both to non-shooting collectors.

I almost did lose on another Colt SAA. It was near closing time once at a big gun show and I hadn't bought a single thing. So instead of coming home empty handed I grabbed a well-worn Peacemaker .45. At home I found this gun wasn't as well worn as I had thought. Removing the ejector rod housing I found no finish under it either, indicating the blue had been removed chemically and not by honest use. Also, the cylinder didn't have the correct bevels for the Colt's time frame as indicated by its serial number. I had paid a decent amount of bucks for a parts gun.

Ever heard of turning something negative into something positive? I did that by sending that Colt .45 to a well known "firearms restorer" (John Schultz, P.O. Box 357, Lawton, IA 51030; e-mail: jschultz45@hotmail.com). He beveled the cylinder properly, had it fully engraved and then silver — not nickel— plated and fitted with ivory grips. It's a show piece of my collection and now at least worth what I have invested in it.

WOBBLY WEBLEY

New interests can also lead you into the unknown. These last few years I've been putting together a collection of World War II firearms, so I grabbed the very first Webley Mark VI I came across at a gun show. But I had totally spaced out the fact very many of those imported to these shores had been converted to .45 ACP. That one indeed had been converted, but luckily I had a friend who was looking for just such a gun. Then I searched around until finding one still an original .455.

The above are a few of my screwups, but alls well that ends well. Next time I come up on deadline time without a good topic I'll tell you about the guns I should have bought — but stupidly didn't. Is there a trend here?

SHOOTINGIRON™

Mike "Duke" Venturino

A Handgun Hunting Class?

To be blunt, I've always been a bit dubious about handgun hunting. My thoughts are that it ranges from difficult to idiotic. So, when invited to check out a Thunder Ranch Handgun Hunting Class, I was intrigued. I've attended many TR rifle and handgun classes, and even instructed a Black Powder Cartridge Rifle one back in 2003. I've always come away far better off than before; both in regards to knowledge and proficiency. But how do you teach handgun hunting?

Simply stated, first by teaching marksmanship, and secondly by constantly stressing ethics. In regards to the first point, after watching the class shoot, I was impressed. I even told them, "You guys could be gun'riters. You already shoot better than most of us." But, perhaps the stress put on the second point was more important. Clint and his assistant instructor for this class, and my long time friend, Ray Coffman, drilled the following into everyone's minds. "The primary idea isn't to just shoot an animal. It's to do so cleanly and efficiently."

As always one of Thunder Ranch's classes encompasses plenty of shooting, and since all class members but one brought .44 Magnums, I expected the students' level of precision to decline abruptly after a few dozen rounds. Clint had planned for that, telling everyone to bring a supply of full-house magnums and also special-type loads. The two types of ammo were alternated.

ZERO FIRST

Most hunters had S&W .44 Mags with Leupold scopes.

The first morning was spent in getting everyone's handguns perfectly zeroed and that also satisfied my first bit of curiosity — what sort of handguns do people bring to a handgun hunting class? Except for Anna LeMaster's S&W Model 327PD .357 Magnum, everyone had one form or another of a S&W .44 Magnum. That was except for Tony Miele, then Smith & Wesson's business manager and currently head of their Performance Center. He arrived with X-frame monsters: a .500 Magnum and a .460 Magnum so the class members could experience this new generation of hunting handguns. Also of interest was the sighting equipment on each of the revolvers. One and all were mounted with Leupold scopes.

Never satisfied to just sit around and be eye candy, that first morning I manned a spotting scope to help with the sighting-in chores. That's when I realized these class members weren't just warm bodies off the street. They could handle these revolvers pretty darn good. From sandbag rests at 50 yards, there were plenty of five shot, 3" groups. And not just in the beginning, but toward the end of the day too. Besides the skill and determination of the class members I also attribute such continued good shooting to excellent ear protection, and those rubber grips with which all the S&W revolvers were equipped.

A special "atta-boy" goes to Lynn Lee. I was also at the Thunder Ranch Revolver Class in the spring of 2005 when Lynn fired her very first rounds from a revolver. To see her less than two years later handling that big .44 like she had done it forever was impressive.

Clint didn't have them do all their shooting from that one position. At times the rests were moved to 25 yards and sometimes discarded altogether. Shooting was done standing two handed, kneeling with shooting sticks, and even semi-reclining with the revolver braced against the knees. Groups may have opened up some but they sure didn't get wild.

Anna with her Blackbuck, 30 yards with a S&W Model 327PD .357 Mag.

Final Test

As a graduation finale the class went hunting. Instead of Oregon, this particular Thunder Ranch class was held at a familiar location — the old Thunder Ranch site in Texas, now called the Flagler Ranch. It's a game ranch with several species of exotics from which the class members could pick. I couldn't stay long enough to see everyone put their skills to use, but was there when Anna LeMaster showed that Clint's talks about ethics had taken root.

Anna had decided she wanted a Blackbuck antelope, and was positioned in a tree stand, with her husband Dale and Ray Coffman in a blind about 50 yards distant. A group of Blackbuck came within 30 yards of Anna's position early one morning, but she held her fire for a considerable length of time. Ray and Dale couldn't understand why she didn't shoot because there was a nice buck in the bunch. Finally she let go with her .357, knocking the buck down but giving him another bullet when he still showed signs of life. Ray and Dale's questions were answered when Anna told them that from her elevated position she didn't have a perfectly clear shot. Not many hunters have that sort of patience when a nice buck is in their sights.

My attitude about handgun hunting was revised after what I saw in Texas. I still think it's a difficult endeavor, but it's certainly not idiotic — if skill and ethics are involved.

23

SHOOTINGIRON™

Mike "Duke" Venturino

Photos: Yvonne Venturino

In Duke's gun culture when there's a break in a match's action it's a fine time to visit with one another.

MY GUN CULTURE

Plenty of kids and dogs are about. No one has to worry about either being mistreated.

Recently, while browsing DVDs in a rental store, I saw one that labeled its movie as a "Look at the dark underside of the gun culture." And in the wake of the Virginia Tech killings, the news media has made its usual references to "America's gun culture." Essentially, those with the rigid mind-set of so-called liberals love to portray people with our interests as "on the edge" just itching to put bullets into live tissue, or some place bullets don't belong.

That stuff drives me up the wall because I've been an active member of the so-called gun culture now for 40 years. Let me tell you about how I see it. In my gun culture words like honor and integrity are not obsolete, and other peoples' property is still sacred. In my gun culture someone's word is still their bond. When I came aboard this magazine three years ago, editor Roy asked me if I felt we needed anything in writing. He and I had been friends for some years already at that time and I said, "No. I know you will do exactly as you say you will, and I hope you feel the same about me." Evidently he did.

TRUST

As for the idea that other peoples' property is still sacred, consider this. Several years back at the big yearly cowboy action shoot called "End Of Trail" (held in Southern California back then), I managed to drop my wife's brace of holstered Colt SAA revolvers off of our gun cart right smack in the middle of the parking lot. This wasn't just the competitors' parking lot, but the one open to the general public. Then in my fatigue I managed to not miss them for over an hour. When it finally clicked in my mind I had lost about $2,000 worth of handguns, my heart was in my throat as I retraced my steps. The guns were nowhere to be found. Then I thought of the lost and found booth and sure enough they were there. The finder didn't leave a name, so I couldn't even personally thank him or her.

The same is true for our weekend Black Powder Cartridge Rifle Silhouette matches held here in Montana. People travel for hundreds of miles around to attend, and many set up their gear, spotting scopes, range boxes, and various accessories under awnings and just leave them out all weekend. Never has anything disappeared. That's the way it is in my gun culture.

RESPECT FOR LAW

For a dozen years now I've engaged in selling the four books I've penned about shooting guns of the old west. Literally tens of thousands of checks and credit card numbers have been sent to me. Some of the latter came from as far away as Israel, Argentina and Australia. Among all those orders I've experienced precisely one bad check and one invalid credit card number. Interestingly, but perhaps meaninglessly, both of those came from women buying my books for boyfriends. That's the way it is in my gun culture.

Also in my gun culture, people don't shoot up road signs, farmer's gates, rancher's cattle, or anything else that shouldn't be shot. People in my gun culture love to shoot, but they shoot at targets of paper or steel, or at legitimate game animals or varmints. Most people in my gun culture love competitions; not because they have to be top dog, but because competitions are their social events. People in my gun culture look forward to breaks in the games' action or the end of the days shooting so they can visit with others. Then they talk about such things as the width and depth of grease grooves in their bullets, or how many lands and grooves their barrels have or what's the best powder for such and such a caliber or gun.

In my gun culture people pay their bills and pay their taxes. They have an independent nature and don't expect the government to take care of them. At the same time it seems like they're always pitching in to help someone else.

People in my gun culture don't watch Rosie O'Donnell no matter what venue she's gravitated to. Neither do they worry much about who's sleeping with whom in Hollywood. People in my gun culture do speak with reverence when they hear another American serviceman has been awarded the Medal of Honor in Iraq or Afghanistan and they hate it when they hear another of those young men or woman has taken a hit.

People in my gun culture are decent. They don't dump puppies or kittens by the side of the road, mistreat children or hit women. I'm proud to be a member of my gun culture.

Protect us all! Duke shooting a machinegun BB gun, and wearing a Hawaiian shirt. Is nothing sacred?

Photos: Yvonne Venturino

WHO'S SERIOUS?

The only full auto firearm I've ever had a serious yearning to own is the 9mm German MP40 of World War II fame. I even had a chance to shoot 50 rounds through one once, but never could see any sense in putting out the big bucks it would take to buy one. I've been told an original German issue one runs about $15K to $25K nowadays.

I've also been subject to very vivid dreams all my life and a few weeks ago I dreamed of buying an MP40; right down to the dealer it was coming from and its cost. A ridiculously low $6K; like I said it was a dream.

Anyway, just for fun the morning after that dream I surfed the Internet looking at MP40s, and happened upon an outfit selling full size MP40 BB guns. To be exact they were airsoft BB guns, which I had never heard of, but it appears that airsoft BB guns fire their 6mm pellets of some synthetic biodegradable material at only about 300 to 350 fps. That's much lower than the 600 fps velocity of traditional BB guns with steel projectiles. I guess in some locales people arm themselves with airsoft BB guns and chase each other around sort of like paintball. I really don't know anything about that.

This group was about a 30 round full auto burst from the MP40 airsoft BB gun from about 10 paces.

KAPOWWE

The outfit that had these things is called KAPOWWE (www.kapowwe.com) so I called them. The pleasant young lady I spoke to answered my questions thusly, "Yes, they are one-to-one scale. Yes, they are made of metal. Yes, the folding stock does work. And yes we have them in stock." At about $140 I figured it would make a good wall decoration in my walk-in gun vault where I've been plastering one section with World War II flags, helmets and what-not. Believe me I've spent more money, more foolishly in the past.

When my airsoft MP40 arrived I was just plain tickled with it. It's full-sized, and the frame is of steel — or at least it holds a magnet. It doesn't weigh as much as I remember the real one I fired, but its does have some heft to it. There is a selector switch on the frame's left side with options for safe, semi-auto, and full auto. The magazines drop out at the push of a button, also on the frame's left side, and they hold about 50 of the

BBs. It even comes with a little plastic apparatus for loading the BBs into the magazines.

It also came with a battery pack. Now, all the BB guns I used back in my youth fired by means of compressed air or CO2 cartridges. This thing runs on batteries. For all I know there is a little elf in there and he won't wind up and pitch until he gets an electric shock. What I do know is this MP40 will sure fling out those BBs at a fast rate. It takes no time to empty a 50 round magazine. The battery pack will last about 12 hours and then needs recharging, or perhaps the little elf needs a rest. I don't even know where this thing was made. The instruction book that came with it was written by someone who thought they knew English. It's hard to decipher.

Duke's airsoft MP40 BB gun looks and feels like the real deal.

Horses Beware

But one thing I am sure of is my MP40 BB gun is extremely accurate. It doesn't just spray those BBs all over the countryside. They go where aimed, at least out to 20 yards or so. I put up a target and from 10 paces let fly about a 30 round burst. It hit dead center with a perfectly acceptable group considering full auto and handheld firing. I put an ordinary baking potato up at 10 paces and made a mess out of it in short order. Most of the BBs went in it about a half-inch or so and stopped.

What's such a thing good for? I really don't know. I've chopped the tops off a lot of weeds. Also Yvonne likes to let our old horses out in the driveway to eat grass. They in turn like to come up to the house and step on anything valuable. It didn't take long before they started high-tailing it back to the corral when they saw me come out the door with the MP40. I can't wait till this summer's usual infestation of grass hoppers arrives.

When I told Clint Smith about buying it, there was a brief period of total silence on the other end of the phone. Yvonne said I must be entering my second childhood, and I told her I wasn't done with the first one yet. Some writers take themselves seriously. Obviously I don't. Not only did I buy an MP40 BB gun and am telling the whole world about it, but now I'm eying an airsoft "Tommy gun."

SHOOTINGIRON™

Mike "Duke" Venturino

Photos: Yvonne Venturino

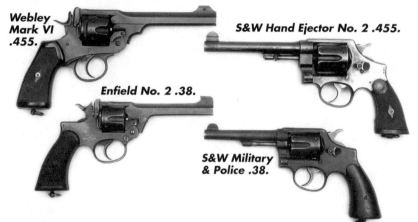

Webley Mark VI .455.

S&W Hand Ejector No. 2 .455.

Enfield No. 2 .38.

S&W Military & Police .38.

The Brit .38s and .455s barely dented. The big caved-in spot was done with a .45 ACP.

WWII BRITISH SIXGUNS

The British have never been ones to march in lockstep with the rest of the world, and a little evidence of that is their choice of handguns in World War II. While most of the world's major military forces had by that time converted to one sort or another of autoloader, the British decided to stick with revolvers.

Mostly they used four types of double action revolver, although in 1940 the British government even bought some Colt Single Action Army revolvers to help arm their home guard. (Today collectors refer to those as "Battle of Britain" guns.) Issued to regular British forces, however, were their domesticly manufactured Enfield No. 2 .38 and Webley Mark VI .455. The Webley Mark VI .455 had been adopted in 1916, and although it had been officially replaced about 1928 by the Enfield No. 2 .38, it was still in common use.

Not having enough of either Webley or Enfield to go around, they also bought many thousands of S&W K-frame Military & Police revolvers chambered for the .38 S&W cartridge. And furthermore, they still had and consequently used many S&W N-frame (Hand Ejector 2nd Models) which they had purchased from 1915 to1917 for World War I.

Their choice of cartridges for these revolvers also seems strange. The .455 Webley had been with them since the 1870s as a black powder cartridge, but their Mark II version of it introduced about 1897 was loaded with smokeless

Duke's S&W Hand Ejector #2 .455 factory letters to the Canadian Government in 1916.

propellant. By American standards, it would be considered "barely loaded." That's because it was rated with 265 gr. bullet at only about 600 fps. In the 1920s the British military determined a .38 caliber 200 grain bullet at about 630 fps gave about the same muzzle energy, and that's what they converted to. Actually the case they chose to use was a twin to the .38 S&W round. That company had been chambering guns for it since the early 1870s, so when the Brits needed S&W to help them out with revolvers in the 1940s.

I've been told by a knowledgeable shooter/collector that prior to WWII the Brits had to reduce bullet weight on their .38s to 178 grains in order to make them full metal jacketed. Otherwise they would have been in violation to the Geneva Convention.

Left to Right: .38 S&W with 190 gr. lead RN, .455 Webley Fiocchi load with 262 gr. lead RN bullet and .45 ACP Black Hills load with 230 gr. FMJ bullet.

NO COMMON SENSE

For some strange reason, probably related to my lack of common sense, my gun trading forays these last few years have netted me samples of the four above mentioned British military revolvers. Two have some minor noteworthiness. The Enfield No. 2 .38 is marked "RAF" (Royal Air Force) and "1936," while the S&W .455 factory letters to the Canadian government in 1916. I was even able to find a 12-round box of FMJ .455 military loads of Canadian manufacture dated 1943 to go with it. British military .38 loads have evaded me completely. For shooting I bought some of the Fiocchi .455 Webley factory loads with a 262-gr. lead bullet and handloaded some Lyman #358430 cast bullets weighing 190 gr. in the .38. Powder charge was only 2.2 grains of Bullseye. The Fiocchi .455s chronographed at 619 fps, and my .38 handloads were 10 fps faster.

So did I "test-fire" these revolvers for accuracy as any self-respecting gun'riter would do? No way. What I did was spent nine bucks at an Army surplus store for an old GI issue steel helmet. Then I set it on a fence post and fired my British WWII revolvers at it from 10 paces. The .38s wouldn't have even given its wearer a headache. They didn't dent it and hardly made it wobble. The .455s did dent it and it wobbled some. Admittedly these were lead bullets and not military FMJs, which might have given more penetration. For comparison, I fired a 230 grain FMJ .45 ACP factory load from a Colt 1917 revolver. It didn't penetrate either but caved in the side of the helmet, and not only knocked it off the fence post but rolled it 20 yards down the road!

Somebody probably knows why the Brits stuck to revolvers in the years leading up to WWII, and even perhaps why they liked such pee-dunkler cartridges— I don't. But they're still interesting handguns, albeit only minor historical footnotes to WWII.

IDIOTS I'VE MET AT GUN SHOWS

Sequoia Blankenship

For 30 years now I've enjoyed gun shows. I've attended ones ranging from less than 100 tables here in Montana to some with over 1,000 tables in Las Vegas. No matter how big or small, it's amazing what neat things you can find at them. Also, every now and then you'll run into some absolutely amazing idiots.

I'm not sure if this first guy was an idiot or just a jerk. As might be expected a gun'riter ends up with lots of extra magazines around the house; the kind you read, not the ones that go into pistol butts. Every few years I'll buy a table at local gun shows and sell off those and other surplus stuff that gathers in my gun room. If I make lunch money out of the magazines, I'm happy. One year I put a stack out with a sign that said "8 for $1.00." Right away this yo-yo came by and said sarcastically, "Those magazines you write for must be in trouble if they're only selling for a buck apiece." To which I replied, "Well they wouldn't do you any good anyway if you can't read better than that. The sign says eight for a dollar." Away he went in a rush and I never saw him again.

"Way Back..."

A couple of years back I was on a kick to own a sample of every N-frame S&W revolver made between 1908 and 1966. At a gun show a fellow had a whole row of tables with some pretty good S&Ws on it, including a 4" Model 57 .41 Magnum. I asked him if I could handle it and was given the okay. Then he launched into a story about how rare that gun was because it was made "Way back in the 1950s." I said, "Boy, I bet it is pretty rare, since they didn't introduce the .41 Magnum until 1964." He went to the far end of his row of tables and wouldn't talk to me anymore.

In my life I've tried to develop a reputation for truthfulness. Not only is it easier to remember what the truth is instead of some made up story, but if you get a reputation for telling the truth, if you're in a pinch and have to lie everyone will believe it. Anyway, at a big Las Vegas gun show I told an out-and-out lie. I was ambling down an aisle when some guy quickly sidesteps and blocks my path. Then without any "hello" or "how de do" he blurts out, "Do you make a lot of money writing those articles?" As I sidestepped him and continued on my way I replied, "Yes I do!"

(Editor's Note: Yes, Duke lied. Lots. Oh, and nice try for a raise, but does the term "In your dreams" mean anything to you?)

PRIME CANDIDATE

But the most brazen of all the gun show idiots I've ever met popped up in front of me recently. He first asked me for a moment of my attention, and then pulled me over to a relatively quiet corner and in a low voice said he had a proposition for me.

I looked at him expectantly, figuring he had a handgun to sell and I was his prime candidate. Instead he went on to say he could tell from my articles I was short of ideas, and he just happened to have a bunch of ideas that would suit me.

That wasn't so bad, but then he went on to say he would give me his ideas for a percentage of what I made for an article. Furthermore he trusted me so we could do this on a handshake; we didn't even need to get lawyers involved. I told him, "Don't call me. I'll call you." NOT!

27

.38 Richards/ Mason Conversion of the Model 1861.

.44 Richards Conversion of the Model 1860.

COLT'S CARTRIDGE CONVERSIONS THAT WEREN'T

A mong avid single action revolver shooters there is a sub-genre of handguns well respected but often misunderstood. Those are the Colt Conversions of cap & ball six-shooters. The interesting fact is Colt's Conversions weren't converted; at least not in the truest sense of the word.

What happened was Colt engineers figured out a way to alter cap and ball revolver designs so they fired metallic cartridges. They didn't actually take existing cap and ball revolvers, tear them down, and rebuild them into cartridge shooters. Colt's Conversions were built of new parts with bored-through cylinders of new manufacture.

No gun company, back then or today, likes to junk perfectly good but obsolete parts, and Colt had tens of thousands of various models of cap and ball revolver parts on hand in the early 1870s. So, rather intelligently, they built them up into guns and "converted" parts into cash.

Two Flavors

T here were two basic versions of Colt Conversion revolvers named after the engineers who figured them out: The Richards and the Richards Mason. The Richards style came first and was based on what we today call the Model 1860 Army. The alteration consisted of fixing a breech plate complete with firing pin and rear sight to the frame, filling in the cap and ball model's rammer recess, and affixing an ejector rod and housing to the right side of the barrel. Who says frame-mounted firing pins are a new innovation?

Later one of Colt's engineers named Mason changed the design somewhat. The firing pin was put back on the hammer and since by this time Colt was running out of cap and ball barrels, new ones were manufactured. Thus there exists no filled-in cap and ball rammer recess on Richards/Mason conversions.

When Colt was building these conversions they actually put them on every style of cap and ball revolver frame being manufactured in the early 1870s. In fact, the most numerous ones were the little five shooters based on the Model 1862 .36 caliber frames. They were made both in .38 rimfire and centerfire models. Approximately 25,000 were made. The larger six shot conversions based on Models 1851 and 1861 Navy .36s were also made both as .38 centerfire and rimfire. About 3,800 of the former and 2,200 of the latter were made. And, although it is possible I could be mistaken, I've never seen one of these .38 rimfires or centerfires that were Richards Conversions. They have all been Richards-Mason Conversions.

Original .44 Colt Richards Conversion of Model 1860. Note the hammer has no firing pin and also note the rear sight on the recoil shield.

Left to right: .38 Short Colt, .38 Long Colt and .44 Colt.

The .44s

W ith the big .44 conversions both methods of alteration were used, but at least as sold by Colt they were all chambered for .44 Colt centerfire. The Richards version was most numerous with about 9,000 made and only about 2,100 .44s were based on the Richards-Mason system. The U.S. Army bought 1,200 Colt Richards Conversions in 1871 and issued them to cavalry units stationed throughout the west. By many accounts they were very well received by the troops.

Although I've owned and/or shot both .38 and .44 caliber original Colt Conversions, I consider them too rare and too valuable to use very often. Therefore, some years back I had a gunsmith (Not named here because I don't think he still makes them.) build both a Richards Conversion .44, and a Richards-Mason .38 on new Colt cap and ball frames. They are beauties, and in fact since this gunsmith had a spare .44 barrel defective near the muzzle, I had him bob it off to 2.75" to replicate a snubby-conversion used by El Paso City Marshall Dallas Stoudenmire in the early 1880s. The switch between 8" and 2.75" barrel can be made in about a minute.

Back when Colt originally made these conversions they left the barrels' groove diameters as they had been for .36 and .44 caliber cap and ball revolvers. Nominally, such were .375" and .451". That necessitated the use of either heel-type bullets or hollowbase ones. I use the former in the .44 and the latter in the .38; both over full cases of black powder. Both are great fun to shoot, and believe me, that little snubby .44's black powder muzzle blast will wake up the neighborhood.

Of course there were other conversions during the 1870s — many frontier gunsmiths did their own. But this is a nutshell-sized story of the ones Colt made and sold.

SHOOTING IRON™

Mike "Duke" Venturino

Photos: Yvonne Venturino

**THUMB BUSTIN'
MUSINGS FROM
THE DUKE**

BLOWED-UP GUNS

A case-full of Bullseye did this Rossi in.

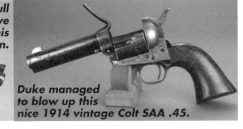

Duke managed to blow up this nice 1914 vintage Colt SAA .45.

Brothers and sisters believe me, when a handgun blows up in your hands it will ring your chimes! That doesn't necessarily mean it will physically hurt you. In fact most of the dozens of blown up handguns I've heard about have done no physical damage to the shooter.

What I mean is having one blow right there in your own two mitts not only scares the hell out of you, it will ruin your confidence in your ammunition and your know-how in general. I can state this will absolute certainty because I have experienced it.

The date was April 1, 1991. I remember exactly because it happened to be our 13th wedding anniversary. Yvonne had a little bit of a head cold and was napping on the couch, so I took a couple of Colt SAA .45s down to my steel target range to plink for a bit at a dueling tree. The first five shots bounced the paddles back and forth as proper. The Colt .45, a 1914 vintage one that had been given to me by Hank Williams Jr. the first time he visited me here at home, was then reloaded with another five handloads. At the first shot the Colt blew with a sound sort of like a FIZZ-BANG. The topstrap detached at the rear and bent forward and the top half of the cylinder just disappeared. It could still be in orbit for all I know. I was unhurt.

RUN AWAY!

As strange and as silly as it might sound my very first impulse upon looking at the ruined Colt was to run; run to nowhere in particular but just to leave that spot. My second instinct was to pack up my gear and quit shooting. I did neither. Instead, I loaded up my second Colt .45 with factory loads that I also had along and shot those 50 rounds slowly and carefully. It was sort of one of those "get back on the horse after he bucked you off" kind of things.

What caused that Colt to blow? To this day I have no idea. That day I had 200 rounds of handloads with me. The bullets of the remaining 194 were pulled and the powder charges weighed. None were abnormal. One "expert" insisted that I had stuck bullet number five in the barrel and then the gun blew when round number six was fired. Ok, dimwit, in that case who smacked the dueling tree's paddle on that fifth shot, the tooth fairy? The most hilarious comment offered was the fellow who said it had to be the air space in the huge .45 Colt case because "You know; air cannot be compressed." Yeah dummy in that case what did you put in your bicycle's tires when you were a kid?

Long ago I gave up trying to figure out what happened because I've heard literally of dozens of other handguns that have blown up. The one single thread running through each and every one of those instances *that I personally know about* is the shooter was using handloads.

I personally do not know of any handgun blowing apart with factory ammo. Could that be why the gun companies only warranty their handguns with factory ammo?

Do I only shoot factory loads in all my handguns now? Nope. I'm an avid handloader and a darn careful one. I don't begrudge the time spent at the reloading benches; consider it quality time spent with precision tools. And I certainly don't reload my own ammunition in order to save money. One fellow I know does just that and is always looking for bargains on powder, primers and bullets at gun shows. He got a bargain alright! It was a can of powder labeled Unique and it didn't bother him that it had been opened. When he loaded up his vintage Colt SAA .38-40 with his usual Unique load, the cylinder split and the topstrap simply disappeared. Lots of savings there, huh? I have nicknamed this fellow Shrapnel.

TRAIL BOSS

Here's one thing I have done with my own reloading, however. With large capacity revolver cartridges — those originally designed for large dollops of black powder — I only use the new IMR Trail Boss propellant now. It is "fluffy" to the point you can't get a double charge in a case, it will overflow. Normal charges pretty much fill up even huge .45 Colt cases to the base of the bullets. That property alone takes a lot of variables out of the handloading mix.

Take my word for it. You don't want to blow up a gun. It will ruin your day — and doesn't do a thing for the gun's value.

A friend of Duke's blew the topstrap off this very nice Colt SAA .38-40 with powder he bought "cheap" at a gunshow.

IWO JIMA PILGRIMAGE

Many people have said to me, "How was Iwo Jima?" To most I just reply, "Wet!" Because on March 12, 2008 the skies opened over Iwo Jima and for several hours rain fell like this Montanan has never seen in his life.

For most, the "wet" comment is something they can relate to. When talking to people who I know are well versed in the history of World War II, I say this. "Iwo Jima was humbling. To stand at the summit of Mount Suribachi exactly where those six men raised the flag shown in Joe Rosenthal's famous photograph and look down on the invasion beaches is chilling."

Anyone even slightly versed in weaponry can see what a perfect killing field the Japanese had. In the first few days of the battle tens of thousands of U.S. Marines were crowded

Duke was both honored and humbled to be able to visit Iwo Jima in the company of these dozen veterans of the battle.

onto the southern part of Iwo. In this area the island is so narrow any of us handgunners could stand in the middle of it and fire a pistol into the ocean on either side. How those Japanese gunners on Suribachi missed anyone is a mystery, except perhaps the incoming fire was so heavy as to make sticking their heads out of their holes certain death.

THERE

Although I have studied the battle for Iwo Jima since a pre-teen, my first view of the island was still a surprise. The pilot of the Continental Airlines Boeing 737 took us low and slow, doing figure eights around the island so both sides of the airplane could look it over before landing. The surprise was the true smallness of Iwo Jima. It's a mere five miles from north to south where the volcano sits and perhaps 2½ miles wide at the northern plateau where the airport is located. I knew the dimensions already but seeing it made it real.

There were about 150 of us aboard that 737 ranging from battle veterans to kinfolk of young Marines killed there in 1945 to history buffs such as myself. During those figure eights I don't recall hearing a sound above a whisper. Although Iwo is just an ugly rock, a mere speck in the Pacific Ocean, we all knew we were about to land on a special place.

Immediately after the battle Admiral Chester Nimitz, U.S. Navy commander in the Pacific was quoted as saying, "On Iwo Jima uncommon valor was a common virtue." To modern ears perhaps that sounds like political BS. After seeing and walking over some of the battlefield I know for sure it wasn't. When the marines landed on Iwo on February 19, 1945 their 4th and 5th Divisions reinforced to about 20,000 men each landed abreast on a two mile stretch of the black sand beaches. (Actually it's volcanic ash.) This was on the island's east side. The 5th Division was on the left, or south, and their first job was to cut the island in two, one regiment, the 28th Marines was then to neutralize Suribachi while the rest of the division fought their way north. The 4th Division's job was to land, and then immediately swing

north and both outfits side by side were then to roll all the way to the north end of the island. Marine Corps planners felt the entire operation would last days, not weeks.

That was the plan. It didn't work. The Japanese were in hundreds of fortified and camouflaged positions and quickly inflicted so many casualties on the two marine divisions two of the three regiments of the reserve 3rd Division were called in to help. Their position was in the center, between the other two divisions.

Looking over the battlefield I could perhaps understand how a young marine faced a day of that fighting. What I can't understand, and never will understand, is how that same marine could climb out of his foxhole in the morning and face the same death and destruction again on the next day. And the next, and the next, until he was killed, wounded, or finally saw the ocean on the island's north shore.

A rain soaked Duke standing (he thinks) right about at the border of invasion beaches Red One and Red Two with Mount Suribachi in the background.

Not An Easy Walk

I walked Iwo Jima from the airport in the central plateau to the invasion beaches. It took me about an hour or so and I'm in poor shape and with an arthritic knee. Fighting on Iwo lasted 36 days, although the island was declared secure on March 14th. It took those young marines two to three weeks (depending on their sector) to conquer the same ground a man in his late 50s, lame and overweight, walked in an hour to an hour and a half.

So yes, I got wet on Iwo Jima but I also discovered what true humility felt like, especially when in the company of Iwo veterans who actually lived what I just described.

SHOOTINGIRON™

Mike "Duke" Venturino

Photos: Yvonne Venturino

THUMB BUSTIN'
MUSINGS FROM
THE DUKE

Obsolete = Ineffective?

Which can be fired fastest, the 1911A1 .45 ACP or the Colt Peacemaker .45?

For at least the first six rounds, the answer might surprise you.

My tattered, old desk dictionary defines obsolescence as "growing out of use." Just above it the definition of obsolete is "no longer in use." Something that often amazes me is how often some shooters confuse obsolete or obsolescence with effectiveness. Just because a handgun has become obsolete does not automatically mean it lacks effectiveness. In fact in practical terms any firearm — shotgun, rifle or handgun — will always remain as "effective" as it ever was. Here's what I mean. Most of my shooting career has been spent with "obsolete" handguns such as Colt Single Actions, Smith & Wesson N-frames, and even older S&W top break Model #3s. A great many people I've associated with in shooting those guns consider them little more than toys. They are not. They are just as deadly as they were the very first day they hit the market. It's just that newer guns are faster to reload, hold more cartridges, or are chambered for newer cartridges that offer absolutely no practical advantages.

Oldie But Goodie

Back in 2004 a couple of young Marine friends just home from the Iraq invasion came by to visit and spend an afternoon shooting with me. After looking over some of my handguns they asked if they could shoot a few revolvers. That request was probably spurred by the fact that they had just seen the western movie Open Range.

They both were packing 1911s of one make or another so after some plinking I asked them if they thought something like my Colt SAA .45 could be fired as fast as their 1911s. "No," they agreed. So with one of them as "judge" the other and I stood side by side and on command fired two shots at a paper target about five paces away. The "judge" said he couldn't tell a difference. So the two Marines switched places and we did the same drill with the same results. They were pretty surprised young fellows. The kicker is that I'm not especially fast with a single action. The trick is to just hold the trigger back with the shooting hand's forefinger and manipulate the hammer with the other hand's thumb. That method is amazingly fast and at only five paces, it's not difficult to keep the bullets close to one another on the target.

Let's carry the matter a step further, back to cap & ball revolvers. They are so obsolete that the average modern handgunner probably doesn't even know how to load one of the things with its loose powder, ball, and caps. In fact cap & ball revolvers aren't even governed by Federal forms or paperwork, and if local and state laws allow, they

can be shipped between individuals. That sort of gives them the aura of "harmless." They are not, as thousands upon thousands of Northern and Southern cavalrymen proved to each other in the Civil War. Would I like to bet my life on say a .36 caliber Colt Model 1851 Navy? Not especially but I'd pick one of them over some of the more modern junk floating around that I know end up next to some peoples' beds. They will shoot an attacker just as dead as they did 150 years ago.

Now let's reverse the idea. Twenty-five years ago it was a rare cop who carried an autoloading handgun — double action revolvers were standard. Now wheel guns are obsolete, but are cops necessarily more "effective" with their semiautos? Fairly regularly the news media has headline stories of one or more cops emptying their high capacity autoloaders with few, and sometimes no, hits on the evil-doers. That doesn't seem very effective even though their handguns are far from obsolete.

Many consider the revolver as obsolete as bi-wing airplanes, but they are just as effective today as they ever were.

WITH THE IN-CROWD?

Over the years I've had many local people ask me what kind of "automatic" they should buy for home defense. My question is, "Why do you need an automatic?" To which they usually reply, "Well, they're the thing now. Revolvers are obsolete." Obsolete maybe, but they are nary a bit less effective than they ever were. Unless the questioner shows signs of becoming an avid handgunner my stock answer is, "Get a double action S&W, Colt or Ruger .38 Special revolver with anywhere from a 3" to a 6" barrel." They are relatively inexpensive, easy to learn to shoot adequately and certainly as effective now as they were 100 years ago.

And for heaven's sake, don't ever let yourself think of those old single actions or cap & ball sixguns as toys. I've personally known a couple of fellows who let their guard down with them and paid the ultimate price.

The old: Colt Model 1851 Navy .36 caliber cap & ball.

The new: Glock 23 .40 S&W.

9mm LUGER

War II vintage British STEN Mk II submachine gun he bought.

As strange as it may sound coming from someone known for a big bore sixgun affliction, I've come to be a 9mm fan. Such a feeling certainly doesn't come from considering it a super duper defensive handgun cartridge. I know very little about such things. My newfound acceptance of the 9mm stems from a historical perspective.

Consider this: we Americans are proud that our Colt Model 1911 pistol is about to hit its 100th birthday. The 9mm Luger already did that in 2008 as the German Army's handgun cartridge, and the German Navy actually adopted it two years earlier. It is arguably the world's most popular handgun and sub-machine gun round, period. Under the title 9X19mm it is currently NATO's official handgun caliber. That includes the U.S. It's also worth noting, as adopted by the Germans over 100 years back, it was called the 9mm Parabellum. That word is Latin meaning "for war." Here in America it got the "Luger" moniker because so many of that design of pistol were captured and brought home by our soldiers in two world wars.

Although I've owned a few 9mm Luger handguns starting with a S&W Model 39 in 1977 and have had a Taurus PT92 around here for at least 20 years, I paid scant attention to it until this year. As I've shown in previous issues I've been putting together a collection of all sorts of World War II firearms. Naturally, that has included a couple of 9mm handguns; specifically a 1938 vintage Luger and a 1943 marked P38. I've also included 9mm sub guns in that collection: a 1941 vintage German MP40 and a 1943 vintage British STEN Mk II.

RELOADING

Owning these guns has led to a considerable amount of 9mm Luger reloading. In order to feed my sub guns I mounted a Dillon Square Deal B press dedicated to 9mm. I picked the Square Deal press for two reasons. First, it's one of the smaller progressive type presses so I've been able to put two, side by side, on one end of my reloading bench (I have several). Second, the auto-indexing feature makes it virtually impossible to double charge a case. Since mounting and adjusting the Dillon press I haven't touched either its powder measure or its dies and have loaded several thousand rounds of 9mms in these past few months.

Duke learned early on not to get careless in handloading the 9mm.

What? More?

And here are two more reasons the Dillon Square Deal is indispensable. It has a carbide sizing die so there's no need to lube the brass and the seating die is a taper crimp type. That last feature is really important and here's why: back in 1977 with that S&W Model 39 I owned I didn't have a taper crimp die and my reloader merely rolled the case mouth back against the side of the bullet. That worked most of the time — until I got a bullet that wasn't locked tightly in the case. When the round jumped from the magazine, up the feed ramp and into the chamber, it pushed the bullet down on top of the powder. The result was a blown out case head with the escaping gas spitting both grip panels and stinging my hand. Luckily the gun itself was ok. With a working pressure in excess of 30,000 copper units the 9mm round is not a cartridge to do sloppy reloading with.

Duke finds it easier to simply keep a Dillon set up for each caliber he needs.

For this current 9mm reloading the only powder charge I've used is 4.3 grains of Hodgdon's HP38; a fast burning pistol powder ideally suited for the 9mm's small capacity. Over that powder charge goes either 115 or 124 grain Hornady FMJ roundnose bullets or 124 grain hard cast, .356" round-noses from Oregon Trail Bullet Company. Now, there are those who will tell you cast lead alloy bullets are not suitable for reloading the 9mm. In truth, many types are not. When I've tried .355" bullets in a few 9mm pistols the results on targets showed as patterns — not groups. However, with very hard cast 9mm bullets of either .356" or .357" diameter I've had pretty good luck with them from both the P38 and Luger. The two sub guns digest them like they were designed around them.

Years ago I worked for a magazine whose editor decreed he wanted a 9mm Luger article in each issue. Naturally I ducked my head and avoided even mentioning the name. Nowadays if I sneak a few minutes to go shoot steel with a pistol it's usually with the P38. I wonder what that editor will think if he sees this column?

SHOOTINGIRON ™
Mike "Duke" Venturino

Photos: Yvonne Venturino

THE ULTIMATE HANDGUN ACCESSORIES
BUYING FULL-AUTO

These are four examples of Duke's new passion. From front to back: German MP40 9mm (1941); American Thompson M1 .45 (1942); British STEN Mk II 9mm (1943); and the North Korean PPsh41 7.62X25mm (1950).

After publicizing in these pages my new found passion — World War II and Korean War vintage submachine guns — several readers have asked about the difficulty in legally obtaining such full autos. Some asked if I got a "full auto license." Others said "isn't that $200 a year fee kind of hard to handle if you're going to buy several as you have done?" And I can tell you this starting out; Nearly everyone I've talked to prior to buying their first full auto nearly balked at the thought of going through the government's red tape necessary to own National Firearms Act items. Besides full autos, such include silencers, rifles with barrels shorter than 16" and shotguns with tubes shorter than 18" among other items. I nearly balked the first time too, for to the unknowing the process seems intimidating. But after the first purchase you realize it's not that big a deal, especially when you get to own and shoot such a fascinating piece of history.

The Red Tape

Duke literally having a blast with his PPsh41.

Here's what it takes. First off, not all states allow ownership of full auto firearms, but perhaps surprisingly, most do. For example, here in the northwest, Montana, Wyoming, Idaho and Oregon do allow them. Washington does not. So you need to know that detail first. Second, you can buy a full auto from an individual in your own state or from a dealer in your own state. You don't need a special license.

Here's how you proceed. The seller fills out the Bureau of Alcohol, Tobacco, Firearms and Explosives' Form 4 and gives it to the buyer in duplicate. All BATFE forms can be printed right off their website at www.ATF.com. The buyer then must supply a duplicate set of finger print cards. The finger printing can be done at your local police or sheriff's department for which they will probably charge a small fee. Also the buyer must affix to the Form 4 two current 2 x 2" photos of himself. Passport photos will suffice. A single Certificate of Citizenship must accompany the Form 4. Again that can be printed from the above website.

This next point might be the most difficult in some locales. The chief law enforcement officers for your place of residence must sign off on the Form 4. Here that factor was a no-brainer. I live out in the country so I needed the Sheriff to sign. Not only is he an avid shooter but a friend of many years. Conversely, I have heard that some chief LEOs of big urban areas won't sign Form 4s for anyone as a matter of policy.

Anyway, after filling out the Form 4s in duplicate and affixing your photos, supplying the fingerprint cards in duplicate, filling out a single certificate of citizenship, and getting that chief LEO's signature, all you have to do is put in a $200 check made out to the BATFE and send the whole shebang to the address on the form. The $200 is a one time fee. It's not a yearly thing. Then you wait.

When the BATFE approves your Form 4 they will mail it back to the firearm's seller. If that is an individual or dealer in your state then you can go to them and take possession of the gun. The BATFE wishes the buyer do that as quickly as possible. So far in my transactions the wait from the day I mailed the Form 4 until the sub-gun was in my hands has been between two to three months.

Somebody is asking right now, "But what if the full auto I want to buy is in a different state?" Then you have to find a Class III dealer in your state to receive the firearm. That initial paperwork goes between the two dealers. Then when the item arrives at the Class III dealer in your state, you and that dealer have to go through the Form 4 procedure as outlined above.

AND ANOTHER THING

Here's another variation. Some full autos are included on the BATFE's list of curios and relics. Most curios and relics are considered firearms older than 50 years. However, in regards to full autos they have to specifically be on the BATFE's C&R list. Therefore a holder of a C&R license can actually receive a full auto from a dealer outside the state, or from another C&R licensee located in another state. Again that's after the Form 4 is approved by the BATFE.

Essentially that's all it takes to buy a full auto firearm. Of course there are many more details. One concern to many is about inheritance upon the owner's death. The firearm can be passed on to a designated person without charge but they must pass the BATFE's examination. Also important is the buyer need be aware he can travel with his full auto inside his home state (obeying all state and local regulations too) but cannot take it outside his home state without another BATFE form.

Once I made up my mind the government's red tape wasn't too difficult, I've now bought several submachine guns without a hitch and without regret. Simply put — they're great fun!

SHOOTINGIRON™

Mike "Duke" Venturino

Photos: Yvonne Venturino

THUMB BUSTIN'
MUSINGS FROM
THE DUKE

The .44 RUSKIE

This is Duke's Navy Arms 3rd Model .44 Russian. He did not even consider selling it during Duke's Great Gun Sale in 2008.

After writing a feature for this issue on why the .44 S&W Special isn't so special, now I'm going to detail why I do like its ballistic twin, the .44 S&W Russian. At least I like it in this one particular revolver. That's the Navy Arms' replica of Smith & Wesson's Model #3, 3rd Model .44 Russian.

Circa 1872 the Russian Government wanted to start buying Smith & Wesson's new top break Model #3 revolvers. Very important to the company was the fact they were willing to pay in gold. But the Russians wanted nothing to do with Smith & Wesson's own .44/100 cartridge because it used a heel-type bullet. That's where a reduced diameter shank fits inside the cartridge case while the full diameter of the bullet is the same as the outside of the cartridge case. Just look at a round of .22 Long Rifle. They're still made that way. The Russians explained if the bullet fit *inside* the cartridge case with revolver chambers bored accordingly things would work much better. They certainly did, and still do. Of course with all that gold in the balance Smith & Wesson said, "you bet!"

The result was the .44 S&W Russian. Smith & Wesson's own cartridge then gained the name of .44 S&W American. Case length for the Ruskie one was set at .97" with bullet diameter at .429". Through the decades the .44 S&W Russian was loaded with bullets as heavy as 275 grains over black powder charges as heavy as 23 grains. By the smokeless powder era in the early 1900s, factory loads were standardized with a 246-grain roundnose bullet at about 755 fps. And when the .44 S&W Special came along in 1908 it was given the exact same bullet at the exact same speed but in a case 1.16" long.

Left is Lyman #429478 (200 grains) and at right is Lyman #429383 (248 grains).

Picky Russians

In its first 30 years of existence the .44 Russian cartridge gained a superb reputation for accuracy, of course as fired in the several versions of Smith & Wesson top break revolvers. (*See my .44 Special article in this issue for an explanation of why cartridge accuracy reputations are myths.*) It's recorded some notable handgun target shots were able to keep five .44 Russian bullets inside a 3" circle at 50 yards. That's probably true, and it should be emphasized not many handguns made today will do that even with smokeless propellants.

Between 1872 and 1874 the Smith & Wesson Model #3 went through three revisions as requested by the Russians. Collectors named them 1st, 2nd and 3rd Models. With each, the Russians asked for design changes altering the Model #3's appearance so much the company started to grouse — despite the gold.

By the 3rd Model .44 Russian, the S&W Model #3 had a "knuckle" at the top of the grip resulting in a saw-handle shaped grip frame, and that odd spur hanging off the trigger guard. Many theories have been thrown out as to the purpose for the spur. The most likely one is Russian Cavalry tactics called for horse mounted troopers to charge with their revolvers cocked and with the trigger finger resting on the spur. That likely saved a lot of horses from being shot in the back of the head as Lt. Col. George A. Custer did to his own horse once when chasing a bison. I've found the spur makes a dandy finger rest for two-handed shooting and the saw handle grip keeps the hand positioned on the revolver exactly the same from shot to shot.

Why the odd hook on the trigger guard?

Good Guns

At one time I owned a sample of each of those vintage S&W .44 Russian revolvers but hardly ever fired them because they were very fragile and also very valuable. So when Navy Arms announced their replica of the 3rd Model .44 Russian about 10 years back, I jumped on it. While it is not an exact clone of the old S&W 3rd Model .44 Russians, it's not bad, and the differences are minor. The Navy Arms' version has a 7" barrel as opposed to the original's 6½", and the original had a front sight forged integral with the barrel while the replica's is pinned on. Oh, and some dimensions are slightly different by a few hundredths of an inch. So what.

My Navy 3rd Model .44 Russian is extremely accurate with either smokeless or black powder loads. I've settled on two loads: 248 grain roundnose bullets (Lyman #429383) or 200 grain roundnose bullets (Lyman #329478) over 4.0 grains of Bullseye or 19 grains of Swiss FFFg blackpowder. Its point of impact is about dead on with the latter bullet and about 2" higher than point of aim at 50 feet with the former. Despite its tiny sights I've gotten one hole groups at 50 feet from a sandbag rest, and standing with two hands I can keep dueling tree paddles swinging. It doesn't gum up with black powder fouling for at least 50 or so rounds.

When I had Duke's Great Gun Sale in 2008 and disposed of 50 seldom used firearms, all my original S&W .44 Russian revolvers went. Putting the Navy Arms 3rd Model .44 Russian on the auction block was never even considered.

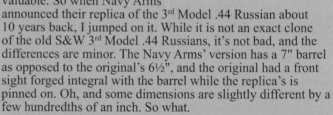

SHOOTINGIRON ™

Mike "Duke" Venturino

THUMB BUSTIN'
MUSINGS FROM
THE DUKE

Photos: Yvonne Venturino

THAT GNARLY NAGANT
BUT WHY?

The Nagant revolvers load and unload through a gate on the frame's right side just as traditional American single action revolvers do.

After writing my article on World War II handguns a few months back a few readers questioned why the Russian Model 1895 7.62mm Nagant revolver was left out. The reason was because it is a silly little excuse for a revolver! Do you ever wonder why someone invents a widget that is decidedly inferior to somebody else's already existent widget? The only emotion I can dredge up about a Model 1895 Nagant is, "why?" By 1895, revolvers of superior design had been around for decades. Of course the vast majority of these were the products of American brains and factories. Regardless, a Belgian named Leon Nagant set about dreaming up an excellent solution to a non-existent problem.

For some reason Mr. Nagant felt that gas leaking between the barrel/cylinder gap of revolvers was a big detriment to their performance. So he figured out a complex revolver system where the cylinder was cammed forward every time it was rotated so its chambers actually fit over the butt end of the barrel. That prevented gas leakage. So naturally to cope with that sort of operation the ammunition had to be special. Bullets had to be seated deep in the cartridge case. Not flush with the case mouth like today's full wadcutter target ammunition but deep as the photo shows.

The odd design of the 7.62mm Nagant cartridge is evident in this photo. Shown lying down, the deep-seated bullet is visible. Next it's shown standing up so the extra length is evident.

Then come some contemporary rounds: .38 S&W, .38 Special, .455 Webley, and .45 ACP.

Then the case mouth had to be crimped inward over the bullet so it too could fit inside the rear of the barrel. For that reason the cases had to be made long, as were the firing pins that had to reach way-forward because that's where the cylinder had gone when the hammer was cocked.

All that machining, fitting, and special ammunition manufacture allowed the 98 grain 7.62mm Nagant bullet to be propelled all of about 1,000 fps. Now hold that thought for a moment. By 1895, it was well known that although a revolver leaked a bit of gas through the barrel/cylinder gap it was really not a big deal. Everything still worked fine. Rounds like the .45 Colt or .45 S&W or .44 S&W Russian shot big bullets at about 750 to 900 fps and were noted man-stoppers.

Duke borrowed this 1943-manufactured, Model 1895 Nagant 7.62mm from a friend. As Forrest might say: "stupid is as stupid does."

SISSIES

Evidently the entire world's military forces back in the 1890s were hit with a plague of "pantywaist-ism." In 1892 America adopted the puny .38 Colt, which shot a 150 grain bullet at about 725 fps. It became famous for getting people killed — not the people being shot but the shooter himself because then the "shootee" really got mad and hacked him up with something sharp. The Brits at least stuck with a big .455 Webley using a 260 grain bullet, but had it moving along at a lazy 600 fps.

By 1895 both Colt and S&W made revolvers that automatically dumped all cartridges either when opened (S&W) or with a single stroke of an ejector rod after the side-swing cylinder was opened (Colt). The Smith & Wesson line of revolvers also had single actions offering simultaneous cartridge ejection. The Model 1895 Nagant still loaded through a gate on the frame's right side but to eject the empty cases an ejector rod system had to be rotated to come in line with the chambers. I would guess the Nagant revolver was made a seven-shooter to compensate for all that rigmarole. It was made in both single and double action versions.

Now here's the ironic part. The major user of the Nagant revolver was Russia and later the Soviet Union. In fact they kept it in at least partial service until 1947. Why is that ironic? Because in the 1870s Russia bought several hundred thousand beautiful quality Smith & Wesson Model #3 top break .44 Russian caliber revolvers. In other words they had far better revolvers already in hand when they adopted the Nagant. They couldn't even use "national pride" as an excuse for adopting a crummy design because it wasn't theirs anyway. At least they got license to manufacture it at their own Tula Arsenal. And here's an interesting little tidbit — Russian officers got the double action version but enlisted men were issued single action ones.

In all honesty I've only fired one Model 1895 Nagant belonging to a friend, a double action one. That was enough. Its double action trigger pull was awful and its single action pull wasn't so great either. I popped one round of Fiocchi factory loads at a surplus U.S. Army steel helmet on a fence post from about 20 feet. It barely wobbled it and hardly left a dent. Being a lifelong handgun enthusiast, when holding the Nagant revolver I thank my lucky stars I was born American!

A WRITER'S WORST NIGHTMARE

Duke's only pretending here — he's actually not bored. Okay, maybe a little when it comes to SAAs.

A full time writer's worst nightmare is (or should be) boredom. If he becomes bored, his writing will be boring. At best, what a writer has going for him is not especially his knowledge, it's his enthusiasm and the ability to infect a reader with it.

And one thing is for sure, enthusiasm can be a fleeting thing. Even the most ardent passions can become dimmed. For instance, take me and the Colt SAA. That revolver was my first true love. I bought my first one, a 2nd Generation .45, in 1968, and I've owned scores in the ensuing 41 years. At one point I owned 36 in a wide variety of calibers, but now I'm down to about a third of that number in only four calibers. The first book I wrote was titled *Shooting Colt Single Actions; In*

All Styles, Calibers and Generations and it has been a great success for me. Yet in the last couple of years I've not taken any Colt SAA out and shot it except for use in an article. In fact as I started writing this column I noticed that in my gun vault where my Colts set on an open shelf many are dusty. I'll clean them someday.

DUKE WAS YOUNG?

Back in my youth when I spent time riding around Montana's mountains on horses I usually carried my pre-Model 29 .44 Magnum with 5" barrel. It's as dusty as those Colts. But

perhaps that is a clue to this boredom/enthusiasm thing. That could be defined as purpose; as in having a purpose for a handgun or type of handgun causes enthusiasm to be generated. During the time I carried that .44 Magnum into grizzly bear country, I fired it often and even if I do say so myself, I was pretty good with it. Likewise with the Colt SAAs. When Yvonne and I actively par-ticipated in cowboy action matches we both shot single actions fairly well.

People call and write to ask me what their Colt SAA or N-frame S&W is worth. I have to say, "To be honest I don't have a clue because I haven't kept up with them for a while." The last gun show I spent any time at did I pore over the many tables holding Colt SAAs, or big bore S&W magnums? Nope, when I finally spent some money that day it was for a 1943 vintage German P38 9mm. How many .45 Colt, .44-40 or .44 Magnum cartridges have I handloaded recently? Nary a one, although I've assembled thousands of 9mms. They are not only for a couple of World War II vintage submachineguns I bought in 2008, but also for the P38, a 1938 vintage Luger and three 9mm Browning Hi-Powers also made circa 1943/1944.

Duke's enthusiasm led him to this Inglis Hi Power 9mm with wooden shoulder stock/holster.

At the same time he searched out and bought this FN-made Hi Power with Nazi markings also made during World War II.

Hi Powers And Stens Oh-My

What's my purpose with these 9mms? To learn; because I knew virtually nothing about P38s, Lugers, Hi Powers and World War II submachine guns. Aside from having an actual shooting purpose for a gun, which generates enthusiasm, personally for me ignorance generates enthusiasm. Hence with the purchase of the Luger there also came purchases of books on Lugers. Along with the vintage German MP40 submachine gun several books were searched out about them. Now I quest for literature about Hi Powers and STENs.

When I told my mother-in-law so far I've written about 1,500 columns and articles for gun magazines she replied,

"How do you keep coming up with ideas?" Well, it's that enthusiasm thing again. If I have enthusiasm then I will dig into the history of certain guns, along with shooting them, and reloading for them. Within each of those facets there are article and column ideas.

When I came aboard this magazine the only direction His Editorship Roy gave me was, "Don't be afraid to step outside the box, Duke." I don't know that "stepping outside the box" is the right phrase to describe what I do. Perhaps it should be called "meandering down a crooked path" or "letting my nose follow my enthusiasm." Hopefully, as I strive to avoid boredom, I won't become boring.

GUN BRUTES AND LOUTS: NOT!

Lucy

Doing The Good

This column doesn't concern handguns. It's about one three-year old girl and hundreds of decent, gun owning, human beings. Our leftist news media loves to portray we "gun people" — as I prefer to call us — as nut cases. At best we're considered louts who go around shooting up road signs while swigging beer. At worst, the public in general is told we're dangerous brutes just looking to shoot somebody.

Let me give you an example of what real "gun people" are like. A company familiar with all Black Powder Cartridge Rifle (BPCR) shooters is Montana Vintage Arms. They are manufacturers of high quality sights and telescopes used on such rifles. An employee there, Lars Waldeisen, has a beautiful daughter named Lucy. During her three-year checkup Lucy was found to have a rare form of cancer. Treatment for Lucy's ailment has required traveling from Montana to places as distant as New York City. Of course that means considerable expense for the entire family.

In the spring of 2009, Montana Vintage Arms, together with Shiloh Rifle Manufacturing organized a benefit raffle. The prize consisted of one of Shiloh's beautiful recreations of a Sharps Model 1874 .45-70 rifle fitted with both Montana Vintage Arms' target grade metallic sights and one of their telescopes. Along with it came a custom wooden box for the telescope by Kansas woodworker Harold Forcum and a bullet mould by Montana custom maker Steve Brooks. The most modest prize was a hardbound copy of my book *Shooting Buffalo Rifles*. Retail value of the prizes was put at $4,500.

Raffle tickets were priced at $50 each, which in today's economy is not an inconsiderable sum. As match director of the Montana Regional BPCR Silhouette Championship in June 2009 I took 20 of those tickets to the event. I had fears about being able to sell many, again due to the state of the economy which our wonderful news media never tires of harping about. Those 20 tickets didn't last the first day. Then we had to take people's money and addresses with a promise to mail their ticket stubs to them. Be aware that my match was a small one. We could only accommodate 64 shooters total.

Other BPCR matches did the same and word was spread about the raffle. Checks for tickets came from far and wide, even from other countries. Drawing for the raffle was set for July 16th during the awards ceremony for the BPCR Silhouette and BPCR Target National Championships. That was at the NRA's Whittington Center outside of Raton, New Mexico. Ticket buyers did not have to be present to win.

Now get this part. Several other people and I traveled to the "nationals" with many ticket stubs belonging to other people. One and all those people had given these instructions to us. "If I win, then I want you to go up on the stage and auction the prizes to the highest bidder with all the money also going to Lucy." That was the sentiment of all these "gun crazy louts and brutes."

This was the prize, although we think Lucy is the real prize! A Sharps Model 1874 .45-70 rifle fitted with both Montana Vintage Arms' target grade metallic sights and one of their telescopes went to the lucky winner.

MOIST EYES

And I want you to soak up this part too. When Jim Gier, president of Montana Vintage Arms took the microphone at the time of the raffle drawing, he informed us that 500 of those $50 tickets had been sold. That figures to $25,000 with every single penny of it going to the Waldeisen family. The cheer raised from the crowd was enormous and looking around I saw many grizzled looking middle aged and older shooting competitors with glistening eyes. Keep in mind too the BPCR crowd is a relatively small one compared to the numbers participating in other shooting sports.

I don't know the fellow who won the raffle, nor even where he came from. What I do know is that we "gun nuts, brutes and louts" as a group are honorable, decent human beings. And I'm sick and tired of being portrayed as anything else!

SHOOTINGIRON ™

Mike "Duke" Venturino

Photos: Yvonne Venturino

You Know **You're A Gun'Riter** If ...

If you would rather be casting bullets while everyone else is watching the Super Bowl then you are probably good gun'riter material.

Many times I've been asked by other "gun guys" if I thought they might be "gun'riter material." Mostly they mistakenly believe writing a few articles insures them free hunts to the "Three big As." That is Africa, Australia or Alaska. Not to mention all the free guns and accessories that go with the big bucks gun'riters make. Sure! Right! Dream on!

Being a fan of Jeff's Foxworthy's "You might be a redneck if ..." comedy routines, I've decided to paraphrase him so you can judge yourself as to whether you are gun'riter material.

If your folks bribed you into going to the senior prom with the loan of their car and some cash but then you took your date home immediately after the dance and then drove to the nearest city with a gun store so you could spend the money on bullet moulds, powder and primers — you may be gun'riter material.

If during college you didn't buy the prescribed school books and instead spent the money on gun magazines, and more bullet moulds, powder, and primers, then you may be gun'riter material.

If in college you majored in journalism although you seldom read a newspaper, then you're shaping up to be good gun'riter material.

If the college you attended mandated a student have a minimum 2.00 grade point average to graduate and you had a 2.10 average, and your friends still chide you for being an overachiever, then you were probably heading down the gun'riter career road from the very beginning.

If you met the perfect girl and decided to get married but had to sell some guns to afford traveling to your own wedding, then you are getting close to becoming a gun'riter. That's especially true if over the next 30 or so years you never let her forget the sacrifice you made for her.

Ball Games?

If you have never had any trouble remembering your wife's birthday or your wedding anniversary because your mind is practiced at remembering numbers because since your early teens you have memorized calibers, powder charges, bullet mould numbers and so forth, gun'riting is probably in your blood.

If you have absolutely no interest in any games that involve balls — football, basketball, baseball, tennis, golf, soccer, ping pong or whatever — you have the gun'riter spirit.

Likewise, if your TV has never played any game involving any of the above mentioned balls and you only have a fuzzy idea as to what a Super Bowl is but your DVD Library contains movies like *Quigley Down Under* and *Band of Brothers* then you are looking like good gun'riter material.

If a dinner conversation with a table full of friends centers around the number of grease grooves on your favorite cast bullets, along with their shape, alloy temper and sizing diameters, you may be a boring individual, but likely good gun'riter material.

If you are at a gun show, gun store, or shooting match and loudly pronounce to your companions you have all the guns you have ever wanted and then a few minutes later they catch you shelling out money for a new gun, then you are most certainly gun'riter material.

Shelling out money after all.

If You've Ever ...

Thought having 200 pounds of pig lead ingots on the dining room floor is a good idea ...

If you've ever been excited buying a gun at a gun show and when you get home you see you already have one in your safe ...

You find yourself digging deep into your gun safe (safes?) and regularly saying, "Hey, I forgot I had this!" ...

If you find yourself saying, "But honey, 5,000 rounds of .308 isn't enough!" ...

When you honestly think reading 35 year old *GUNS Magazines* — *you* bought on the newsstand 35 years before — is a really fun way to spend an evening ...

When you move you need to hire a 28 foot Penske truck just to haul your ammo ...

If your desk is cluttered with hundreds of bullets and cartridges that you "need for photo props," then it's likely you *are* a gun'riter and a pretty good one.

And lastly, if your last thoughts at night before you fall asleep are about the shape of the next cast bullet you want to design and not about your wife's shape, then it is likely you have been a gun'riter for a long, long time. Maybe too long?

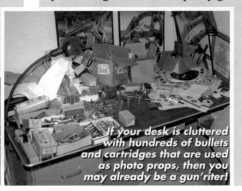

If your desk is cluttered with hundreds of bullets and cartridges that are used as photo props, then you may already be a gun'riter!

SHOOTING IRON ™

Mike "Duke" Venturino

Photos: Yvonne Venturino

THUMB BUSTIN' MUSINGS FROM THE DUKE

GROUPING

GROUPIES

Group shooting in and of itself is meaningless. It has taken me over three decades to fully realize that fact. The purpose of a handgun is not to shoot groups, and in fact nobody ever shot anything with a group. The sole purpose of a handgun is to direct a bullet to a specific point, whether it is a paper target, a tin can or flesh. Each shot is an individual act.

So how did groups become the be-all and end-all in some people's minds? It happened because groups are shot to determine the level and consistency of a handgun's precision. But group shooting is fraught with the possibility for errors. Most all of us avid handgunners have a group or two taped to our gun room walls. But there is one indisputable fact. A single group is only a record of what *that* handgun did with *those* five, 10 or however many shots in *that* specific instance.

Consider the following. A superb 5-shot group can be, and often is, a fluke. A superb 10-shot group is less of a fluke, and a superb 25- or 50-shot group actually begins to give an indication of what that *specific load delivers from that specific handgun.* Four or five groups of five shots are a better indication of a handgun's precision, just as four or five 10-shot groups or four or five 25-shot groups are "more better." But who in the world has the time or gumption to do that? So, most "gun tests" use the lazy man's five shot groups.

And then there is the shooter-factor to consider. By shooter-factor I mean how well the trigger was pulled and the sights aligned, with the understanding that muscle and eyesight fatigue are related factors. Obviously a shooter is going to be capable of firing a better group at the beginning of a session than he will after an hour or two of constant shooting.

After a handgun is made to shoot like this, meaning it is sighted in and shoots tight groups, then more group-shooting is superfluous. After that it's time to build marksmanship skills.

AMAZING PRECISION?

I recognized that fact early on in my career and began using machine rests. Those devices minimize shooter fatigue. The flip side of that coin is they give no indication of the "shootability" of a handgun. In other words, a handgun which delivers amazing precision from a machine rest may be completely incapable of hitting anything when put in a human's hands. Again let me explain. Perhaps the two greatest drawbacks to shooting a handgun with precision — meaning we are attempting to direct a *single* bullet to a *specific* target — are the visibility of the sights and the quality of the trigger. There's also the factor of where the handgun sends the bullets in relation to where its sights are pointed.

A handgun with a 10- or 12-pound trigger pull will shoot groups from a machine rest just as tight as a similar model with a two- or three-pound trigger. Likewise, a revolver with modern high profile sights will be easier to hit with than one with the old fashioned half moon front and a small groove down the topstrap for a rear sight. However, both revolvers might shoot groups just as small when mounted in a machine rest. And since a handgun mounted in a machine rest is not only anchored to that heavy apparatus of table and rest, rounds fired give absolutely no indication of where they will impact when the same handgun and ammo are fired handheld. In other words, machine rest groups give no indication of a handgun's "shootability." They only indicate mechanical accuracy.

For the best results in shooting groups, Duke has relied on pistol machine rests (like this Ransom) for over 30 years.

While his 1917 revolver and 1911 both shoot great groups from a machine rest, Duke can only actually hit the target reliably with his 1911 due to ergonomics.

ERGONOMICS TOO

Now consider this. I own two Colt .45 ACP handguns from the World War I era. One is a 1911 and the other is a Model 1917 revolver. The former has a 5-pound trigger pull and the latter has a 7-pound trigger pull (single action). Both shoot respectable groups from machine rest with a variety of loads — say in the 2" range at 25 yards give or take a half-inch or so. Both handguns hit point of aim at 50' with my chosen loads. However, I can actually hit something with the 1911 pistol much more reliably than I can with the 1917 revolver. Why? Because of ergonomics. The pistol fits my hand and the revolver feels like it was designed for someone with gorilla length fingers. Its actual grip is small yet the distance my finger has to stretch to reach the trigger seems immense. I don't shoot that particular revolver well despite its potential for good groups.

Nowadays I don't shoot groups near as often as in most of my previous years. Instead when a new handgun ends up here I shoot it at paper or steel from 30 to 75 feet. Its type and purpose dictate the range. Self defense/concealed carry handguns are fired close, others are shot farther. Then I see how well I can actually *hit* with that handgun shot to shot, when it's held in my own two hands — because that's the only thing that really counts.

39

SHOOTINGIRON ™

Mike "Duke" Venturino

Photos: Yvonne Venturino

Drift adjustable front sights, such as found on Duke's German Luger and German P38, are moved in the opposite direction to where you want the bullet to impact. Note both of these are a bit off-center after Duke zeroed the pistols.

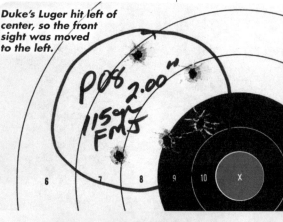

Duke's Luger hit left of center, so the front sight was moved to the left.

P08 2.00"
115gr FMJ

SIGHTING-IN SECRETS

One of the most frustrating experiences I had as a fledgling gun'riter was caused by a nitwit editor. He rejected an article of mine about sighting in fixed sight handguns saying, "It's no big deal to hold off." If you actually want to hit something with a handgun, yes it definitely is a "big deal" to have it sighted in. Later after I gained a "name" that same editor wrote me asking for articles. I threw his letters in the trash.

All handguns should be sighted in to hit point of aim at some distance determined by its owner and its specific purpose. Personally I use 50' for mine, and here's a tip: sight them in by shooting them in the manner in which they are likely to be used. That is one handed, two handed, or however. Quite often a handgun sighted in from a solid sandbag rest will have a different point of impact when fired unsupported.

Handguns with adjustable rear sights are sublimely simple; merely move the rear sight in the direction you want the point of impact to move. Say the handgun's point of impact is to the right. Then move the rear sight to the left. If it is hitting low just raise the rear sight. It's no more difficult than being able to manipulate a screwdriver.

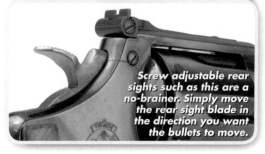

Screw adjustable rear sights such as this are a no-brainer. Simply move the rear sight blade in the direction you want the bullets to move.

Sorta' Adjustable

The next level of complication is sights that are what I call "semi-adjustable." With my current fiddling with World War II handguns I've run into a few of these. The German Luger makes a fine example here. Its rear sight is a simple blade mounted on the toggle. Into it is cut a V-shaped notch. There is nothing remotely adjustable about that rear sight. BUT, the front sight blade is dovetailed into a barrel stud near the muzzle. My personal Luger hit right on for elevation at 50' with 115 grain FMJ factory loads but it printed several inches left at that distance. No problem there either. I put the Luger in a padded vise, took a small brass punch and whacked its sight blade in the dovetail so it was *left* of center. That brought point of impact to the right and so now it's sighted in. And I can shoot it pretty darn good even if I do say so myself.

Now let's carry things one step further. After buying the Luger I just had to have a German P38 as well. Those clever Germans also saw fit with that model to put the front sight blade in a stud near the muzzle. My "new" P38 not only printed left but shot way low too. I prevailed on my gunsmith buddy Tom Sargis (28 Lake Drive, Livingston, MT 59047) to order in a small array of P38 sight blades from Numrich Arms. We picked out one that looked substantially lower than the issue sight, and dovetailed it in so it set slightly left of center. Bingo! After our first attempt some shooting showed the P38 now hit right on at 50', again with 115 grain FMJ factory loads.

1911 FOIBLES

US Army Ordnance officers were not as smart as the Germans when developing the US Model 1911 and Model 1911A1. On those pistols the rear sight is dovetailed into the slide and drift adjustable for windage. However, the front sight is a tiny blade staked into the slide. It cannot be easily replaced with a higher or lower one, as the case may be. Unless you are a talented gunsmith the elevation you get with an issue 1911 is what you must live with.

There's an "unless" that can go with that last statement. Elevation in handguns can be manipulated to a modest degree with ammunition. Simple physics cause the following: heavy bullets impact higher than lighter bullets with all other factors the same. That's because recoil begins immediately as the bullet starts to move. Therefore heavier bullets cause a handgun's muzzle to raise more by the time the bullet exits. Thus some adjustment of point of impact can be accomplished by trying different bullet weights.

Speaking of ammunition, I said my Luger and P38 were sighted in with 115 grain FMJ factory loads … what about handloads? To maintain their zero, it's my duty to load my 9mms to equal said factory load's ballistics.

Next issue we'll get into the really difficult sighting in chores — handguns with fixed sights that are not adjustable by screwdrivers nor are dovetailed on.

The Gun'Riter's Burden

For this column I am sharing this note sent to me via my gunsmith buddy, Tom Sargis. Spelling, punctuation, and grammatical errors belong to the writer, not me. Oh, and I withheld his name since I have some kindness left in me, in spite of what he has to say!

HEAVY WEIGHT

Brothers and sisters, this is a prime example of what I call "The Gun'riters' burden." About the only thing this yo-yo got right is that it's a "free country." I can write pretty much about anything I chose. If readers like it then that great eminence in Missouri, Editor Roy, will keep printing it. If not, well then I'm history. Several things in this fellow's note can only cause other gun'riters to smile. Here's a few, " ... *made all his money.*" What money? If someone finds a bag of money labeled "Duke" please get it to me

Perhaps Duke did turn his back on single actions. After all, this one is jammed into a hip pocket.

quickly. If a gun'riter has a pile of money he didn't make it writing for gun magazines!

"*He did become famous.*" If I'm famous where are all my paparazzi? I can move about the world freely without being stopped by autograph seekers. "*He is selling books and making a killing.*" That one is just great. I wish! My "killing" on those books every year is just about enough to finance my attending a season's worth of BPCR Silhouette matches — precisely the thing Mr. Dimwit says I've turned my back on. And if I turned my back on it, how did I finish seventh overall at the 2009 NRA BPCR Silhouette National

"*Oh,* while I have you on the line I looked on Mike Venturino's site, as I had something I wanted to let him know. I have sold all of his books that I bought, I am no longer a fan of his, as I think many others feel the same way. It has to do with his abandoning his cowboy stuff, which he made all his money on, and built his fan base on, and taking up the dress and armaments of our enemies, past or present. I am a veteran, and can't help but feel betrayed when I see him with a full auto mp40, with a german helmet on, or with some russian sub gun. I know it is a free country, and he has a right to morph into what ever he likes but he did become famous, and make a lot of money writing articles about big bore single shots, lever guns, colt saa's, and all the other 'guns of the old west' he is still selling books and making a killing, but has dropped all that stuff. One reader in a magazine a while back made the comment that when he saw Mike wearing that krout helmet, he was shocked, and said that he thought Mike was on our side! My sentiments exactly. He conveniently has no link to contact him on his own site. I don't mean to drag you into this, Tom, I am not mad at you at all, really. It is just that you are the point of contact for Mike. Tell him how I feel. That is why I sold all of his books because that is the way I feel about what he is doing. I won't read another article of his, or buy another book he writes, either. That's too bad, too, as he was originally a big reason that I got into the old west guns in the first place. Times change, and I guess people do, too. Just my thoughts.* " — Name withheld*

Championship? Heck, that was my best ever finish.

Perhaps the most absurd complaint in that note is about that photo of me wearing a too small German helmet while cradling a World War II vintage German MP40 submachine gun. And I might add, while also wearing a Hawaiian shirt. Wake up, Ding-Dong! It was a clown photo. It was meant for laughs. If you didn't laugh at that one, you've got your buttocks pinched way too tight, and there's gotta' be something wrong with you.

Life Is Perfect

Back in college in Psychology 101, we were taught a basic tenet of mental health. It was that humans need new experiences to keep their heads screwed on right. I still have a rack of Colt SAAs, S&W N-frames, Winchester lever guns, and Sharps and Remington Rolling Block single shot rifles. To them, in the last few years I've added World War II handguns, rifles,

carbines and most recently a modest collection of World War II submachine guns. The basic thread running through all but a few of the firearms there in my vault is they are historical. I have not become a "demon of darkness" or a "cornfield commando." I am a "shooting historian."

And I might add I'm having a blast in learning about all those firearms. My mental heath is great, my head is screwed on just about perfectly, and my buttocks aren't cramped from over-pinching!

Recently, I had a serious, life threatening health problem, which hospitalized me for many days. (That bag of money labeled "Duke" would really come in handy right now, by the way). To the doctor in charge I said, "Doc, you got to get me through this because my life is perfect." He looked at me oddly for a moment and replied; "No one has ever said that to me before." And I was not exaggerating one bit. I can bear that "Gun'riters' burden."

41

PLIERS AND FILES

Duke left these plier tracks on the front sight of a Colt SAA .45 when bending its front sight. They bother him not at all.

In the spring of 1984 I was preparing to fly to Southern California to participate in my very first *End Of Trail* cowboy action match. I had only one misgiving. That was that my 3rd Generation Colt SAA .44-40 with 4¾" barrel put its bullets about 4" left of where aimed at 25 yards. Such a thing is very annoying and likewise very common with single action revolvers.

Being impetuous by nature and letting annoyance transcend into anger I said to the Colt, "I'll fix you!" I frequently talk to inanimate objects. Whereupon I rummaged through the pickup's glove box until a pair of pliers was found. Then sans any sort of padding to protect it I gripped the Colt's front sight and bent it to the left. I was surprised at how soft the sight's steel was and one tweak had the .44-40's point of impact matching point of aim. It still does too. A friend owns it now and takes great pleasure in showing the "plier tracks" on its front sight to anyone who will look, while telling them who mutilated it.

Other handgunners have said to me in wonder, "You actually bent the front sights of revolvers?" You bet I have. I'd take a hammer to them if that was needed to get them sighted properly.

However, I freely admit the front sight on the second Colt SAA I did that do was of considerably harder steel and took much more effort to bend.

Actually bending front sights on revolvers wasn't my original idea. The late Charles Askins once wrote that while a member of the Border Patrol in the 1930s that outfit received a shipment of Colt New Service .38 Special revolvers, most or all of which likewise placed bullets left of where aimed. He said he bent all their front sights until they were on. I copied him. At least one very annoyed reader copied me and wrote me saying his front sight came off when he tried that. So I guess the moral there is don't copy me, like I copied Charlie?

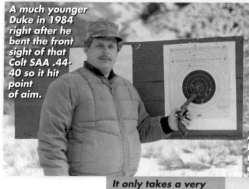

A much younger Duke in 1984 right after he bent the front sight of that Colt SAA .44-40 so it hit point of aim.

A gunsmith once brought a portable vise to Duke's home range along with his barrel turning blocks and they sighted in about a dozen single actions in one afternoon.

Tool Savvy

If you have the least bit of handiness with tools in your makeup there's a better method, and keep in mind this for *single-action revolvers* only. Drill a hole slightly smaller than the barrel diameter of your revolver through a block of hardwood. Then saw it in two directly down the center of the hole. Get some rosin from a hardware store and coat the blocks so they'll grip the barrel. Dismount the single action's ejector rod housing and lock the barrel in the blocks with the cylinder removed. Get a long piece of hardwood such as a broken shovel handle, insert it in the cylinder's recess and then give the frame a gentle tweak. Key word here — gentle.

Now pay attention. You want to move the front sight in the *opposite* direction you want the bullet's point of impact to move. Move the front sight *towards* where the bullets landed. Usually only a very slight tweak is necessary to move point of impact several inches at 25 yards. Moving the barrel counter-clockwise is most commonly necessary and that's good because that's tightening the barrel. Moving it clockwise is loosening the barrel, and just a tiny bit of movement in that direction goes a long way. Once a gunsmith no longer with us brought his portable vise to my home range and we sighted in every one of my single actions needing it. At least those not already suffering from bent front sights.

Now, I am so mechanically inept I don't even do this myself anymore. The reason is my gunsmith buddy, Tom Sargis lives only a five minute drive away. With his barrel twisting setup permanently in place, I just run up there with any new single action needing adjustment.

It only takes a very slight bit of lean on a single action's front sight to move point of impact.

TOO TALL?

What about elevation? If the revolver shoots low then the remedy is filing off some of the front sight. That should be done very slowly, at the shooting range, test firing often. Elevation can also be adjusted slightly by changing bullet weight. As a rule, heavier bullets impact higher, lighter ones impact lower. If your revolver hits high, then you have a more of a problem. I've actually seen gunsmiths squeeze a single action's front sight in a smooth jawed vise to make it taller and then file it to shape. Of course it gets narrower in the process. You'd better be very handy with tools to do that!

And here's one last bit of common sense. Before you go to the trouble of sighting in your fixed-sight single action, have your load all figured out. If you change the load, then you risk changing the revolver's point of impact. Then you get to do it all over again!

SHOOTINGIRON ™

Mike "Duke" Venturino

Photos: Yvonne Venturino

**THUMB BUSTIN'
MUSINGS FROM
THE DUKE**

HIP POCKET HANDGUNS

When practicing, Duke draws from his hip pocket these days. His S&W Model 442 might show a tiny bulge there, but you'd really have to be looking for it to notice it.

C lint Smith will probably want to give me a knock on my noggin for this column, but having a hard head, I'll proceed anyway. For a variety of reasons too involved to discuss here, I've not worn a belt for a couple of years. That means — no belt no belt holster. The most comfortable manner of packing a handgun I've ever experienced was with one of the Milt Sparks Summer Special inside the pants holsters. With that arrangement I've carried full size 1911s all day without a problem. The belt binds the gun against the body, which in turn keeps its weight from pulling downwards. But like I said — no belt no belt holster. Also for the very reason I'm built very broad I find shoulder holsters most uncomfortable. Also here in Montana for most of the year you need to wear a winter coat, which of course inhibits access to a shoulder holster anyway.

So nowadays, when I want to exercise my concealed carry right my hip pocket is my holster. That means carrying a full size 1911 is out. Actually it means carrying a full size anything is out. In movies the hero is always shown just slipping a 1911 in the small of his back inside the waist of his jeans or trousers. My jeans are hard enough to keep up anyway so I'm not going to stress them more with the weight of a full-size 1911 pressing down back there. And for the same reasons mentioned above I'm not going to discuss, I don't wear suspenders anymore either. Nor do I wear button up shirts tucked into trousers or jeans: instead favoring pull over shirts and sweaters. Get them long enough and they'll cover a hip pocket handgun.

Duke shot these 10 rounds from the Model 442 at 10 feet. Five of the bullet strikes in center were fired slow fire.

Duke's "hip pocket handguns."

At left is a S&W Model 360 and at right is a S&W Model 442.

J-FRAME HAPPINESS

M y solution is very light, very small .38 Special revolvers. Specifically these are Smith & Wesson J-frames with alloy frames. One is the aluminum alloy frame Model 442, the so-called hammerless version, which likewise means it fires double action only. The other is their newer scandium alloy frame Model 360, which is capable of single or double action firing.

Right now some sharp eyed reader is saying. "Duke is sure dumb! That S&W Model 360 is a .357 Magnum." Well, it's chambered that way because some marketing genius at Smith & Wesson decreed it be so. If you can stand to shoot full-bore .357 Magnum loads through it there's something wrong with you. I tried that; one round was fired and I ejected the other four. It's a .38 Special in practicality if not in precise reality. But it did work on the marketing side of things, I suppose.

NO MAGIC NEEDED

U nloaded, the Model 360 weighs a mere 12 ounces. The Model 442 is 4 ounces more. Neither one is apt to pull someone's breeches to half-mast suddenly while in public, even without a belt or suspenders. Five rounds of ammunition add about 2.5 ounces to that. Even though it's a little heavier, I prefer the Model 442 because not having an exposed hammer it isn't likely to hang up on clothing.

Nor do I think that some sort of

magic ammunition is necessary for these two lightweights. With the reduced velocity possible from their stubby 1⅞"barrels I feel that no sort of jacketed soft point or jacketed hollow-point bullet is going to expand reliably. In fact both of these little .38s are filled with Black Hills .38 Special, 158-grain semiwadcutters. I chronographed five rounds from each revolver. The Model 442 gave 760 fps and the Model 360 gave 707 fps. Will .38 Special cases in the .357 Magnum length chambers of the Model 360 give those annoying carbon rings? Yes if enough of them are fired without cleaning.

Can I hit anything with these .38s?

Firing two handed, double action, slow fire and aiming from 10 feet I can keep five rounds inside about 3". Speeding things up I can still keep five rounds on one of John Taffin's hats at that range (Sorry John, just using that example to help illustrate a point …) and the PACT Mk IV timer said I was getting the five rounds out in 1.75 seconds.

Some smart aleck is now thinking, "But Duke lives in Montana. How does he get to a hip pocket handgun when wearing a heavy coat in winter?" Well, that's pretty easy. I just slip the little snub noses into a coat pocket. And maybe you should too?

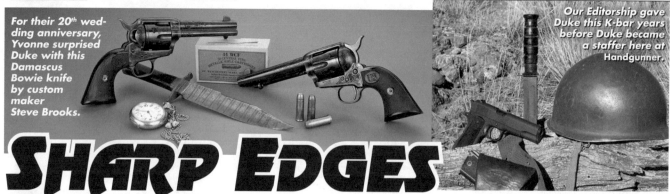

For their 20th wedding anniversary, Yvonne surprised Duke with this Damascus Bowie knife by custom maker Steve Brooks.

Our Editorship gave Duke this K-bar years before Duke became a staffer here at Handgunner.

SHARP EDGES

Recently there was a letter printed in these pages bemoaning the fact *Handgunner* sometimes prints knife articles. That caused me to give a moment's thought to my own sharp edges. I said to myself, "I'm not much of a knife guy: I'm a gun guy. That is except for my Spyderco folder and my Steve Brooks Damascus Bowie. And except for a couple of Damascus hunting knives. And except for the British Commando dagger I stumbled onto. And except for that big box full of bayonets that go with my military rifle collection. And except for my replica US Model 1860 cavalry saber and oh yeah, I can't forget the newest one: a genuine Japanese World War II officer's saber."

Well, I guess the bottom line is I *do* have a lot of sharp edges. Some of them, like the hunting knives, have seen their share of use. Others, like the replica US cavalry saber, are used only as photo props.

Steve Brooks is a Montana based custom knife and bullet

mould maker and a friend for over 20 years. His beautifully crafted Damascus knives bring hefty prices, but about 15 years back I finally afforded one for myself — a modest sized hunting knife. Then for our 20th wedding anniversary Yvonne knocked my socks off. She surprised me with a beautiful Brooks' Damascus Bowie knife. It has an 8" blade and a handle made of buffalo horn. Bowie knives are not the most practical of items nowadays but I treasure mine for obvious reasons.

Two of my knives have my name on them. One is a Damascus hunting knife with deer antler handle that has my name scrimshawed on its base. It simply arrived in the mail one day with a letter. Its West Virginia maker is a reader and since I was born and raised in that state he said he made that knife for me as a friendly gesture. The other one carries my nickname "Duke" engraved on its blade and was a birthday present from a friend. Again for obvious reasons I treasure them too.

USELESS EDGES

To a civilian bayonets are just about as useless as swords, which today are perhaps the most useless of all edged weapons. Still when I began assembling a collection of military rifles it seemed natural to obtain bayonets to go with them. I have a couple of the triangular type bayonets going with late 1800s rifle/muskets, a similar one fitting a Winchester 1873 .44-40 musket and other blade-type bayonets fitting Krags, Garands, Springfields, Enfields, Mausers, Arisakas and more.

Another rather useless edged weapon of military origin was one I found on one of my numerous road trips in a pawnshop in Fort Collins, Co. It's a dagger of the type the British issued to their Commandos in World War II. I believe they are called Fairbairn-Sykes fighting knives. This one has a 6" blade and grooved hilt of some sort of non-ferrous metal. Its only markings are "England" on the handguard and the numeral "1" near the end of the hilt. Besides dressing up an occasional photo with it, the only purpose it sees is in opening boxes. Its edges aren't that sharp but that point is wickedly so.

This replica cavalry saber is good for one thing — as a photo prop!

Uh-Oh, here we go again. Duke with a helmet and weapons! This time he's showing off a genuine Japanese World War II officer's sword recently given to him by a friend, and a Nambu. If you don't laugh at this, there's something wrong with you!

SWORD SILLINESS

And lastly there are the swords. I say they're the most useless of all edged weapons today because swords have absolutely no other practical use than in fighting. Guns serve much better for that. The replica cavalry saber is inexpensive and came from Dixie Gun Works. Except as a photo prop the only thing I've ever done with it is to tie a long piece of ribbon from the hilt. Then I've jammed it in the ground at the firing line of a silhouette match to serve as a wind-flag. That got laughs from my buddies.

The Japanese officer's sword is special to me. A few months back when I arrived at one of our Montana BPCR Silhouette events a friend walked up and handed me this "Samurai sword." He said, "Here add this to your World War II collection." It had Japanese writing under the hilt, which turned out to indicate it was handmade by a rather well known sword maker during World War II. That one will be with me forever.

Oh yeah, I almost forgot. Years before our editor Roy was my boss, I was visiting at his home. He gave me a K-bar like the US Marine Corps has issued for decades. It's not going anywhere either. I guess I am sort of a knife guy too.

THE COLT MODEL 1903 .32

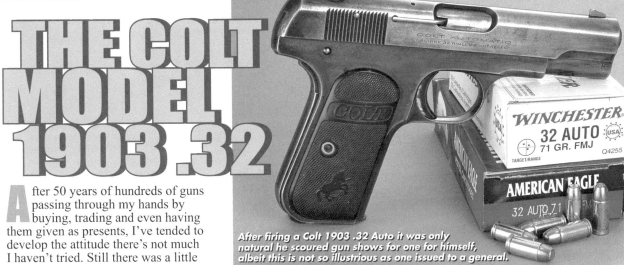

After firing a Colt 1903 .32 Auto it was only natural he scoured gun shows for one for himself, albeit this is not so illustrious as one issued to a general.

After 50 years of hundreds of guns passing through my hands by buying, trading and even having them given as presents, I've tended to develop the attitude there's not much I haven't tried. Still there was a little autoloader that always intrigued me even though I had never even fired one until 2010 — Colt's little Model 1903 .32 Auto Pocket Pistol.

Why the attraction to an obsolete pistol chambered for a dinky little cartridge? Because anyone who looks at a Colt Model 1903 has to see it was ages ahead of its time. In fact, in regards to pocket pistols, it's still ahead of its time, except for the dinky little .32 Auto chambering. And John M. Browning and Colt addressed that issue in 1908 by making another version chambered for .380 Auto.

Why do I think the Colt Model 1903 was ahead of its time? Look at the photos: no exposed hammer, a grip safety, very thin and not a sharp edge anywhere on it. Today gunsmiths get paid actual money to "melt" the edges of autoloaders. That means make them curved and smooth. The Colt Model 1903 came right from the factory already "melted." And show me a modern "pocket pistol" as thin as an '03 Colt. The gun itself is only .80" wide but the grips make it 1.10". Look at pocket pistols designed much later than the little Colt and you will see exposed hammers. Examples would be Walther's famous PPs and PPKs which appeared in the late 1920s. Certainly Walther's designers recognized the problem with exposed hammers on pocket pistols because those handguns got burrs instead of spurs to help prevent snagging on clothing. Better yet to not have one showing at all.

Right now someone is saying, "Yeah but those Walther pistols had double-action triggers and the old Colt was single action only." So what? The Colt 1903 had a grip safety and a thumb safety meaning it could be carried with a round chambered. There's no way the thing can go off until a hand firmly grasps it, which incidentally is when the thumb lays right on the safety. I've shot DA pocket pistols and I think the Colt '03 can be put into action just as fast as any double-action pocket pistol.

Duke Likes It

Back in the spring of 2010, I got my first chance to fire one of these little .32s, and what a specimen it was. It belonged to a friend here in Montana named Bill Smart, whose father, Jacob E. Smart just happened to retire from the US Air Force as a four star general. For many decades, and possibly still for all I know, when an American Army or Air Force officer attained general rank he had his choice of at least three handguns. Those were either a Colt Model 1903 .32, a Colt Model 1908 .380, or a US Model 1911 .45. General Smart picked a .32, and friend Bill let me introduce myself to the model by shooting his father's.

Consequently, it was only natural at the very next gun show I attended my eyes were searching tables for Colt Model 1903s. If there is any good at all to come from the downturn in this nation's economy it's that gun prices have dropped a bit. I was able to buy one cosmetically worn but mechanically fine for a darn good price.

Colt introduced this model with a 4" barrel but that was soon reduced to 3.7". Grips started out as hard rubber and evolved to checkered wood about 1924. Mine wears hard rubber grips. Weight is about 24 ounces. As usual for pocket pistols, sights hardly exist. The front sight is a little nub and the rear is a dovetailed blade with a tiny notch. When I can actually see them my '03 hits point of aim at 20' with 71-grain FMJ factory loads. Also as befits the *Shooting Iron* title of this column the entire gun will hold a magnet.

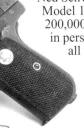

The US Government bought many thousands of the little Colt Model 1903s.

According to the *2005 Standard Catalog of Firearms* by Ned Schwing, between 1903 and 1945 Colt made 572,215 Model 1903s for the commercial market. About another 200,000 were sold to the American military. To put that in perspective more Model 1903 .32s were made than all the 1st Generation Colt SAAs and Colt New Service double action revolvers combined. With that many in circulation it's amazing more are not seen on used gun racks in stores or at gun shows. I guess I'm not the only one who likes them.

Duke's first firing of a Colt Model 1903 .32 Auto was with this general officer's version belonging to a friend.

SHOOTINGIRON™

Mike "Duke" Venturino

Photos: Yvonne Venturino

THUMB BUSTIN'
MUSINGS FROM
THE DUKE

DUKE'S LUCK

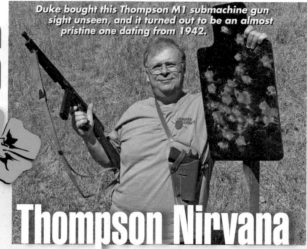

Duke bought this Thompson M1 submachine gun sight unseen, and it turned out to be an almost pristine one dating from 1942.

Thompson Nirvana

My luck in games of chance is absolute zero. Once in my early 20s I tried my hand at blackjack. After about 20 minutes the lady dealer said, "Mister, you have the worst luck of anybody I've ever seen. You shouldn't gamble." I've pretty much adhered to that advice ever since.

Also when it comes to hunting I bear a curse. That curse can range from prairie dogs to African game. Fellows have invited me to hunt the former with them saying, "The ground will appear alive there are so many of them running about." Then I've sat in the hot sun for hours firing perhaps a half-dozen or so rounds.

Africa is famous for its plenitude of game. My professional hunters told me usually on the first day or two they take their clients after warthog or impala in order to get them over their jitters. In 14 days we saw precisely one warthog, running away for all he was worth. Then we hunted for several days *just* for an impala buck without getting a single shot. One fellow said to me, "Yeah, but I've been in your office/gun room and there are antlers and African mounts on the wall." Certainly there are. Occasionally I've run into critters having worse luck than mine.

By the time my M1 Thompson arrived I had a book titled *American Thunder* by Frank Innamico. Sitting down with my new "Tommy-gun" I gave it a full examination. Duke's Luck! It was precisely as it had been made in 1942, right down to the inspector's stamps. The buttstock with reinforcing cross bolt was a later M1A1 version, but using my much-vaunted luck again I found a proper M1 cross bolt-less stock.

Back in the early '70s when I was struggling to finish college, one of my professors insinuated my grade in a tough but necessary class could be better if I helped him find a certain gun he had been searching for with no luck. He was awestruck when I had it the next day. Duke's Luck scored a good grade that day!

Just recently his majestic Editorship Roy wanted a special gun for La Belle Suzi's 2010 Christmas present. I told him "no sweat" and found what he wanted pronto and at a good price I might add. Duke's Luck strikes again and keeps his editor happy at the same time.

Someday I'm going to write a column about my luck in finding a wife!

Duke's luck benefited La Belle Suzi Huntington with this fine Colt Python.

Gun Magnet

Now to the other end of the spectrum. When it comes to finding good used guns I have few peers. Fellows have said to me, "If I could just follow you around and get the good used guns you pass up, I'd be happy."

My new quest for assembling a shooting collection of World War II firearms also has seen such luck. At a gun show in Bozeman last year I had just said to a friend, "Well my money is safe. There's nothing here I want." Then I looked down at a table to see a really nice US Army marked Colt Model 1911 .45 of 1918 vintage. A holster with it had a previous owner's name carved into it, along with the US Army's Signal Corps insignia and the year 1931. In better light I found the same name was visible on the bottom of the magazine.

Not only did I get it for a darn good price, but I can shoot it more accurately than any 1911 I've ever ownead.

That luck held when I started adding some full-auto submachine guns to my World War II collection. The second one I hunted for was a "Tommy-gun." But I wanted only the M1 or M1A1 version made from '42 to '44. I felt it was more the quintessential Thompson submachine gun of World War II fame. A friend told me about an Internet site called *Guns America* that listed items for sale. Sure enough, there was an M1 Thompson on there. The price was enough to take your breath away, but having sold a bunch of unused guns I could afford it. Also as with buying full-autos, you must make the deal, then wait while the government paperwork for transferring ownership is processed. I figuratively held my breath for the months while that happened, hoping I hadn't bought a "pig in a poke" as my father used to say.

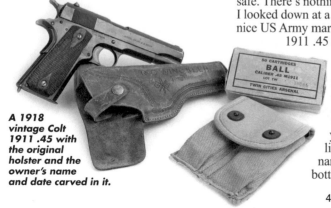

A 1918 vintage Colt 1911 .45 with the original holster and the owner's name and date carved in it.

SHOOTINGIRON ™

Mike "Duke" Venturino

A LIFETIME OF HATS

In my 6-plus decades I've worn many hats, speaking literally not figuratively. They have never been for adornment, never has there been a "Sunday go to meeting" hat hanging by my door. All have been for keeping my head warm, dry, or protected from the sun. If head protection wasn't called for then my hat was left at home, because I was (and still am) likely to just misplace it.

One sunny afternoon 40 years back, while working as a dude wrangler in Yellowstone National Park I let a pretty girl wear my wide brimmed hat while we rode horses. That evening my face was burned lobster red. After that girls had to furnish their own headgear. Except for baseball type caps, which just seem to grow around here, I've never built an assortment of

any kind of hat. If one disappeared it was replaced.

Way back in 1973, a friend and I got it in our heads to ride horses from Bozeman, Mont. through the mountains to Jackson, Wyo. The second day out while leading my horse in a terrible rain and windstorm, my hat blew off into the horse's face. He went nuts and bolted. In trying to hold onto the reins, I was whip-lashed into a rock filled ditch. My partner caught up the horse and said, "You should have seen that hat go! It never hit the ground the entire time it was in sight." He was totally uninterested in my lumps and bruises. Winds like that make stampede strings on hats handy. As soon as possible I bought another Stetson. I still have it.

HAT PRIZES

I like well-worn handguns, especially if I've owned them since new. The wear simply means I probably have gotten a considerable

Left: The Military Historical Tours group gave Duke this ball cap during the trip he made to Iwo Jima in 2008. The trip was a life's dream come true. Middle: Suzi Huntington once gave Duke this fur hat and he's never far from it during those Montana winters. Right: Duke bought this Stetson in 1973 after another hat blew away in a windstorm. He still has it. It does look a little disreputable doesn't it?

amount of pleasure from life while using them. The same goes for hats: I don't mind dirty, dusty, sweated, soaked and/or frayed. That means they were on my head while going about interesting pastimes. That western hat I bought back in 1973 is a good example. Its blemishes range from beer foam to blood and other bits of some critter's internals, put there because I'm not the most careful of knife users when dressing game. One friend's wife actually suggested I leave that hat outside when coming into their ranch house. I don't think she was kidding.

A couple of my prized pieces of headgear are indeed baseball caps. I have a Thunder Ranch one that I take better care of than most of my hats because it also says "staff" on it. Clint Smith has asked me a couple of times to help with classes there at the school and so he gave it to me. I'm very proud of that hat.

Another baseball cap of mine shows plenty of dirt and sweat stains because I wear it so often. It also says "Iwo Jima Reunion of Honor, 2008." Such a baseball cap was given to everyone who made that year's trip to the island to commemorate the 63rd anniversary of the battle. Visiting Iwo Jima was one of my life dreams come true.

My oddest hat is what I call a Norwegian fisherman's hat. It is brown leather and looks like something a deck hand on a North Sea fishing trawler would wear. That's probably exactly what it was because I found it under a bed in a hotel room in Oslo, Norway when there in 1993.

Lifetime Supply

Here's some irony. My most practical Montana winter hat was given to me by someone living in Southern California at the time. That was Suzi Huntington, who's the editor of our *American* COP magazine and wife of Editor Roy. We were at a Thunder Ranch get together in Texas one December, when an unusually fierce wind was blowing from the north. I don't know how Suzi came to have a rabbit fur hat with her but when she placed it on my frosty head she made a fan for life. It gets plenty of use around the place here every winter.

I have several original and replica steel military helmets hanging up in my office and gun vault and sometimes it gives me pleasure to do a "clown photo" with one for these pages. Some readers like those pictures and some think they're silly. Regardless I've not done my last helmet photo. At the same time I'm glad I've never had to wear one of those things for real. The respect I have for people who have done so is immense.

Aside from ordinary wool caps of the type I lose so often — to Yvonne's exasperation — I'll probably never buy another hat. I've got a lifetime's worth still hanging around my office on deer antlers and such and there's a lifetime of memories connected with them.

47

A Shoulder Holster THAT ISN'T

Duke with his 7X Leather "shoulder holster that isn't." The collie's name is Brady, and he's Duke's constant companion.

The rear has a simple adjustment system, which adds to the comfort.

I've been searching around for a good method to carry a handgun if I'm not wearing a belt. I haven't worn one for several years, for reasons too long to detail here. As I described in a previous *Handgunner* article, most shoulder holsters aren't a viable choice for someone as broad as me because I'd need gorilla length arms to reach the handgun. But photos showing the type of holster issued to American tankers in World War II intrigued me. Those guys were forever climbing in and out of hatches; in turn they couldn't have a belt holster hanging up every time they did. Instead, the holsters placed their 1911s in front, on their chests. In fact, I even bought a couple of replicas of such and found they make good photo props, but really didn't suit my needs. Besides they were fairly "cheesy" in quality.

Last winter at a gun show here in Montana, I met a young saddle maker. His name is Wes Daems and he does business as 7X Leather. Along with being a horseman, Wes is also an avid handgun shooter and wisely carries a big-bore revolver with him on his family outings into the Montana mountains. As I also learned four decades back, he realized packing a handgun around day in and day out, especially while riding a horse, can be an awful nuisance. Worn on the hip, it catches on everything from tree limbs to packhorse lead ropes. And big handguns can be very tiresome when packed in traditional shoulder holsters. It gets to feeling like you're toting a goose by the end of the day.

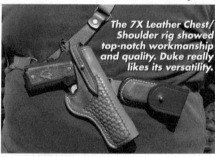

The 7X Leather Chest/Shoulder rig showed top-notch workmanship and quality. Duke really likes its versatility.

Convenient Carry

On our visit, Wes showed me a holster of his own design. I call it: a shoulder holster that isn't. It could also be called a cross draw holster — that isn't. It could be termed a chest holster, which for me, is what it is. Actually, it can be all three with the proper strap adjustment. After Wes showed me his rig, I asked him to build a rig for me. He asked, "For what handgun?" Well, I'm not likely to ride about the mountains on a horse ever again so instead of making it for a big sixgun I told him to build it for a full-size 1911. That way it can accommodate one of my several, ranging from a Les Baer Thunder Ranch Special .45 to a Kimber Pro Compact .40 S&W.

Let me say up front, Les Daem's holster idea isn't so much for concealed carry as for *convenient* carry. For outdoorsmen in cold weather, his holster rig can be worn under a coat. For open carry in summer garb, an outdoorsman can adjust the straps so the holster is lower to the offside position, much like a cross draw. Conversely, the straps can be adjusted to position the holster right in the middle of the chest, over the heart. That's proven best for me. Another benefit is various holsters and magazine pouches can be substituted in the same basic harness. I think my next holster will be for my little Colt 1903 .32 and we'll see if the rig can function for concealed carry.

A Proper Holster

Workmanship on this rig is top notch. The holster and spare magazine pouch are made of sturdy saddle leather and the straps are much lighter, pliable leather. One thing I was happy to see that Wes and I agreed about was there are no snaps in the rig because, in my experience, snaps often cease snapping. Instead he uses snubs and split holes for safety straps.

Just last weekend, I was finally able to give my new holster its first workout while attending a vintage, bolt-action military rifle competition. Some of the stages required the competitor to first fire a handgun, so I took along a 1911-A1 .45 in the new holster. It was worn for hours, getting on and off an ATV, getting in and out of various positions for rifle shooting and getting the pistol in and out to be fired. Not once, not ever, was this leather rig an inconvenience or uncomfortable. And when I took it off at the end of the day there wasn't a sigh of relief. I've found the proper holster for me at this stage of my life.

A LIFE SPENT RELOADING

At the time of this writing, Duke actively reloads for all these handgun cartridges.

L ist making is an exercise in mental relaxation for me. Recently, I set about listing the handgun cartridges for which I currently handload, and that ballooned into how many different ones I've reloaded in my lifetime. It's a list with some odd twists and turns.

The total was 32, with handguns and die sets for 21 still on the active list. For semi-auto pistols they have ranged from .30 Luger to .45 ACP. For revolvers, on the small side they were .32 S&W Long, to .454 Casull on the big end. At this writing the smallest handgun cartridge for which I'm actively reloading is .32 Auto. The largest in volume is .45 Colt, but the largest in regards to bullet diameter is .455 Webley.

Like so many other reloaders of handgun ammunition, my career started with the .38 Special. That was in December 1966. Being a list keeper even at that age I jotted down the quantity assembled after each session at the bench. I quit doing that in 1980, by which time the total of .38 Specials had passed 60,000. Remember that was before the advent of commonly available progressive presses. On the other end of the spectrum are .357 SIG and .454 Casull; both calibers for which I have loaded only a few hundred rounds. They were fired in borrowed guns solely for the purpose of writing articles and I wasn't impressed with either round.

By the fall of 1968, I was reloading

for .44 Special, .44 Magnum and .45 Colt. At that time I also began assembling my first autoloading pistol cartridges. Naturally that was .45 ACP. Here's one of those odd twists. Over the decades, I have handloaded tens of thousands of three revolver cartridges, but perhaps only a couple thousand .45 ACPs. I seldom take those .44- or .45-caliber revolvers off the shelf now, but have fired many thousand .45 ACPs (and 9mm Luger) these past few years. That's because in building my World War II firearms collection, a couple each of .45 ACP and 9mm submachine guns have landed in my vault, along with handguns for same. I have one progressive press dedicated each to .45 ACP and 9mm Luger.

Duke's most recently reloaded oddballs are the 7.65 French Long for their Model 1935A and the Japanese 8mm Nambu for their Type 14 pistol.

Over the years, things change and so has the handgun cartridge for which Duke does the most reloading. Now .45 ACP and 9mm Luger are at the top of the list.

Duke Cussing?

H ere's an odd turn. The most cussing I did at a handloading bench was the first time I tried loading .44 WCFs (.44-40s) for a Colt SAA revolver. None of my rounds would chamber in a friend's 1890 vintage revolver. Reloading manuals said to use .427" bullets, but cartridges carrying them were too fat for the chambers. With research I discovered that early .44 WCFs used .425" bullets and sure enough, when my cast ones were sized that they fit perfectly.

With such a start it's probably odd that now .44 WCF (.44-40) is my favorite for revolvers. Reloading them requires a little bit of finesse and an eye for mating bullet specs to barrel and chamber mouth dimensions. When that is done my Colt and U.S. Firearms "Frontier Six-Shooters" are tackdrivers.

Speaking of tack drivers, there are four handgun cartridges I think are the inherently most accurate of the 32 which I've handloaded. Those are the .38 Special, .41 Magnum and .44 Magnum for revolvers and .40 S&W for pistols. In my experience, it's difficult to reload an inaccurate combination for them.

ODDBALLs

I n 45 years of handloading, I've seldom shied away from tackling oddball cartridges. In earlier years, some such were .38 Colt, .41 Colt, .44 American and .44 Colt. All of those were introduced with the so-called "heel-type" bullets fitting inside a cartridge case, as do .22 LR bullets, and carried their lubrication on the outside. Later .38 and .41 Colt evolved into "Long Colt" versions using hollowbase, inside-lubed bullets. I've handloaded them both ways and prefer the latter method.

I'm still not scared of tackling oddball cartridges. The most recent ones added to my list have been the French 7.65mm Long and the Japanese 8mm Nambu. The semi-auto handguns both are part of my World War II collection. I also handload for a 7.62x25mm Tokarov, although there has never been a handgun for that cartridge in my collection. Those cartridges have been fed to a PPsh41 submachine gun. Still I count it among my life's list of handgun cartridges reloaded.

From my vantage point, I can't see adding to my list in the future. In fact, just yesterday I made arrangements to sell my only .38 Super pistol, so I'm actually down to 20 handguns cartridges actively being loaded. That's still enough to keep me busy — especially since I cast bullets for all.

SLUGGING IT OUT

Recently a reader sent his Editorship, Roy, a request for a specific column about how one goes about "slugging" barrels. Since I've been doing that for decades, I got elected to detail the process. First, a word about why anyone would want to "slug" a barrel. The sole reason is to determine its size, or more precisely, its interior diameter. Why? So the proper size bullets can be sent through it. With most American made handguns of modern manufacture, slugging a barrel is likely not necessary. Tolerances today are that good. With handguns of yesteryear, or modern ones of foreign make, it's possible their barrels can measure all over the map.

Also, there's this to consider. If you are going to only handload factory jacketed bullets in your handguns, or fire only factory loads, I say don't bother. You will be restricted by the diameters available anyway. However, if you're going to cast your own bullets or fire commercially cast bullets, then it pays to know what diameter you need.

Duke's USFA .45 single action's barrel measures right at .451" in its grooves.

Tap the lead slug through the barrel, taking care it lands somewhere soft. You don't want to damage your slug.

Get The Lead Out

First off you'll need pure lead "slugs." For that purpose I bought a wide variety of pure lead round balls for muzzleloaders as sold by Hornady and Speer. For the slugging process I pick one much larger in diameter than the barrel to be checked. For instance, if it will be a .357 Magnum then I use a .375" pure lead round ball. If it's a .45 caliber then I use a .490" one.

Next you need a non-metallic hammer, like a leather or wooden mallet or a weighted rubber hammer. Don't use a metal hammer of any sort to pound a slug into a barrel! Trust me, you'll mess up the crown. Also you'll need a short piece of hardwood dowel a bit longer than the handgun's barrel.

Lay the pure lead round ball atop the barrel's muzzle. It doesn't hurt to put a squirt of oil on it. Then pound it in flush with the muzzle using your non-metallic hammer. See why now? By hammering in a much larger size ball, there will be a lead flange around the muzzle. That's okay, just toss it aside. Now the slug in the bore will have parallel sides easily measured. Using the piece of hardwood dowel, tap the slug all the way through the barrel. Here's a tip learned from hard experience. If the barrel is permanently mounted, as with a revolver, place its butt on something soft so you don't chip the grips. Of course if the barrel is easily dismounted, like a 1911, take it out of the handgun for slugging.

POTENTIAL GLITCHES

With many older guns it may just fall through once started. Don't worry, that's a sign of a tapered bore. With some other guns you may notice the slug slides through very smoothly. That's a sign of fine manufacturing quality. With some guns you may notice tight and loose spots. Again that's not a great cause for worry. It's a sign of modern manufacturing quality, which often does not equal bygone years. Here's another tip. Be prepared to catch the slug as it exits the barrel. There's no sense in going to this trouble and then have the soft lead slug deformed by hitting a hard floor.

Now, all one need do is measure the slug with a set of calipers or a micrometer. Is it really that simple? Yes, it is if the gun in question has an even number of grooves. You just measure the opposing ones and that's your barrel's groove diameter. Conversely, that's not possible with barrels having an odd number of grooves. For instance all Smith & Wesson revolvers have 5-groove barrels. What to do then? Well that requires a bit extra and we'll detail that in the next issue.

I like to give an example of what is detailed so my USFA "Custer Battlefield" single-action .45 was slugged as Yvonne photographed the process. I was sure it would measure .451" and sure enough, that was precisely what happened. That's all there is to it. I could have slugged a half-dozen barrels in the time it took me to write this description, so don't be afraid to give it a try.

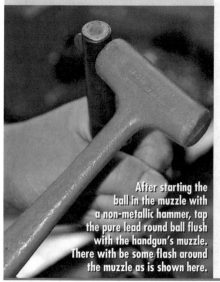

After starting the ball in the muzzle with a non-metallic hammer, tap the pure lead round ball flush with the handgun's muzzle. There will be some flash around the muzzle as is shown here.

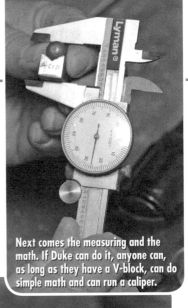

SLUGGING IT OUT: PART 2

In the last issue, I wrote a "How-To" about slugging handgun barrels. I finished it by saying measuring a slug from a barrel with an odd number of grooves is more difficult because the grooves don't oppose one another. Let me begin with a brief overview of slugging a barrel for those who might not have read the last issue.

A great many handguns have barrels with actual groove diameters varying from their nominal specs. This was common in bygone times, but still is with some foreign pistols and revolvers. Forget all about it if you're going to only shoot factory-made jacketed bullets because you can't vary from the sizes manufacturers offer anyway. The place slugging is beneficial is with lead alloy bullets, especially those made yourself. Commercially sold lead alloy .45-caliber bullets can be commonly had measuring .451", .452" or .454". If you're casting them yourself you can also size them to .450", .453" or .455".

Slugging a barrel is ultra simple. It consists of merely pounding a piece of lead down the handgun's barrel and measuring it. There are a few caveats to consider. First, use only pure lead for your slug. Second, tap it into the barrel's muzzle with something non-metallic, such as a weighted rubber hammer or a hardwood stick. Next, tap it on through with a piece of wooden dowel. Don't use a metal cleaning rod! And don't let the slug bounce off the floor as it exits the barrel as being so soft it will be deformed.

Next comes the measuring and the math. If Duke can do it, anyone can, as long as they have a V-block, can do simple math and can run a caliper.

To begin slugging a barrel, you'll need something non-metallic to hammer with, and a pure lead slug significantly larger than the bore to be slugged. Duke likes to use round lead balls.

Duke's Secret

And here's my own personal tip. Pure lead round balls as sold for cap-and-ball pistols make perfect slugs, but use ones considerably larger than the barrel to be measured. This way the slug gets a good length of parallel sides to measure. For instance, to slug .44-caliber barrels I always start with a pure lead round ball measuring from .451" to .457".

For a demonstration, I slugged the barrels of a S&W revolver because, to the best of my knowledge, all that company's revolvers have 5-groove rifling. This sample was an N-frame .44 Special, 2nd Model Hand Ejector made in 1929. I had never slugged it previously, having been satisfied to accept S&W's nominal spec as .429".

A .457" pure lead round ball was tapped through the .44's barrel. Now this is where the skill of a machinist and knowledge of mathematics comes into play. By the way, I don't have either one. Once, after writing I was unable to measure a slug accurately because it came through a barrel with an odd number of grooves, I received an e-mail from a reader named Ken Caldwell. He has both machining skill and math knowledge and he offered to make me a V-block so I could measure barrels with an odd number of rifling grooves. What a V-block consists of is a small piece of steel with a V-shaped trough cut into it. The slug rests in that.

Once nestled in the V-block, a formula is used to determine the slug's diameter. "A" is the measurement from the bottom of the block to the top of the slug. "C" is the distance from the bottom of the V-shaped trough to the bottom of the block. "C" is subtracted from "A" to get the value of "B." "B" is then multiplied by the constant .8944 to get the diameter of the slug. Ken also told me "C" is always unique to each V-block, but I don't know how to determine it!

A V-block like this one is needed to measure slugs from odd-numbered rifled barrels.

AND THE ANSWER?

For the .44, my "A" measurement was .826". My V-block's "C" measurement is .34658". Subtracting "C" from "A" gave a figure of .47942". That multiplied by my V-block's constant of .8944 gave the measurement of the slug as .42879". Since my calipers are only hobby grade, which can safely be rounded off to the nearest thousandth — or .429"!

MORE REVOLVER ACCURACY VARIABLES

Forcing cones are important too. Many vintage revolvers have rifling coming right to the butt-end of the barrel such as this 1907 Colt New Service .38 WCF (.38-40). Note the leading caused by no forcing cone.

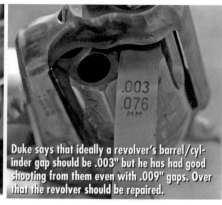

Duke says that ideally a revolver's barrel/cylinder gap should be .003" but he has had good shooting from them even with .009" gaps. Over that the revolver should be repaired.

In the last two issues I've detailed how to slug handgun barrels so lead alloy bullets of the proper size will be used in them. However, that's just one of the factors involved in handgun accuracy — especially revolver accuracy.

Revolver cylinders add about another five to eight dimensions to the mix, depending on how many chambers are there and how uniform they are. Long ago I learned just matching a lead alloy bullet to a revolver barrel's groove diameter did not insure it would be delivered to the target with precision. For instance, I slugged the barrel of a 1960s vintage Colt SAA .45 right at its nominal .451". Therefore, I loaded my .45 cast bullets to .451" and got disappointing groups.

For many years, I just blamed it on the .45 Colt as being a cartridge of inherently poor accuracy. That was nonsense.

Finally I figured out the problem was Colt .45s of that vintage (and today) have notoriously large chamber mouths. I just took a break from this keyboard and measured all six chamber mouths of my 1967 vintage Colt SAA .45. — they were all .456".

If you start a relatively hard .451" bullet out in a .456" chamber mouth it's going to get slammed into the barrel's forcing cone cocked off its axis. My solution has been twofold. If .45 Colt bullets must be hard (Brinell hardness number 12 or above) then I size them .454". Conversely, if they can be soft, say of 1-20 tin to lead alloy (BHN of 10) and used at speeds under 1,000 fps, then they can be sized .452". The pressure of powder ignition will cause softer bullets to obturate or fill the chamber mouths.

GAPS & CONES

Things like this impair accuracy: one chamber mouth at .453" and another at .455". Cylinder from a 1990s vintage 3rd Generation Colt SAA .45.

Another measurement anyone shooting revolvers should take note of is the gap between the barrel and the cylinder. If it gets too large the revolver will be spitting particles of powder and bullet, which is downright distracting. When excessive, the loss of powder gases will substantially reduce velocity. I've actually seen revolvers with large-barrel/cylinder gap deliver good precision, but it's still a thing to avoid. So what's excessive? In my opinion, barrel/cylinder gaps should run from .003" to about .006". Up to about .009" isn't uncommon, and a revolver with gap that large can still be serviceable. Revolvers with gaps larger than that should be taken to a good gunsmith or returned to their manufacturers for repair.

There's one other important factor in revolver accuracy hard to quantify. That is the smoothness and angle of the barrel's forcing cone. The forcing cone of a revolver barrel should act like a precision funnel, allowing the bullet to enter it, and then center it with the barrel. Forcing cones should not be abrupt or rough, and they often are on newly manufactured revolvers. Heck, they often are on vintage ones too! As the photo shows, my Colt New Service .38 WCF (.38-40) has no forcing cone at all. The rifling comes right to the butt-end of the barrel. Rough revolver forcing cones are evident by the amount of lead fouling accumulated in them.

The Fix

Brownell's, the gunsmith tool and goodie supplier, sells forcing cone reaming kits. I'm told by those who know more than me the optimum forcing cone angle is 11 degrees. My gunsmith buddy Tom Sargis has that kit and has cut many of my revolvers with it. With some I've noted a definite increase in precision. With others I've noticed no change at all. What I have *never* encountered was a decrease in accuracy after a revolver's forcing cone was cut and smoothed.

While on the subject of measuring tools, to check cylinder chamber mouths I bought a set of plug gauges from machine a tool supply outfit called ENCO. There are 250 in a set, in .001" increments from .250" to .500" and cost me less than a hundred bucks delivered to my door. As for measuring barrel/cylinder gaps, the common feeler gauges used for setting spark plugs are available at any automotive parts store and work just fine.

If you're a handloader, especially one using lead alloy bullets, and you take note of your revolver's dimensions and prepare loads accordingly, your results will almost always be very satisfying.

MACHINE RESTS

LOVE AT FIRST SIGHT?

I love pistol machine rests!

Handguns can't be sighted in properly when mounted in a Pistol Machine Rest. Their recoil dynamics are totally different than when handheld.

My job would be much more difficult without them. The alternative to a pistol machine rest is to shoot handguns from a sandbag rest. Although never very good at sandbag shooting I can do it — for a short period. After a bit my eyes blur, my hands get sore, and I tend to start jerking triggers. Then I never know if flyers are caused by me or by a fault of guns or ammo. My limit for group shooting from sandbag rest is perhaps two score rounds of light to moderate power (.22 LR to .44 Special) and not more than a dozen full-bore loads from magnums.

On the other hand, when using a machine rest I've fired several hundred rounds in an afternoon, and figure the results are as valid for the last cluster as for the first. The hitch is changing targets, as in it's a time consuming 50-yard roundtrip after every group. On my luckiest days I've conned Yvonne into being my target changer, but usually can only prevail with considerable whining about my bum knee.

Before I had my own home range, a Lee Pistol Machine Rest was handy. It needs no permanent mounting because the handgun actually isn't anchored to the rest. It's a sort of brace affair. The handgun, sans grips, is mounted between aluminum grip adaptors, which are then pushed against stops in the base plate. Although still handheld, it's aimed the same each time. Back in the '70s I made up a portable bench out of an old redwood picnic table. Then I would find a suitable backstop on secluded public land and be able to start shooting in a matter of minutes. Too bad Lee Rests have been out of production for decades now. It was a good idea.

THE RANSOM

Once I owned a permanent place to shoot I transitioned to a Ransom Pistol Machine Rest. With this setup the pistol is clamped into the rest, which means the entire apparatus must be solidly anchored. Recoil from powerful handguns is nigh on an irresistible force. Get a finger between a bench top and big revolver's butt when it's fired and you'll agree.

So, when I had my shooting house built some years back the contractor put in a beam for the Ransom Rest as part of the construction. It does not shift. Still you cannot bolt the handgun into its grip adaptors and start testing with the first round. To mount up a pistol or revolver in the Ransom Rest first its grips are taken off. Then its bare grip frame is put into special aluminum grip adaptors lined with a dense synthetic material. Those are fastened into the machine rest, the handgun's sights aligned on target, and shooting starts.

The sights won't stay aligned where you started. Recoil will cause the handgun's grip frame to settle into the grip adaptors, which causes the bullet's point of impact to climb. Personally, before paying attention to groups, I fire at least 20 rounds of fairly hot loads to settle the handgun in. Then test shooting commences.

Duke at work with Ransom Pistol Machine Rest with a S&W Model 23 Outdoorsman mounted. He can shoot all day like this with little fatigue.

38-40 1¼"
TRAIL BOSS

When time allows, Duke likes to shoot 12-shot groups from revolvers so each chamber (of sixguns) is used twice.

9   10   9   8

THINGS YOU CAN LEARN

When in a hurry to meet a deadline I'll often settle on 5-shot groups because it saves time both in reloading chores and shooting. On occasions when I get my life planned a bit in advance, I prefer 12-shot groups from sixguns or 10-shot groups from autoloaders. A dozen rounds through a sixgun means every chamber is fired twice. If one chamber tends to throw flyers it's immediately evident. Flyers from the same chamber don't happen often, but on occasion I have seen one chamber giving better precision than the other five.

Once I mounted up my old Smith & Wesson Military & Police .38 Special of 1940s vintage and fired five, 5-shot groups from each *chamber* using factory 148-gr. wadcutter ammunition. All chambers averaged less than 1.50", but *one* of them averaged less than 1".

Now here's a solid fact although I've read differently on the Internet: You cannot sight in a handgun when it's mounted in a machine rest. Having it bolt into that apparatus changes recoil dynamics. In other words, a handgun does not recoil as freely as when handheld. In my experience most, if not all, shoot much lower than where their sights are aimed when machine-rest mounted.

Admittedly most handgunners do without a pistol machine rest, but I dearly love mine!

Duke's Hungarian PA63 9mm Makarov using Western Powders Accurate #2. Range was about 50'.

POWDERS FOR PISTOLS

For the first time in 45 years as an avid handloader I find myself loading more cartridges for pistols than for revolvers. At this moment I'm set up to reload these nine pistol calibers: 7.65x25mm Tokarov, .32 Auto (aka 7.65mm Auto), 7.65mm French Long, 8mm Japanese Nambu, .380 Auto (aka 9mm Kurz), 9mm Parabellum (aka 9mm Luger), 9mm Makarov, .40 S&W and .45 Auto.

You might think it would be easy to settle on one propellant to use in all nine cartridges, but nope, it's not. Granted all those autoloading cartridge cases are of small volume, so the slow-burning powders associated with magnum revolver rounds can be discounted immediately. Still, we're left with dozens from which to choose. Lyman's *Reloading Handbook 49th Edition* has a fairly comprehensive list of today's available propellants. Generally speaking those suitable for autoloading pistols range in burning rate (fast to slow) from Norma's R-1 at number one to Alliant's Blue Dot at number 43.

Even someone as enthusiastic as me cannot claim to have tried every one of those propellants. I can say I've used the majority of them at one time or another and to one degree or the other. In 1968, when I started handloading for my first

Duke uses these five powders for reloading his nine semi-auto pistol calibers.

pistol cartridge, the .45 Auto, the only handgun propellants available to me where were Bullseye and Unique. Therefore, I've burned scores of pounds of those two over the decades, with much of it fired in autoloading pistols. Conversely, the only time I've used Western Powder's Accurate #2 in autoloaders was a reloading project on pocket pistols a couple years back. To my pleasant surprise Accurate #2 gave best results in .32 Auto, .380 Auto and even 9mm Makarov.

LAZY RESEARCH

With two of the listed calibers, I've only ever tried one propellant. Those were the 7.65mm French Long for a Model 1935A, and 8mm Japanese Nambu for a Type 14. Why have I not tried others? Mostly because of fear. You see, there's just no data available for reloading those two very oddball cartridges. In fact one of the powder companies contacted me to see what I was using for my 8mm Nambu.

The sole propellant I've tried with them is Hodgdon's Titegroup, and what I did was start out low and then work up a couple tenths of a grain at a time with my chosen bullet weights until perfect functioning was achieved. That happened with 3 grains under 81-grain .313" cast bullets in the French round, and 3.5 grains under 106-grain cast bullets in the Japanese round.

A natural question would be, "Duke, why did you start out with Titegroup in the first place?" Simply because it was the closest suitable powder can to where I was sitting, and I was too lazy to get up and hunt for anything else! I've been perfectly happy with the results and doubt if I'll ever bother to experiment further.

LEAST FINICKY

Duke is currently handloading for these nine semi-auto pistol cartridges. Left to right: 7.62x25mm Tokarov, .32 Auto (aka 7.65mm Auto), 7.65mm French Long, 8mm Japanese Nambu, .380 Auto (aka 9mm Kurz), 9mm Parabellum (aka 9mm Luger), 9mm Makarov, .40 S&W and .45 Auto.

Opposed to that has been the work I've done with .40 S&W using my Kimber 1911. I've tried many powders with a wide variety of cast and jacketed bullets in that pistol, with considerable test shooting done from my machine rest. I've yet to find a powder in burn rate between Bullseye and Unique that didn't give fine accuracy and perfect functioning. I think the .40 S&W has to be one of the least finicky autoloading cartridges I've ever experienced.

The same can be said for .45 Auto. There must be at least 40 powders good for the old .45. I started back in '68 with 5 grains of Bullseye and 225-grain cast bullets, and still like that load. However, upon dedicating a bench to a pair of Dillon Square Deal B presses in 9mm Luger and .45 Auto, I settled on W231 (aka HP38) for both. With 115-grain jacketed 9mm bullets and 120-grain cast ones, 4.4 grains is my *always* charge, and with lead 220- to 230-grain FMJ .45s, it's 5.4 grains.

One Powder? Never.

My autoloading "handgun" for 7.62x25mm Tokarov is a semi-auto only copy of the Soviet PPs43. It has a rather heavy bolt needing high-pressure loads to get it to cycle 100 percent. Perfect functioning only came when I coupled 6 grains of Unique with Hornady's 86-grain jacketed soft point bullets.

Those five powders cover my autoloading pistol needs. Still, a fellow asked me, "Duke, what would you do if limited to only one powder for all, as is the case in some highly restricted European nations?" My immediate answer was, "I would leave there."

Duke always considers it near magical that shiny bullets can be made from grungy looking lead.

LYMAN'S CAST BULLET HANDBOOK
4TH EDITION

I've written this many times but I'll say it again. When I started handloading late in 1966, at that time and in my locale casting bullets wasn't an option — it was a necessity. An older gent in the local target pistol shooting club sold me a gas-fired lead pot and another sold me a Lyman bullet mould for a .38 Special wadcutter, Lyman #358432. From the very beginning it fascinated me I could take grungy-looking lead alloy, melt it, pour it into a bullet mould and upon opening the blocks a shiny bullet would drop

out. Not only did those new bullets look good, they were accurate enough I eventually became reasonably proficient with my S&W K38 revolver.

In those days solid information on how to produce good cast bullets was not overly abundant. There did exist a book called *Handbook Of Cast Bullets* printed by the then-named Lyman Gunsight Corporation. It was copyrighted 1958 and full of information. Neither was it found in great abundance, but a third member of that pistol shooting club loaned me his copy to read, stressing he wanted it back.

That book was greatly admired by me, but it was so rare about three decades passed before I finally obtained a copy of my own. In the interim, Lyman published two more editions. Neither of them are dated, but by my memory the second edition appeared in

the early 1970s and the third in the early 1980s. Their tattered condition is physical proof I've used them heavily.

Then late in 2009 there occurred the greatest compliment ever bestowed on me during my gun'riting career. The now-named Lyman Products Corporation asked *me* to be the primary writer for the informational chapters of their *Cast Bullet Handbook 4th Edition*. I say "primary" because of 18 informational chapters, I wrote 15. Three specialized chapters were contributed by others. Still in the book's table of contents I'm listed as author, which is a source of great pleasure to me every time I open it.

I won't say it was my brain that dreamed up those 15 topics. Lyman listed a general idea and then let me tackle it with no interference. Writing it during the winter of 2009/2010 was also one of the most pleasurable events of my career.

THE BOOK

Here's a brief synopsis of what the *Cast Bullet Handbook 4th Edition* offers you. Cast bullet date-ranges for handguns begins with the .30 Luger (aka 7.65mm Luger) and goes to the .500 Smith & Wesson. In between are 32 other pistol and revolver cartridges. Some are as new as the .480 Ruger and .45 GAP, while other rounds covered are quite old and have been given new leases on life by the popularity of the cowboy action sport. Examples are the .44 S&W Russian and .45 S&W Schofield.

Also as a departure from previous Lyman cast bullet manuals, this new 4th Edition does not present data only on the company's own designs. There's also data on Lee, Redding/SAECO and RCBS cast bullet numbers.

Duke has all four editions of Lyman's cast bullet handbooks. Duke is pleased to be listed as the author on the newest edition.

OBVIOUS TRENDS

Having all four of Lyman's cast bullet books on my desks allows me to see some of the changes in the firearms industry since 1958. Regarding smokeless propellants, the first cast bullet handbook mentions only Bullseye, Unique and 2400 along with a couple other long discontinued types. In the fourth edition, there are 13 smokeless powders listed for .44 Magnum, 15 for .45 Colt and a total of 19 different types for .45 ACP. I wish I could claim some credit for the data sections but alas that cannot be. Rightly so, Lyman garnered that information from their well-equipped laboratory in Connecticut. None of it came from my shooting range (aka: horse pasture) in Montana.

With the immense increases in prices of factory jacketed bullets, and likewise increases in the cost of shipping factory-produced cast bullets, I foresee strong incentive for people to take up bullet casting as was necessary a half-century back. For those who would be interested in learning about casting and those already casting but needing fresh data, I recommend taking a look at Lyman's new *Cast Bullet Handbook 4th Edition*. And I confess, I'm proud of the final product!

Duke is still an avid fan of casting bullets, even after 46 years of doing it.

This group of about 3" was fired at approximately 10 feet with the VOCO FP45, and it was the only group Duke was willing to fire!

VINTAGE ORDNANCE COMPANY

CAN YOU SAY OUCH?

Photos: Yvonne Venturino

The VOCO FP45 comes complete with facsimile waxed cardboard carton, a small cardboard box for extra .45 ACP rounds as did the originals, and even a small piece of wooden dowel for ejecting empties.

LIBERATOR .45

Clandestine organizations can come up with some weird ideas. In regards to World War II and weapons the United States' FP45 has to be one of the weirdest. It was a one pound, single shot, all-metal, unrifled pistol taking the .45 ACP round. Its purpose was for dropping behind enemy lines in both Europe and Asia so resistance groups could use them to shoot armed German or Japanese troops. Then the shooter could make off with the dead soldier's better weapon.

Evidence this wasn't one of the brightest ideas military minds dreamed up is that according to the Wikipedia website, there is not a single documented case of one being used for its intended purpose. That's not too hard to accept considering armed enemy soldiers weren't often encountered alone, and also the noise a .45 ACP makes is apt to bring running all other enemy soldiers in hearing distance. There was one other thing for the shooter to consider. A .45 ACP bullet fired in an unrifled barrel was only going to be effective at close range. *Very* close range!

Never mind the feasibility factor the United States Army had a million FP45s produced in mid-1942. Manufacturer was the Guide Lamp division of General Motors, which up to that point had produced headlights for the automotive industry. Guide Lamp was also the maker of the later M3 submachine gun commonly called the "grease gun." Cost of the FP45s was said to be $2.40 each. When the Office of Strategic Services (OSS) was organized to serve as America's first clandestine warfare organization, the army turned the FP45s over to them.

FP45s came in a waxed cardboard box complete with a 10-round pack of .45 ACPs and even a small piece of wooden dowel to punch out the empty case after firing. More usable was a sheet of instructions in cartoon drawing-form showing how to load, fire and unload the FP45.

Despite the huge number of FP45s made in 1942 originals are very rare today. I've seen the pistol alone priced at over a grand and have never seen one with an original box, much less the paper instruction sheet.

This facsimile of the original cartoon-like instruction sheet issued with US Government made FP45s comes with VOCO's replica FP45.

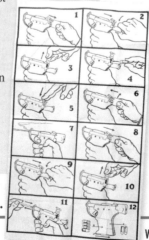

Rifling And...

But, all things about World War II have become popular so a small company named Vintage Ordnance (VOCO) has seen a market for new FP45s. Although I don't have an original FP45 in my collection to compare this sample to, it does appear identical to all photos I've seen of them.

The card accompanying VOCO's reproduction says their FP45s differ in two regards. One is the barrel must have rifling. Smoothbore pistols are proscribed by Federal regulations. Also mandated by the Feds are serial numbers and company markings. The first is printed in the front of the grip and the latter is beneath the barrel, inside the triggerguard.

Each of the VOCO FP45s come in a facsimile of the original waxed cardboard box, complete with another small cardboard box in which 10 rounds of .45 ACP will fit, the wooden dowel and the sheet of instruction art. Also worthy of note is VOCO can supply non-firing dummy versions or ones capable of only firing .22 blanks. The information card also says VOCO's FP45's barrel, tube strap and breech block are made of 1050 medium carbon, cold rolled steel while the cocking piece is cast of dense zinc alloy.

SHOOTING IT?

Test shooting of VOCO's FP45 was the briefest I've ever done. On-hand were some US military .45 ACPs dated from 1953. I loaded the pistol, and from 10 feet took aim at a paper target. The muzzleblast was loud and the recoil of a 230-grain FMJ bullet from a 1-pound pistol was bad! My hand hurt. Two more shots were fired and the group formed as shown in the photo. Then I was done — my hand was bleeding. I should also mention I figured a double tap with an FP45 took about 90 seconds. No wonder nobody tried to use them for their intended purpose.

Still, a collection of World War II military handguns will have a small gap without an FP45. That is the intended purpose of this replica — not an afternoon's plinking session!

HANDGUN ESTHETICS

Even a pistol as utilitarian as the US Model 1911A1 can be gussied up with finish and grips to make it look good, like this Les Baer Thunder Ranch Special.

Why are so many of today's handguns ugly? Do handgun manufacturers test design applicants for a sense of esthetics and then not hire any who have it? Used to be at movies I would annoy Yvonne endlessly by identifying whatever model of handgun someone on screen was using. Such as, "That guy's got an S&W Model 19 with 2½" barrel, or that Japanese officer has a German P38 instead of the Nambu he should be packing." Now if someone asked me what handgun anyone on screen was holding I'd have to say, "Don't know but it was big, square-shaped and black.

I blame a lot of this on Europeans. They hardly ever had a lick of sense about what a handgun should look like, especially the British. Europeans had one bright spot among handguns. It was what we know as the Luger, although there never was a Luger factory as such. Someone might ask, "But what about the Browning Hi-Power made in Belgium? They're decent looking handguns." My point exactly; they were designed by American John M. Browning.

When I was going to movies as a kid, if the bad guy was a European he usually pulled out a Luger before falling to an American good guy shooting a S&W Military & Police .38 or Colt Model 1903 or 1908 Pocket Pistol. Going back even farther to black and white movies on late shows, European or Asian bad guys sometimes would pull out Broomhandle Mausers. They were ugly too, but at least you wouldn't mistake one for any other handgun.

American Panache

Compare those to American-designed handguns. Sam Colt got his early cap-and-ball sixguns a bit blocky, but by the 1860s they were extremely graceful. By 1873, with the Colt Single Action Army there was hardly a right angle anywhere. Smith & Wesson Model #3s weren't quite so esthetically pleasing but still not bad. By necessity, Misters Smith and Wesson were swayed by Russian gold into redesigning their Model #3 for large sales, but they certainly complained about how ugly their revolvers became. By 1878, they returned to their natural American inclination and brought out the much more visually satisfying New Model #3.

American revolvers from the 19th century: A Colt Model 1861 "Navy" (left) and a Colt Single Action Army.

The Austrians started our dilemma of soulless handguns with the Glock. Black, lots of synthetics and square as a brick. Now everyone else has had to copy them. I get it. They work. They shoot every time. They don't rust. All that is important. Even my own wife chose one as her packing pistol. My complaint is this — can't synthetics be used to build pistols that still look *good*? Can't a pistol be built today with graceful lines and still be reliable? Couldn't polymers be molded into rounded parts such as the slide on a Colt Model 1903 Pocket Pistol? Does every new pistol have to hold a bazillion rounds so its grip is as big as a beer can?

Used to be "gunny" sorts of men took great personal pride in their handguns. There are plenty of well-used Colt SAAs around that were ordered factory engraved. I emphasize well used because the buyers of those fancy revolvers didn't just set them in a drawer somewhere; they packed them in holsters. Same with Colt 1911s and Smith & Wesson N-frames. Ever wonder why the above types of handguns were so often sold in nickel-plated versions? It was because they looked great! Ever notice how handsome a handgun is if the grip material contrasts with the metal finish? Even a utilitarian design like the 1911 can be gussied-up quite a bit with a little imagination.

Duke says about the only time Europeans got handgun esthetics right was with the Luger.

SOME FLASH?

In fact, fancy after-market grips were probably the most common way professional gun-toters of a past era personalized their handguns. Used to be I always took note of what cops were carrying in their holsters, whether they were giving me a traffic ticket or just sitting at a donut shop. Those wearing stock, as-issued handguns, I would have bet couldn't hit a bull in the butt at a dozen paces. When I saw a cop's handgun with fancy grips, my estimation of their ability grew a notch or two. If the handgun was engraved or had some sort of fancier finish then I figured he must be a "pistolero." I might have been wrong but those were my initial impressions. I'd like to know what our Editorship, Roy, packed in his 20-year career. Might be interesting, eh? *(Check out the* Insider *in this issue! -Roy)*

Nowadays, all cops have big, square, black pistols. No fancy finishes, no custom grips, no pride of possession. Nothing to indicate which of them might even be a good shot. Well, some carry 1911s nowdays and I'll bet some of those are gussied-up a bit. Usually a cop with a 1911 in his holster is a gunnie. As far as handgun esthetics goes, I'm glad I grew up in a bygone era.

WHAT'S WRONG WITH

RELIABLE AND PREDICTABLE

Duke picked up his 1940s vintage .38 Special S&W Military & Police Smith & Wesson for $65 the same year he and Yvonne were married.

A .38 SPECIAL?

Let me stress heavily I'm no self-defense expert, I'm no guru on home defense handguns and my total law enforcement career consists of being deputized in 1982 for all of 8 hours. Never, not once, have I had to resort to any firearm in a crisis situation. That said, to some family friends and even distant relatives I'm the only "gun-guy" they know. So it's not easy to fend them off when in this current political climate I'm asked what sort of guns they should buy for home defense. That puts me on the hot seat because I don't think novices to firearms should buy *any* gun unless they include some sort of training as part of the picture — and I stress that to them.

Even so I know some of the males think, "Yeah, yeah, just give me some info, I'll figure out the rest for myself." The Daniel Boone Syndrome is not dead. And, I know they will never go to the effort to get training or perhaps not even visit a range to gain experience further than taking their new gun to see if it actually goes off.

My stock answer to someone wanting to buy their first home-defense handgun is, "What's wrong with a .38 Special?" Some people, mostly those with just a grain of knowledge, have acted downright offended and say. "Why, that's not state of the art!" Here's where it gets hard because they have to be told, "*You're* not state of the art either."

Both state-of-the-art: Duke's 1940s vintage S&W and and the Springfield Armory XD.

In my honest opinion, double-action .38 Special revolvers may not be "state-of-the-art" but they are *stable in the art*. To me, it's a no brainer. Double-action .38 Special revolvers are easy handguns to train with. Opening one for loading consists of no more than pressing a latch or button and swinging the cylinder out. There's no trick to getting chambers charged since cartridges can only fit in one direction. I've actually seen novices try to load semi-auto magazines with the rounds backwards. Then the cylinder is pushed closed till it clicks in place. That's all there is to it.

A double-action revolver requires merely pressing the trigger to fire. There's no safety to remember, and no moving slide to bite fingers. Most double actions can also be fired single action, which is an aid when gaining familiarization with the handgun, or weak hands, even if not optimum for a potentially deadly situation.

Then there's the ammo factor. Some semi-autos can be amazingly finicky about ammo. I own one .40 S&W that will not feed certain types of factory ammo, yet runs 100 percent with others. That fact may not have even revealed itself to me if not for having access to many different types of factory ammo due to my occupation.

Conversely, a .38 Special double-action revolver always works if it's in good repair. They're about as foolproof as a handgun can get. Good quality factory ammo ranges from very light full wadcutter loads meant for target shooting, to +P types meant for personal defense. The .38 Special might have a bad rap among those who see nothing less than big bores as effective, but effective only counts if hits are made. Almost anyone can learn to handle a .38 Special with proficiency. That's not true of big-bore handgun calibers.

THE HANDGUNS

What about the exact .38 Special handgun? I almost always say, "Get a Smith & Wesson Model 10 with 4" barrel." Those are built on Smith & Wesson's medium (K) frame and are heavy enough so recoil is mild. A 4" barrel doesn't deliver intimidating muzzle blast like a snubnose. The lighter .38 Special double actions, such as Smith & Wesson's variations of Chief's Special on their light (J) frame, are better suited to experienced shooters. This is even truer of the new breed of extra-light polymer double actions being put out now by Smith & Wesson, Ruger and Taurus.

Inquisitors have sometimes thought they would trip me up by asking, "You recommend a .38 Special for us but what do you have for yourself?" It's true a Kimber .40 S&W resides in my sock drawer, but even closer is a 12-gauge shotgun. That said, a S&W Model 442 goes with me nearly everywhere when traveling in-state, and I have at least two other .38 Specials (one a Model 10) placed strategically in our home. There's nothing wrong with a good .38 Special revolver.

COLT'S SAA IN BATTLE

As both a student of Plains Indian Wars history and enthusiastic handgunner I've paid special attention to documentable instances where revolvers saw action circa 1860-1890. Although standard US Army doctrine had each cavalryman issued with saber, carbine and handgun, surprisingly few mentions of sidearms in combat against warriors exist.

An exception to that happened on the afternoon of June 25, 1876 at the Little Bighorn Battle. That day the US 7th Regiment of Cavalry was divided into four distinct battalions. Five companies under the direct command of Lt. Col. George A. Custer were wiped out to a man, making "Custer's Last Stand" the most famous of all Indian fights. However, lesser known is that seven companies of the 7th Cavalry survived the battle, albeit with considerable casualties. Their siege on a Montana hilltop is one of the US Army's epic stories.

Colt Single Action Army .45 caliber revolvers played a significant role in allowing many 7th Cavalry troopers to get to the top of that hill. Every one of the approximately 600 troopers riding into the valley of the Little Bighorn that day packed one.

Every trooper of the 7th Cavalry carried a 7½"-barreled, .45-caliber Colt SAA revolver when they rode into the valley of the Little Bighorn.

THE GUNS

The Colt .45s issued to the 7th Cavalry were all of a type. They had 7½" barrels, 1-piece walnut stocks, color case-hardened frames with the remaining metal blued. Sights were a mere groove in the frame's topstrap, with blade front sights. Their ammunition consisted of 250-gr. lead bullets over 30 grs. of black powder; giving perhaps 800 fps velocity. Officers were allowed to carry personally owned sidearms, and Marcus Reno had a nickel-plated Colt, otherwise the same as issued ones.

Oral history left by young Cheyenne warrior Wooden Leg, says he and friend Little Bird closed to either side of a trooper and lashed him with their whips whereupon the soldier pulled his handgun and shot Little Bird in the thigh. Wooden Leg then clubbed the cavalryman off his horse. That was the prevailing tactic used by warriors. If they could get a soldier to fire all six chambers they closed in for hand to hand combat. Troopers who kept their wits in this melee were able to keep warriors at bay by picking their shots.

One of Custer's favorite scouts, Charlie Reynolds, became dismounted when his horse tripped or was shot as he galloped across the prairie dog town. Reynolds tried to make a fight of it with his six-shooter, but was killed after firing only a few rounds. Civilian employees such as scouts, interpreters and mule packers packed their own weapons, so it's lost to history as to what sort of revolver Reynolds used.

Besieged on that hilltop for another two days the cavalrymen had little more use for their handguns because most subsequent fighting was at distance. Their worth in getting many troopers to safety, however, had been invaluable.

COLT'S NEW MODEL ARMY METALLIC CARTRIDGE REVOLVING PISTOL

Contrary to common myth, US Government .45 Colt loads of the 1870s carried 30 grs. of black powder, not 40 grs.

2 Cartridges,
for
's Revolver, Cal; .45;
rder, 30 grains. Bullet, 260 grains
FRANKFORD ARSENAL
JANUARY, 1874.

THE BATTLE BEGINS

On the fateful afternoon three companies, comprising one battalion, under Major Marcus Reno along with both Indian and white scouts were ordered to charge the southern end of a huge Sioux and Cheyenne village. Their charge quickly deteriorated to a stationary skirmish line, then to a defensive position in a heavily wooded bend of the Little Bighorn River.

With hostiles crowding troopers in the timber, unit cohesion was lost, quickly turning the fight into a rout. The spark igniting it happened when Bloody Knife (an Arickaree scout) got his brains blown into Major Reno's face by an attacker's bullet. Severely shaken, in quick sequence, Reno shouted for troopers to mount, dismount and mount again. Then he led a headlong rush across a large flat containing a prairie dog town, to the river and up the steep bluffs on the other side. It was an "every man for himself" situation.

As wolves chasing down prey might do, the Sioux and Cheyenne fell upon the panicked soldiers. One officer, Lt. Charles Varnum, related warriors rode to both sides of the straggling column of cavalrymen, using Henry and Winchester repeating rifles laid across their horses' withers — "pumping lead into us."

For rifles, troopers were armed with .45 Government caliber single-shot Model 1873 "Trapdoor" carbines. Their sabers were stored back at a base camp. Their primary means of self-defense during a half-mile run across prairie dog town, into the river, and up steep bluffs were their Colt revolvers.

And at that they only had six chances for salvation. As anyone knows who has loaded a Colt Single Action or ridden a horse at full gallop, recharging the revolver then would be an impossible feat. The only instance I've encountered of a trooper reloading his Colt during this fight was a Private William Morris who did so while his horse slowed when wading the belly-deep river.

59

HAVE A GUN...

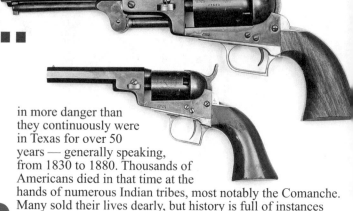

In the 1850s, Jacob Haby saved his horse and possibly his life without firing a shot. The clicks of his new "six-shooter" being cocked scared away an Indian warrior sneaking up on him. At that time, his six-shooter could have ranged from the tiny .31-caliber Colt Baby Dragoon to a full-size .44 Dragoon.

It's probably safe to say the number one rule of gunfighting is to have a gun. It's easy to see in our modern society where that can be problematic. Even in areas where carrying guns — concealed or unconcealed — is permissible, there are still regulations and social mores to be considered. It's understandable good people often end up as defenseless prey.

What is not so easy to understand is how people let themselves be defenseless prey on our American western frontier of the mid to late 1800s, where going armed had no negative social connotations, and even less regulation.

Nowhere in the history of our nation have settlers been in more danger than they continuously were in Texas for over 50 years — generally speaking, from 1830 to 1880. Thousands of Americans died in that time at the hands of numerous Indian tribes, most notably the Comanche. Many sold their lives dearly, but history is full of instances where the victims knew there were depredations happening all around them yet remained oblivious to their own peril.

DUMB VS. SMART

Did it make sense in an area full of hostile Indians in 1873 to wander away unarmed from a column of cavalry when every one of the hundreds of troopers was carrying a Spencer carbine, a Colt's revolver and a saber?

A man named Ezra Sherman decided to take up farming in the western end of Parker County, Texas, and settled there with his wife, Martha, and three children. At that time the locale was suffering some of the worst Indian raids in the state's history. Mr. Sherman did not even own a firearm. On Nov. 26, 1860 the Comanches struck. All the Sherman family could do was run, but Mrs. Sherman, being 9 months pregnant, couldn't keep up. Long story short, she died 4 days later of her wounds and horrible mutilations. She was only one of 23 people killed in a 2-day period by that single band of raiders.

Compare this other Texas story. In the 1850s Indians were raiding around a place called the Haby Settlement, so a settler named Jacob Haby chained his horse to his house's porch where he could keep night watch through the open door. He also kept a newly purchased "six-shooter" in his hand. In the night, the horse became restive which alerted Haby. An Indian was easing alongside the cabin to the open doorway so in preparation Haby cocked his new revolver. The Indian heard the clicks, knew what they meant and skedaddled. No need for shooting.

Consider this one. In June 1874 at the Adobe Walls trading post in the Texas Panhandle, a group of 28 buffalo hunters, skinners, storekeepers, blacksmiths and bartenders, plus one wife, gathered for mutual protection. Several hundred rampaging Comanche, Cheyenne and Kiowa warriors were known to be in the area. The night of June 26/27 was hot, so several of the men slept outside, but they took their sixguns and cartridge belts along. One of them was later to become famous as "Bat" Masterson.

At dawn the Indians charged on horseback and were into the settlement before anyone could respond. The defenders' salvation was their handguns. The ones sleeping outdoors fought their way into the buildings with them. Then as the Indians were trying to batter down doors with rifle butts, revolvers were fired between chinks in the logs and from broken windows forcing warriors far enough away so the defender's buffalo rifles could be brought into play. The battle was touch and go for the first 30 minutes, but after that, the issue was never in question. Being armed and with at least a modicum of mental preparation made the difference. Archaeology at the site has proven at least some of those revolvers were Smith & Wesson #3 .44 Americans and .44 Colt Conversions.

EVEN CUSTER'S MEN

It wasn't only civilians who got into trouble by being unprepared in an area known to contain danger. In the summer of 1873, a portion of the US 7th Cavalry commanded by Lt. Col. George A. Custer escorted surveyors in eastern Montana. They knew hostile Sioux and Cheyenne Indians were shadowing them continually. Yet their regimental veterinary surgeon, John Honsinger, and an accompanying civilian settler named Baliran, wandered only a few hundred yards from the marching column. Both were unarmed despite a plentitude of weapons in the expedition. Indians hiding in the brush killed both men and made their escape before anyone knew what was happening.

Everyone involved in firearms training will say this: "Possession does not equal competency." But at least at a time and place where going well armed was possible, and even encouraged, some people still ignored it, to the detriment of their lives. Maybe having a gun isn't a bad idea at times?

1st Model (Triple Lock) with 4" barrel

2nd Model with 6.5" barrel

3rd Model (Model 1926) with 6.5" barrel

These four versions of S&W Hand Ejector .44 Specials also spanned the era from 1908 to 1966. All these .44s have standard fixed sights.

4th Model (Model 1950 Military or Model 21 after 1957) with 5" barrel

EARLY S&W
.44 SPECIALS

Over the years in these pages, I've made no secret of my opinion there's nothing really special about the .44 Special. It's a fine old low-velocity, big-bore handgun round no better and no worse than several others. With that said, I'll never be accused of mouthing anything but praise about the revolvers which Smith & Wesson chambered as .44 Special. They were exquisitely made handguns.

Spanning the era from 1908 to 1966, there were four basic ones — simply labeled by collectors as 1st, 2nd, 3rd and 4th Model Hand Ejectors. The 1st Model .44 Special was a milestone in two regards: it was the introductory vehicle for the .44 Special cartridge and it was also the first S&W revolver based on the large N-frame.

The 1st Model is often called the "Triple Lock" because S&W engineers designed an extra lock on the crane meshing with the frame upon cylinder closure. All swing cylinder S&W revolvers had front and back locks. No one seems to have given 2nd Model .44s a special name, but the 3rd Model was also called the Model 1926 for its year of introduction. The 4th Models had even more names. They were also called Model 1950 Military and Model 1950 Target. Starting in 1957 they became the Model 21 and Model 24 in the same order. It's worth mentioning the first three models were also available with adjustable, target-grade sights. Fixed sights were the usual S&W half-moon front with groove in the topstrap for the rear.

Standard catalog barrel lengths of these .44s were the same throughout 58 years of production, with one small exception. All were offered in 4", 5" and 6.5" lengths except the Model 1950 Target/Model 24. It was cataloged only with 6.5" barrels. Understand one thing though; it's possible to encounter non-standard barrel lengths because in those bygone days it was not uncommon for gun companies to accept special requests.

Introduced in 1908 along with the Hand Ejector 1st Model (Triple Lock) the .44 S&W Special (center) was derived from the .44 S&W Russian (left). The .44 Remington Magnum (right) followed the .44 Special.

EJECTOR ROD SHROUDS

Hand Ejector 1st Model .44s started out with shrouds beneath their barrels to protect ejector rods. Legend has it Smith & Wesson dropped the ejector rod shroud and crane lock at the behest of the British Government who claimed they would foul in the mud of World War I's trenches. According to Roy Jinks, Smith & Wesson's historian, those changes were already underway because the company desired to reduce the .44's selling price. As introduced, the Triple Lock cost $21. In his book *History of Smith & Wesson,* Jinks writes both fixed and target sighted 1st Model .44s sold for the same prices. Eliminating shroud and extra lock enabled 2nd Models .44s to sell for $19. Presumably both target and fixed-sight versions were still priced the same.

The 2nd Models began production in 1915 but manufacture stopped for a couple years due to World War I's demands by both the British and

American governments. It started again in 1920 and ran till 1940. The 3rd Model (AKA Model 1926) was produced concurrently with the 2nd Model until 1940. In reality the 3rd Model was the same revolver as 2nd Model except the ejector rod shroud was reinstated, but not the third lock. Both 2nd and 3rd Model 44s were dropped during World War II, but in 1946 3rd Models returned until the 1950 versions appeared.

BIG-BORE FIGHTERS

It seems these big-bore handguns were most popular in areas of unrest during their time of manufacture. For instance, it was a Texas based firm named Wolf & Klar that instigated the return of the ejector rod shroud by placing a huge order for them. Texas was still a pretty wild place in the 1920s. At the same time West Virginia's Mingo County was the site of the vicious Coal Mine Union Wars. Growing up there in the '50s and '60s I was no stranger to S&W .44 Special revolvers. Used gun cases in pawnshops were full of them, although at that age I couldn't tell a 1st Model from a 4th Model.

Over the decades I've owned multiple samples of all four versions of S&W HE .44 Specials in a variety of barrel lengths — even a super rare 4"-barreled "Triple Lock." Most of them have been passed on to other owners now. The only two remaining in my vault are a target-sighted "Triple Lock" and a 2nd Model that factory letters to a West Virginia hardware store in the '20s. Both have 6.5" barrels. I get them out once in a while just to remind myself of how good old double-action revolvers were.

These four versions of Smith & Wesson Hand Ejector .44 Specials spanned the era from 1908 to 1966.

1st Model (Triple Lock) Target

2nd Model

3rd Model (Model 1926)

4th Model (Model 1950 Target or Model 24 after 1957).

Duke's inexpensive 9mm Makarov pistol groups well at 10 yards.

9MM MAK RCBS-CAST 3.3 GR ACC#2

THE 9MM MAKAROV:
AN ODDBALL CARTRIDGE

Duke's Hungarian-made PA-63 9mm Makarov cost him a single C-note. Some 20 years later, it serves a unique purpose. Holster by Thad Rybka.

My friends say I've never met a $100 bill I didn't like. That being said, I've never regretted the single C-Note handed over about 20 years ago for a Hungarian-made PA-63. It's an unashamed knock-off of the Walther PP, but chambered for the 9mm Makarov, a cartridge that I knew virtually nothing about at the time of purchase. Ignorance of oddball cartridges has never been a stumbling block for this Handloading Loonie (To paraphrase John Barsness' "Rifle Loonie" term). Instead, I consider them a learning opportunity.

Never doubt the 9mm Makarov is an oddball — at least by American standards. For one thing, it has no commonality in bullet size with what we normally think of as a conventional 9mm round. Jacketed bullet size for 9mm is .355". All American jacketed handgun bullet manufacturers use this diameter.

However, our "Big Three" of handgun bullet manufacturers — Hornady, Speer and Sierra — each differ in the size of their 9mm Makarov bullets. This is according to the most recent reloading manuals published by each company. For 9-Mak bullets, Hornady lists .365", Speer says .364" and Sierra says .363". This makes them actually about 9.2mm bullets.

SIMILARITIES & DIFFERENCES

The 9mm Makarov is usually listed as being midway between .380 ACP and 9mm. In case length it might be true, but not in power. In round figures, case lengths of the three cartridges in question are: 17mm, 18mm and 19mm. However, in actual velocity, the .380 ACP and 9-Mak are much closer to one another than to the 9mm Luger. Again, only generally speaking, the .380 and 9-Mak will give about 1,000 fps with 95-gr. bullets. The 9mm beats 'em both by 200 fps with 125-gr. bullets.

You might also tend to think these three rounds share the same basic case, differing a bit in length (I thought so too in the beginning). The 9mm Makarov and 9mm Luger are actually close in nominal specs — close enough to share the same shell holder. The .380 ACP actually has a smaller diameter in both case rim and case body, requiring an entirely different shell holder from the other two. Starline, the Missouri-based brass manufacturer, sells 9mm Makarov cases.

As always, when setting up to begin reloading for a new handgun cartridge, I buy at least one bullet mould to fit it. The one I ended up with was RCBS-made and labeled 9mm-100-MAK. Mysteriously, it does not appear in their current catalog — neither does Lyman catalog a 9mm Makarov cast bullet design. Redding/SAECO does have their #340 for a 100-gr. Round-nose, meant for sizing to .365". My old RCBS mould also drops a 100-gr. roundnose, which I size to .365".

From left to right: 9mm Makarov factory load by Hornady with 95-gr. JHP. Next is a 100-gr. cast bullet from a special order RCBS mould, shown with a loaded round. At right is a 95-gr. FMJ Speer bullet, also shown with loaded round.

Ready For Reloading

Most reloading benches will not have tooling able to be shared if you decide to take up 9mm Makarov handloading. It will require dedicated dies, jacketed bullets, a cast bullet mould — if desired — along with special cast bullet lube and sizing die.

None of this daunted me and I've had fine results with 9mm Makarov handloads in my little PA-63. For one thing, with reloads containing properly-seated bullets — regardless of cast or jacketed — and taper crimped in place, my little semi-auto has never failed to function.

With case volume so limited, only the fastest burning pistol propellants are suitable for 9-Mak reloading. The ones I've used are Bullseye, Titegroup, W231, Accurate #2 and Unique. The highest velocities have come with Unique, the best accuracy with Accurate #2, but I've determined 3.4 grains of Titegroup or 3.5 grains of W231 will be my standards with either the 100-gr. cast roundnose or 95-gr. jacketed bullets. Those loads break 1,000 fps and show no signs of excessive pressure.

So what sort of accuracy can one expect from a *good* 9mm Makarov pistol with home-built ammo? My PA-63, which indeed is a fine little pistol, will group five bullets inside a silver dollar at 10 yards — and I can't see any reason why anyone would need to shoot it at further distances.

Something else my friends say about me is that I'm not mind-melded to guns: sometimes selling ones owned for decades with nary a look back if I have no further use for them. This isn't about to happen with the PA-63. It often travels with me, and fills a niche in my pistol needs.

TAPERS AND ROLLS?
CRIMPING DE-MYSTIFIED

Different types of crimps Duke applies to his World War II handgun loads. From left: 7.62x25 Tokarov, roll crimped; 7.65 French Long, taper crimped; 8mm Nambu, roll crimped; 9mm Parabellum, taper crimped; .380 British Revolver, roll crimped; .45 ACP, taper crimped and .455 Webley, roll crimped.

Over the years I've done reloading seminars for cowboy action shooters. There seemed to be a universal lack of understanding when it came to crimping. If there's one thing I'm sure of regarding handloads for revolvers or autos, is there must be *some* sort of crimp applied.

There are two basic ways to accomplish this. With cartridges that don't headspace on the case mouth — revolvers or autos — a roll crimp is standard procedure. With semi-auto rounds headspacing on the case mouth, a taper crimp is normal. A taper crimp can be applied to revolver cartridges, although it might not be sufficient to keep a bullet locked in place with heavy magnum loads.

Actually, there's a third way of crimping bullets, but to the best of my knowledge it can only be done at the factory on the assembly line. Those are called stab-crimps and are actually a spot where a hardened pin or rod has pressed against the cartridge case at different points around its circumference. This pushes a bit of the case into the side of the bullet. Stab-crimps are mostly seen on military ammunition.

Here's a factory loaded Romanian 7.62x25 Tokarov and a US .30 Carbine. Note the stab-crimp on the Romanian round. The .30 Carbine must be taper crimped because it headspaces on the case mouth.

THE TRUTH

The purpose of any crimp is simply to lock the bullet solidly in the cartridge case. The results and possible dangers of not crimping are several. With revolvers, if a bullet moves forward in the cartridge case it can end up protruding from the chamber — which will tie up the cylinder. That's the *best* case scenario. Worst case scenario is the bullet moves forward, in effect increasing case capacity. If the propellant used is one of the hard-to-ignite types then the load might misfire — or even worse — squib. A squib is when the powder partially ignites, then it's possible for a bullet to only go partway up the barrel, creating a block. Firing another round then could lead to disaster!

With autoloading pistols a loose bullet moving in the *other* direction can also be dangerous. There must be a taper crimp on the bullet to keep it from getting pressed *into* the case as it travels from the magazine, up the feed ramp and into the chamber. When this happens, case capacity is diminished, pressures rise and the result can be a ruptured case, releasing high pressure gas into the pistol. That's a recipe for disaster.

Almost all bullets designed for revolvers have a crimping groove or cannulure so case mouths can be roll-crimped into them. Yet, almost all bullets designed for autoloading pistols are completely smooth sided. Taper crimps press case walls against the smooth bullet's side, and taper crimp dies are minimally adjustable to help gauge that pressure. Usually the proper procedure is to set the die so the shell holder comes up against its bottom. Then the full amount of taper crimp is applied.

This is what can happen when a bullet is pushed down inside a case.

High pressure gas escaping from the ruptured case can destroy a pistol, and damage the shooter or bystanders.

DON'T CRUMPLE

Roll crimps can be adjusted from barely turning the case mouth toward the crimping groove — or cannulure — to rolling it in so far the case crumples. How much crimp is enough? At those cowboy action seminars I always told the cowboys, "Run your index finger from the bullet of your loaded round down and across the case mouth. If your finger nail hangs up on the case mouth — you don't have enough crimp!"

Sometimes the seating/crimping die in a standard die set is substandard. It will roll crimp the case mouth properly on one side — but hardly touch it on the other. Some reloading tool companies have come out with specialized crimping dies to address things like this. Lee has their Factory Crimp dies and Redding has their Profile Crimp dies. I've used both with total satisfaction, and to be honest, the roll crimp dies in about 98 percent of the die sets I've used for the past 47 years have been fine too.

To paraphrase Mr. Spock, "Crimp heavily and crimp tightly — so you will live long and prosper."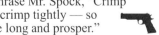

ACCURACY VS. PRECISION

Duke says his accuracy potential with Model 1911's is limited, due to their drawing blood from his hand. If that area of his hand is pre-bandaged he can shoot 1911's accurately for long periods of time.

When the human factor is removed from handgun testing then the tester is determining its "precision" capability — not its accuracy.

We American shooters have some of our terms confused, and I blame it on gun'riters — myself included. Here's the gist of it. We often talk about how accurate our pistols and revolvers are. That is a misnomer. The pure mechanical ability of a pistol or revolver to place one bullet closely to another with little or no human influence is actually its precision capability. A subfactor to that is the quality of ammunition you feed it. To paraphrase computer-speak: It's "junk in/ junk out" in regards to ammunition, whether it be handloads or factory loads.

Accuracy is the ability of the shooter to actually place a bullet to the spot at which he aimed. In simple terms — hitting with it. Factors to be considered in accurate shooting are the quality of the handgun and ammunition, but also the fit of the grip to a shooter's hand, recoil and noise, ability to see the sights and the level of skill possessed by the shooter.

If I'm shooting an issue Model 1911 model, it's a fact its hammer will draw blood from the web of my shooting hand time after time. The time frame with which I will shoot accurately with that pistol is limited to how long I can stand hammer bite. Conversely, if I wrap a piece of tape — even a Band-Aid — over that area, I can shoot a stock 1911 all day without becoming inaccurate with it.

A revolver like Freedom Arms' .454 Casull is a similar but different matter. Those big 5-shooters are incredibly precise when fired from a bench or machine rest, but I'm able to get about two rounds out before I become hopelessly inaccurate with one. Their immense recoil and noise take their toll on me quickly, even though I've been firing centerfire handguns since 1966.

Groups?

It's my feeling "shooting for groups" probably came about in the 20th century. I have never found a reference to shooting groups — either with rifles or handguns — in first person accounts from the 19th century. In fact almost all references to shooting handguns accurately from that era talk about firing them offhand — standing and using only one hand. In fact, at least until the Korean War and likely longer, I know US Army and Marine Corps troops were trained to shoot their handguns 1-handed, standing.

Without proof to back me up — but with over 50 years of studying the matter — I think the idea of group shooting came about when people started writing about guns in periodicals. There needed to be some method by which they could evaluate the quality of the test gun. To stand up and shoot a newly introduced handgun with one hand didn't prove much about it unless the shooter was a world-class shot, and the readers knew it. Most writers were not world-class shots, so group shooting evolved as a way to quantify one part of the overall quality of a gun.

STAND AND DELIVER

When embarking on my gun'riting career over 40 years ago, one of the first accessories I bought was a machine rest. That was because I knew trying to fire big bore, especially magnum big bore handguns, from a sandbag benchrest would gain me no usable information. I was just not a good enough shot, or better said — the longevity of my skill was not up to lengthy shooting sessions. I tested handguns for their precision but actually wrote it up by referring to the level of "accuracy" they were delivering in terms or 5-, 10- or even 12-shot groups on paper. I just didn't know better.

What is ironic is at that time I was an above average 1- or 2-handed offhand pistol or revolver shot. For recreation in those early years I used to set up paper targets at 25 yards and strive to deliver every bullet into the black bullseye. I even did that practice only loading the handgun (any handgun) one round at a time. Without actually knowing it I was striving to be "accurate" with those handguns.

Of course my writing is not going to switch things around. We're not suddenly going to change terminology. But I'd like to stress an important point. No one ever developed the hand/eye coordination to deliver bullets to point-of-aim by spending hour upon hour behind a machine rest or in shooting groups from a sandbag rest. That skill comes from standing up — and shooting with your hands.

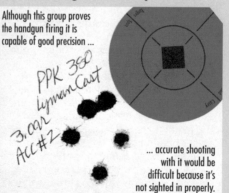

Although this group proves the handgun firing it is capable of good precision ... ... accurate shooting with it would be difficult because it's not sighted in properly.

PPK 380
Lyman Cast
3.0gr
ACC#2

STARTING OUT

Many times people have asked me how I got my "start" — as in, my consuming interest in firearms, followed by my lifelong career writing about them. My stock answer is, "I was born to it." And I think that is a fact.

My mother always said by the time I could go outside to play in our yard without supervision, my first moves of the day were to buckle on my toy gunbelt with its pot metal six-shooter and then slip on my cowboy boots. Was television responsible for that? Hardly! We didn't have one until a couple of years later. A funny note here: When we did get a TV the very first program on was a football game. I've never watched another.

One of my first memories was my initial handgun experience. At about age six I must have pestered my non-shooting father about actually firing a real handgun. He borrowed a nickel-plated, double-action .22 revolver from someone and bought a box of .22 shorts for it. Helping me support the .22, we shot a few rounds into a large fallen tree. Dad then dug the little lead slugs out so I would understand what happened when the trigger was pulled.

Conversely, my mother hated guns. When she was young her drunken coal miner father would get a load of moonshine on and go wild. He always owned handguns — S&W .38's and .44's. He would start waving one about, sometimes even shooting it in the house. She tried to discourage my interests in guns. She might as well have been battling an anvil with a cotton hammer.

Duke's first "real" auto, the French M1935A. Here it compares with the 1911, which was its designer's inspiration.

A PAINTED PISTOL

About the time I turned 12, Dad came home with a pistol in a full-flap leather holster. He gave it to me with the admonition about safety, as in no messing with it when he wasn't there, no taking it out of the house for any reason, etc. I obeyed because it was understood if I didn't, that pistol would disappear as mysteriously as it arrived.

What was it? In the beginning I had no idea. It resembled a .45 Auto, which I later came to know were called 1911's. But it wasn't big enough, and the hole in the end of the barrel was far smaller than a .45. Also its finish wasn't blue like on the .22 rifles I owned by that time. It looked like paint. It turned out it was paint.

Slowly, my education by means of gun magazines — which I started buying at age 13 — led me to understand my pistol was a French SACM Model 1935A chambered for an odd cartridge named the 7.65mm Long. Dad admitted the reason he felt safe giving me that old automatic was no ammunition was available for it. How he knew that remains a mystery because as I said he wasn't a gun-guy. He also eventually told me how he came to have it. Our small town's chief of police was also of Italian descent. Dad said the cop took the French pistol off a drunk and gave it to him. I suspect Dad's job as a bill collector was somehow part of the story, but never found out for sure.

About the time I turned 16, some military surplus 7.65 French Long rounds became available in this country. With Dad's permission I ordered some and finally was able to shoot my Model 1935A. It jammed a lot, but otherwise I have no memories as to its performance. At age 19 I was a full-fledged handloader, bullet caster and member of the local gun club. Needing cash for some powder and primers I sold it to my only shooting buddy for $12.50. It didn't even seem ironic to me he was the son of the same chief of police. My friend soon discovered he could shoot the French pistol with .32 Auto factory loads, albeit only as a single shot. Dad would have been horrified to know that.

FRENCH 7.65 long
25 yds 2 ¾"

Duke's handloads hit center at 25 yards with his current French Model 1935A.

A COMPLETED CIRCLE

There the story ended for 45 years. Not long ago, during my on-going effort at putting together a collection of World War II handguns, it dawned on me I needed another Model 1935A. After all, the French carried some in World War II, and after the Nazis takeover the Wehrmacht issued about 40,000 of them to its forces. I picked one up for $265 from an Internet auction site, along with a couple boxes of nice looking French military surplus ammo. Not a single round of it would fire, and I wonder if that's a social comment too! Space won't allow details of my handloading efforts with it, but I do make my own 7.65mm Long ammo. Unlike my first '35A this one doesn't jam and actually hits to the sights at 25 yards.

By today's standards the Model 1935A isn't much of a pistol, but one darn sure helped me get a start.

32 CARTOUCHES de 7,65 L.
pour pistolets

ÉTUIS LAITON   A.VE   3-53
AMORCES   A.TS -9-51
BALLES LAITON   A.VE   1-52
POUDRE BPₐ (0,4) D1,5 5-51 SL
CHARGE 0,318 g.

A.VE LOT 104-53

The original 7.65mm French Long cartridge with Duke's handloaded version using the 84-gr. RCBS cast bullet #32-84RN.

P35 VS. P38
DOES HI-CAP TRUMP DA MODE?

Contrary to common misconception, when Germany unleashed its blitzkreig on Poland in 1939 precipitating World War II, its military forces were woefully unprepared, especially in regards to small arms. They were just as short of pistols as they were tanks. Of course the "Luger" will forever be identified with Germany's military, and rightly so because it served in their holsters from 1906 when first adopted by the German Navy (Kreigsmarine) and still served as official sidearm of the German Air Force (Luffwaffe) to 1945. Interestingly, the Germans seldom if ever called it "Luger." Mostly it was P08 to them — Pistole 1908.

However, as early as 1938 the

German Army (Heer) adopted a replacement pistol designed by the Walther firm. It was named for that year — P38. Actually Germany's military was not unhappy with the P08's. They were replaced because they were expensive in both money and time to manufacture. When outlining what they required in a new pistol the German ordnance people specified it have both double-action/single-action trigger modes and fired the 9mm Parabellum.

The finished product had those features plus grips of a black synthetic material instead of wood. Early ones were checkered and latter ones merely had lateral grooves. Barrel length was

Duke's World War II P38 was made by Mauser in 1943.

5" and the safety was a sizeable lever on the slide's left side. It is the "decocking" type; meaning if the P38's exposed hammer is at full cock, when the safety is engaged the hammer will fall but is blocked from striking the firing pin. Another notable feature that had to have been appreciated in the dark confines of a foxhole or bunker is a loaded chamber indicator directly above the hammer recess. When a round is in a P38's chamber a small pin extrudes backward. Magazine capacity was eight rounds.

LOTSA' FEATURES

Duke's FN-made P35 with German markings was made in 1944. Below: The target is a good example of how Duke's P38 and P35 shoot with modern Winchester 9mm, 115-gr. FMJ factory ammo.

There are two other features that had to be appreciated by P38 users. I certainly do! One is its sights are large by military standards of that era. The rear is a blade dovetailed into the slide. The second one is a blade front sight dovetailed to a stud atop the barrel. It can be drifted laterally for windage or it can be replaced with taller or shorter ones as the need may warrant.

Mine warranted replacement. It is of 1943-vintage wearing the code "byf", meaning it was made by Mauser. It shot very low with the front sight blade on it. I bought a set of various height sight blades from Numrich Arms. Even then the lowest one had to be filed slightly to make point of aim coincide with point of impact. Also it had to be drifted significantly left to fulfill zeroing.

By May 1940, Germany's Wehrmacht had overrun Belgium, in the process capturing the Fabrique Nationale (FN) factory intact. It was ordered to continue producing military weapons which were then absorbed by Germany's armed forces. One of these was John M. Browning's last creation, the Hi-Power, aka P35.

THE P35

An American familiar with JMB's Model 1911 won't be nonplussed if handed a P35 the first time. Its grip may be thicker but one's right thumb lands right on the smallish safety and if that thumb is pivoted slightly it lands right on the magazine release button. Something else similar to US Model 1911/1911A1 pistols are the P35 sights. But that's not a good thing. The front is a tiny nub staked into the slide and the rear sight is a blade dovetailed to the slide with an equally tiny notch. Windage can be adjusted by drifting the rear sight laterally but elevation is what you get per individual P35.

Whereas the P38 gets an extra "atta-

boy" for its double-action trigger mechanism, the P35 gets one for its magazine capacity. In an era when seven to eight rounds per magazine was normal, the P35's held 13 rounds. Hence the reason for the thicker grip, which incidentally were checkered wood throughout World

War II production.

For my collection, a P35 was hunted down wearing German Waffenamts, i.e. military acceptance stamps. They are tiny eagles holding a tiny swastika inside a circle in their talons. Mine was made in 1944, and its finish shows some tool marks indicating production had been speeded up compared to the beautiful blue on pre-war Hi-Powers.

In shooting my two specimens, the P38 will rarely fail to completely eject an empty case — emphasis on rarely. My P35 so far has never failed to function in any manner. Both are more than adequately accurate. What I have never discovered is what did German soldiers think of the two pistols? Did 13 rounds trump eight? Was DA pull for first shot needed in combat? I'd like to know.

DE-MYSTIFYING .38 SPECIAL MILITARY LOADS

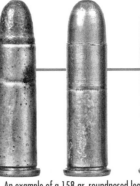

An example of a 158-gr. roundnosed lead bullet. Middle round is a .38 Special with full-metal jacket as issued later (bullet weight unknown). For comparison at right is a .38 Super Police load with 200-gr. roundnosed bullet.

After my recent feature on WWII revolvers appeared in *Handgunner* ("WWII Revolvers," July/Aug 2014), reader Marshall Williams wrote our esteemed editorship Roy, informing him of a significant error in the article. To my chagrin it turns out Mr. Williams was abolutely correct so I would like to thank him for the information.

I wrote during World War II the US Navy and US Marine Corps supplied many Smith & Wesson M&P .38 Special revolvers to air crew. In that I was on-target. However, I also wrote their ammunition held 130-gr. FMJ bullets. And with that I missed the bullseye even though my source was the respected book *U.S. Cartridges and Their Hanguns 1795-1975* by Charles R. Suydam. On page 174 the late Mr. Suydam shows a .38 Special round saying it was the 130-gr. FMJ for military use in WWII.

Mr. Williams had different information which he supplied in detail, but I had to find something to corroborate it. According to his sources, at first aircrew were issued standard 158-gr. round-nosed lead factory loads as commonly used by American police at that time. Of course, plain lead alloy bullets violated international conventions proscribing expanding bullet ammunition. In fact the British had been taken to task about this same subject with their .38/200 grain load for Enfield No. 2 revolvers. Thereafter they issued FMJ bullets weighing 178 grains for them.

After receiving Marshall's letter I consulted every book in my possession to try to prove him wrong and I couldn't do it. *Cartridges of the World, 9th Edition* listed a military load in the .38 Special section of a 130-gr. FMJ bullet with a velocity figure of 950 fps. Next checked was *Military Small Arms of the 20th Century, 7th Edition*. It was certainly off base, giving a .38 Special military load's bullet weight as 200 grs. with a velocity of 750 fps. The book *Military Handguns of Two World Wars* by John Walters ignored .38 Specials altogether. None of my reloading manuals concerned themselves with .38 Special military loads in their informational preludes to load data.

DETECTIVE WORK

Next I spent hours perusing my rather extensive array of cartridges kept for photo props. Considering I'm not a cartridge collector as such, my assortment of obsolete rounds is impressive. I just *knew* there were some WWII .38 Special rounds mixed in with things like .44 Henry Rimfire or .41 Rimfires for Remington Derringers. I *knew* samples had to be there because in the mid-1960's I came into a batch of FMJ .38 Special loads and felt certain I kept a sample or two. Evidently like any good teenager I shot them all away. Besides a few red-tipped tracer .38 Special rounds with commercial Rem-UMC headstamps — as also described in the Suydam book's page 174 — all I could find were some empty cases headstamped WCC71. No joy there.

So finally the next step was one I really did not want to take. That was to consult the Internet. My hesitation stems from the fact there is just so much misinformation online. However, after searching ".38 Special" with World War II, I'm satisfied the details found on Wikipedia are correct.

According to the site, in May of 1943 the government-owned Springfield Armory developed a steel jacketed .38 Special load with 158-gr. bullet. Its velocity was rated at 850 fps from the 4" barrel of a revolver. It does not mention where those loads were produced in bulk. Outfits like Winchester and Remington produced military ammunition during World War II as did many government owned facilities. Wikipedia did mention the steel bullet jackets were given a copper coating and also red tipped tracer ammunition was made with both 120- and/or 158-gr. bullets.

During World War II the US Navy and US Marine Corps issued Smith & Wesson M&P .38 Special revolvers to their aviators. Barrel lengths were 4" or 5", as this one carries.

AH-HA MOMENT!

The 130-gr. FMJ .38 Special loading did not arrive on the scene until 1956 according to Wikipedia. And then it was at the behest of the US Air Force. Its official designation is M41 Ball. It's not rare, and boxes of M41 can be found on firearms auction sites.

Just for reader information I'd like to add one fact. Back in the '60's when shooting up those military .38 Special loads, one was a squib. Its bullet stuck midway in the barrel of my treasured S&W K38 and I remember thinking, "Oh boy this jacketed bullet might be hard to drive out." It was not because its nose was covered by a metal jacket but its bearing surface was lead alloy. I wish it was still on hand to weigh.

So Mr. Williams, we thank you for giving us a reason to dig deeper into .38 Special military ammunition details!

LEAD ALLOY BULLET LUBE

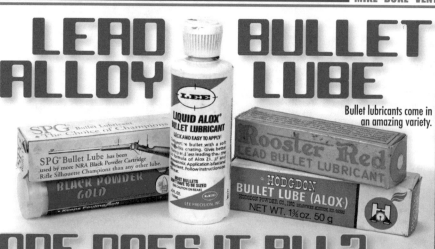

Bullet lubricants come in an amazing variety.

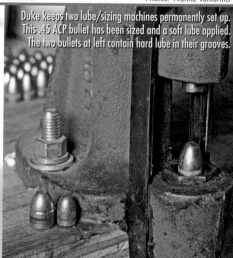

Duke keeps two lube/sizing machines permanently set up. This .45 ACP bullet has been sized and a soft lube applied. The two bullets at left contain hard lube in their grooves.

ONE DOES IT ALL? HARDLY

Whether big or small, fired slow or fast, lead alloy handgun bullets must have lubrication. Some bullet lubes work great at high speeds, others work better at slow speeds, some are proper for smokeless powders while others are optimum for black powder. Now get this: *No bullet lube is great for all alloys, at all speed and with all powders.*

First understand why lead alloy bullets need lubrication. It's because without it they will leave significant remnants of themselves in gun barrels. It's aptly called leading. And let's also get this point straight. Lubricants are not insurance against handgun barrel leading. There are too many other factors involved — barrel quality, bullet temper, bullet size and more. But there is one universal fact: without lubricant, lead alloy bullets are hopeless.

For a couple decades now commercial bullet casting companies have been using hard lubricants on their bullets. Its smell brings back childhood memories of Crayons and in fact comes in a variety of colors. Hard lubes were developed so bullet lube doesn't smear all over other bullets when jumbled together in boxes. To put hard lubes on home cast bullets a special heater must be mounted under the lube/sizing machine to soften it for application.

Liquid alox as sold by Lee Precision is unique in its application as far as bullet lubes go.

A squirt of alox in a bullet box, a vigorous shake, and the balls are ready for loading.

DIFFERENT THINKING

At the other end of the spectrum are soft lubes — mostly intended for black powder cartridge bullets. You see, the duty of a black powder lubricant is extended past just handling barrel leading. It must also serve to keep black powder fouling soft by mixing with it. Otherwise barrels become so hard-fouled bullets are too damaged to fly true. Take note of old bullet designs from the pre-1900 era. They have large deep grease grooves. More modern designed bullets tend to have pencil thin grease grooves because keeping powder fouling soft is not a consideration with smokeless propellants.

The downside to soft bullet lubricants is in hot climates they are apt to melt right out of the lube/sizing machines. Furthermore, if ammunition using soft lubed bullets is left in direct sunlight some lubricants will melt out of the bullet grooves and contaminate the powder.

In those pre-1900 days bullet lubes consisted of natural ingredients. The Sharps Rifle Company recommended a half and half mixture of sperm whale oil with Japan wax. Nowadays many bullet lubes contain petroleum-based ingredients. Alox is one such. It first appeared in the 1960's and took the cast bullet world by storm. Its lubricating properties were such that experts said to use it only in one groove of multi-groove bullets.

MAKE A DECISION

And that brings us to applying bullet lubricants. Almost all cast bullet shooters use one sort or another of lube/sizing machines. Their dies not only size to a specific diameter but will true up any bullet out of roundness while squeezing lubricant into the bullet's grooves. I keep two such machines mounted. With lube/sizers it is no problem to size and lube several hundred bullets per hour.

A variation of this theme is Lee Precision's Liquid Alox. If bullets do not need sizing this type of alox can be applied quickly. You simply put the bullets in a plastic container (empty bullet box) give it a squirt of Lee Liquid Alox and shake vigorously for a few seconds. You then have ready-to-load lead bullets. I've found this method especially handy if a limited number of special purpose bullets are required. For instance, when I load pure lead round balls in .45 Colts they are lubed this way.

Starting in 1966 I've used up many hundreds of sticks of bullet lube. I won't even begin to try telling readers exactly what they need. There are too many choices out there. Lyman sells five types, Redding sells three and RCBS catalogs two. You'll need to pick according to your shooting purposes but at least you'll likely find one that works just fine.

Now in his Medicare years Duke feels the need for bling! The perfect match for his shiny Colt 1911 .38 Super is a fully carved holster from El Paso Saddlery.

BLING?

"Bling" seems to be a modern catchword in American slang. I think it refers to fancy doodads. For my entire life I've avoided bling. In the horseback days of my youth, my handmade, custom-built saddle had no tooling or carving. It was just plain leather. The most bling I had with leather holsters were my initials carved on them. When buying custom grips for many of the hundreds of handguns owned starting in 1966, what I desired most was walnut. To me even rosewood was fancy. Never have I worn jewelry. My wedding ring was on my finger only on that special day in 1978.

Now in my Medicare years, from just out of the blue the need for some bling has struck. Driving down the road one afternoon the thought just popped into my mind I needed a nickel-plated Colt 1911. And it *had* to be .38 Super.

But having one must have been my destiny because within 24 hours of that strange thought I walked into a well-stocked gun store and beheld the shiniest Colt 1911 I've ever seen. It was a .38 Super. I am nothing if not impetuous and quickly counted out the bucks for it.

Obviously, this particular 1911 wasn't your stock Government Model. It did have the usual 5" barrel but not only were its sights taller than normal but they were white-dot types. Also it had no arched mainspring housing, which has been standard on Colt Government Models since the 1920's, and its grip panels were checkered rosewood. Its serial number had the peculiar prefix of "ELCEN" and it carried the words "COLT CUSTOM" rather large on the slide's left side.

Mysteriouser

Neither was it nickel-plated as I thought at purchase. Upon getting back to my computer my searching revealed this pistol was made of stainless steel. Instead of matte stainless steel as usual on handguns, it was polished to a high luster. That was even better to my mind. It definitely has bling, but I'll have no worry about the nickel peeling.

From the rather meager information gleaned from research, it seems the "ELCEN" prefix meant this 1911 was part of a run especially made by Colt for a large distributor who pedaled them south of the border. Thus the .38 Super chambering. Military calibers such as .45 ACP and 9mm are proscribed by law in Mexico. Each run had its own name such as "EL" this or "EL" that. Evidently Colt had some overruns in the "ELCEN" batch, finished them up with the "COLT CUSTOM" marking and sold them in the United States. Mechanically they are said to be the Series 80.

To say my friends understand my sudden need for bling would be incorrect. Those who I have shown my new 1911 to

In his youth Duke wanted plainness. His custom-made saddle had no carving, nor did its saddle bags. He at least allowed his initials to be carved on custom-made holsters.

have had reactions ranging from wide eyes to laughter. One even said I would have to hold it sideways for firing like the "gangstas" of movies. My own dear Yvonne's eyes showed perplexity when I proudly whipped it out of its pistol rug upon bringing it home. At least she just said, "It's pretty, Duke."

DUKE'S HAPPY BLINGED-OUT

None of their reactions bother me in the least. This .38 Super puts bullets where its sights are pointed at 25 yards. That's with 130-gr. FMJ Remington +P factory loads. At deadline time I've not had the opportunity to feed it handloads, but reloading dies and proper bullets are

on hand. Factory ammo has functioned flawlessly so far. My main concern with it is whether I will have it fitted with ivory or mother of pearl grip panels. A fully carved El Paso Saddlery holster fits it perfectly.

When sitting and holding this "pretty" Colt 1911, I can't help but feel

sorry for all those handgunners out there who own black guns. They have no bling at all.

Who ever thought I'd be saying this?

Is a relic like this a classic? The answer is yes, no and perhaps. It depends on where it was found. Near a famous battlefield? Then maybe.

TREASURE — OR JUNK?

Three typical "old guns" I see. The S&W's (left and center) likely have some value as they are clean and work fine. The revolver on the right is from a cheap, mystery-maker and worth about as much as a heavy fishing sinker to savvy gunnies.

When are handguns classic treasures and when are they junk? It's a good question because many uninitiated people think just because a handgun is old it's a treasure. That just isn't so. If it was junk when it was new it's still junk when it's old.

A simple rule to judge them by is brand name. If an old handgun carries a name such as Colt or Smith & Wesson or Remington then it just might be a treasure. The operative word there is "might." A good brand of handgun can still be rendered to junk by abuse.

Some years back a local fellow called and asked me to look at his family's heirloom Colt. He didn't know what it was but since it had that magic word on it he figured it was worth a bundle. He wanted me to tell him just how big a bundle he was sitting on.

It was a pretty small bundle and he didn't like hearing that. His treasure was junk despite the word Colt on it. Specifically it was a Model 1878DA chambered as .44 WCF/.44-40 caliber. That was good. The bad was it was trashed. The cylinder spun freely and the hammer fell back and forth. Those problems could be fixed but deep pits all over the thing were going to be there forever. A normal barrel/cylinder gap is from 0.003" to 0.008". This old Colt's was about an eighth of an inch. I don't even know how that could happen.

WHY SOME & NOT OTHERS?

Just because two handguns *look* like each other doesn't mean both are classics. I'm thinking of late 1800's small-frame Smith & Wesson top-break revolvers. Those were beautifully crafted little .32's and .38's, often nickel-plated and fitted with mother of pearl or ivory grips. In even half-way decent condition they have value. But, there were many copies of those little gems made both domestically and abroad, ranging from okay guns to junk from the day one.

But, even good samples of old small-frame Smith & Wesson or Colt revolvers don't bring the bucks as do bigger holster revolvers of the same vintage. Why? How does a certain handgun become a classic?

Mostly, it's a result of movie or television exposure. Do you think Colt SAA's would have become so world-famous if not for their use in hundreds of movies for over a century? Look through a book of actual vintage photos of people with guns. In holsters you will see S&W No.3s packed in all its permutations, or the big Remington Models 1875 and 1890, or even other versions of Colts, like the double actions. Until recent years did you ever see such a handgun featured in a movie? No, Tom Mix, Roy Rogers and John Wayne all carried Colt SAA's.

The S&W Model 1917 .45 at left is a collectible classic. The new version at right looks just like the early one but so far it's just a shooter.

THE CLASSICS

Handgunners of my age will remember the frenzy for Smith & Wesson Model 29's after Clint Eastwood used one in *Dirty Harry*. For years a Smith & Wesson Model 29 with 6½" barrel brought a premium price. After the sequel *Magnum Force*, there was a run on Colt Pythons.

I'm not immune to such things either. I bought an S&W 6½" .44 Magnum in 1973 even though I already owned a Model 29 with 4" barrel. And I admit in May 1970, after the movie *Butch Cassidy and the Sundance Kid* played in my town, I bought a Colt SAA with 4¾" barrel. Maybe the era of cinema influence on handgun popularity is over? All you see nowadays are black, square-looking handguns. I don't even know what they are, but it does seem gangs and novices do watch movies, as that's what they prefer — not Colt SAA's.

And lastly, survival rates can cause a classic rating. For instance, 50 years or so ago tons of British Mk VI .455 handguns were imported into the US. A huge percentage of them were converted to fire .45 ACP. That means the ones left original are now classics — like the one I bought.

And as a final word, all of the above is why I shy away when someone says, "Can you come and evaluate my guns?"

SHOOTING IRON

THUMB BUSTIN' MUSINGS FROM THE DUKE

MIKE "DUKE" VENTURINO Photos: Yvonne Venturino

THE .38-44 BIG, BRAWNY BRUISERS

These are three of the .38 Special revolvers rated for .38-44 factory loads. From left S&W Model 23 Outdoorsman, Colt SAA and S&W Model 20 Heavy Duty.

High velocity .38-44 factory loads looked no different from ordinary .38 Special factory loads with 158-gr. roundnose bullets, but they were meant only for firing in large frame revolvers.

The first of many "shooting buddies" came in my senior year of high school — 1966/1967. His name was Mike Bucci, pronounced "Butch" and that's what we called him. His father was our small West Virginia town's chief of police, which led to several interesting experiences for me.

First among them was my introduction to the .38-44, one of the more unusual innovations major gun and ammunition manufacturers ever introduced. At the time Butch and I became shooting buddies, I was focused on my treasured Smith & Wesson K-38 and had just taken on bullet casting and handloading endeavors. So Butch could shoot with me his father gave him one of his several Smith & Wesson service revolvers, but initially Butch was a bit disappointed in it. It only had fixed sights whereas my K-38 wore fully adjustable target sights. When I got my first look at his sixgun, I squashed that bit of jealousy because I was honestly impressed.

I said, "Butch, this is a Smith & Wesson Heavy Duty .38-44. It's built on the big N-Frame and meant for extra-hot .38 Special loads." Butch wasn't overly studious and had no idea what I meant, but I had just finished reading Elmer Keith's book *Sixguns* so I was a wealth of information. An older gent in the gun club had loaned me the book and also given me a coffee can of .38 Special brass to begin my reloading. Some of those cases were headstamped .38-44.

So I told him how, in about 1930, S&W brought out a .38 Special revolver built on their .44 frame. Then, extra hot ammo was made only for firing in large frame revolvers. I pointed out my .38 wadcutters gave about 700 fps but .38-44's shot 158 grain bullets at 1,150 fps. He really perked up at that.

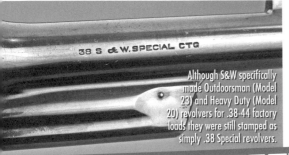

Although S&W specifically made Outdoorsman (Model 23) and Heavy Duty (Model 20) revolvers for .38-44 factory loads they were still stamped as simply .38 Special revolvers.

BLASTING BRICKS

In my inexperience I was probably endangering both of us, but I put together some handloads with 2400 powder so we could experience a .38-44. For some reason there was a pile of old bricks at our shooting range, which Butch and I usually had to ourselves on weekday afternoons after school. I set a brick up on a fence post and popped it with my K-38 with light wadcutter loads. The impact knocked it down but left only a lead smear. Then I had Butch shoot it with his Heavy Duty and my .38-44 duplication loads. The brick shattered. Butch never afterward had a complaint about his handgun.

Back in the 1930's when .38-44 factory loads became available, there were only a few handgun models suitable for it. Those were S&W's N-Frames — the fixed-sight Heavy Duty with 4", 5" and 6½" barrel lengths, and slightly later the Outdoorsman with target sights and only 6½" barrel length. Colt's Single Action Army was strong enough. In fact my 1935 Colt catalog even lists .38-44 as one of its caliber options. And Colt also had .38 Special chambered New Service revolvers in several permutations as respect to fixed and target sights. They were all rated for .38-44 loads too.

Intelligent Shooters

As for .38-44 factory loads the only ones I have ever seen are headstamped REM-UMC .38-44. The only loading I'm aware of was a 158 grain roundnose bullet at 1,150 fps. In appearance the .38-44 differed not a whit from ordinary .38 Special police loads. Evidently back in those days firearms and ammunition manufacturers expected a degree of intelligence from purchasers not seen today, because those .38-44 factory loads were far hotter than our current +P .38 Specials. If you ever encounter them they should never be fired in small frame revolvers!

Over the years I've fired a passel of .38-44 duplication handloads in all the revolver types mentioned above and still own a Smith & Wesson Outdoorsman. It became the Model 23 in 1957 when the company switched to numbers instead of names for their products.

My friend Mike Bucci enjoyed his S&W Heavy Duty .38-44 until he contracted Hodgkins Disease. I was on one of my summer forays to Montana when I got word in July, 1971 he had passed away. I think about him often.

SHOOTINGIRON
THUMB BUSTIN' MUSINGS FROM THE DUKE

Photos: Yvonne Venturino

MIKE "DUKE" VENTURINO

For starting bullet casting for handguns, Duke recommends a bottom-pour lead furnace of 20-pound capacity and multiple-cavity bullet molds. Note exhaust fan in window.

Duke says wadcutters (#1) are the least versatile. Semi-wadcutters (#2) are never a poor choice for revolvers. Roundnoses (#3) are perhaps best for semi-autos but usually are very accurate for revolvers too. Roundnose/flatpoints (#4) are good all-around bullets for all handguns.

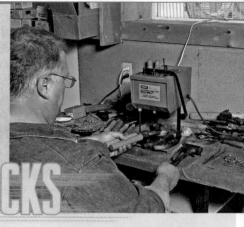

BULLET CASTING TIPS & TRICKS

After the last great ammo-primer-powder-bullet shortage, I've gotten quite a few questions from people about casting bullets for their handguns. I've been pouring my own for 49 years now, so I do have a little practical experience and made most of the possible mistakes along the way.

Think of getting into casting like when you were getting into a swimming pool as a kid. If you dipped a toe in then you likely backed out saying it's too cold. But if you just jumped in the initial shock likely took your breath away but then the water quickly became comfortable.

That translates to this. I've seen guys buy a tiny lead pot and a single cavity bullet mold and then throw their hands up in despair when an entire afternoon's work netted them enough bullets for about 10 minutes of shooting. If you are serious about being the master of your own bullet supply and decide to buy your initial set-up timidly you might as well just add the cost of the Spartan equipment to the amount you will spend later on a truly good set-up. I know!

For starting to cast handgun bullets, here's my take. Buy a bottom-pour lead furnace of 20-pound capacity from Lyman, Lee or RCBS. Why a bottom-pour instead of a ladle-type furnace? Because in casting handgun bullets we're going for quantity. Ladling is for supreme quality.

MOLDS

I recommend handgun casters to buy three or four cavity molds whenever possible. Here's the deal: Lyman offers four cavity bullet molds only for some select, really popular designs. RCBS only offers two cavity molds for handgun bullets, which is a real shame considering they have some excellent bullet designs. Redding/SAECO does offer three and four cavity molds as special order items. Lee goes up to six cavities for some special order molds.

Personally I prefer three-cavity molds when possible because they seem to always turn out three good bullets whereas often with four-cavity mold one or more bullets drop as rejects. I bought my first three-cavity bullet mold from the long defunct Lachmiller Company in 1971 and I still have it.

What really works great is to have a pair of three-cavity molds working together. I borrowed one from a friend and worked them like this. The first was filled and set aside to cool while the second was filled. Then the first mold's sprue was cut while letting the second mold cool, its bullets dumped and then it was filled again. The same process was repeated again with number two. In this manner by actual timing I produced 600 good .44 caliber bullets in an hour.

Because RCBS doesn't make any but two-cavity molds and I prefer three- or four-cavity, I've had to adapt. I buy two molds of the same design and then use the alternate casting method as described in the above paragraph. This nets the kind of production I desire.

To make my casting process smooth, I set a cast iron ingot mold upside down under the furnace's lead spout. Then the mold is rested atop it. When the first cavity is filled I push the mold until the second cavity is filled, and so on. It's a lot easier on wrists and hands than using muscle power to hold the weight.

WHICH BULLET?

Finally there's the question of which bullet design? It's actually an easy question to answer. For semi-auto handguns a roundnose (RN) or roundnose/flatpoint (RN/FP) will usually give 100 percent reliability. For revolvers, a semiwadcutter (SWC) or RN/FP usually suffice. In days gone by, the vast bulk of target shooters used full wadcutters (WC) but in my humble opinion the SWC's and RN/FP's will give precision on a par with WCs.

Also there can be some overlap in regards to bullet designs. For instance, RCBS #45-230CM is an RN/FP meant for the cowboy action shooting crowd to use in .45 Colt and .45 S&W Schofield. It has a rounded ogive so it will slide through lever guns reliably. This also makes it slide through semi-autos as well. I have found it an excellent .45 ACP and .45 Auto-Rim bullet.

Here's another one. The RCBS #40-180CM is meant for .38 WCF/.38-40 revolvers and lever guns. It might be the best ever .40 S&W cast bullet I've tried in my Kimber!

Enough for this installment. Next issue I'll talk about what to do with all those newly cast bullets after they have cooled enough to handle.

The RCBS #45-230CM works well in .45 ACP, .45 Auto-Rim, .45 S&W and .45 Colt, for which it was originally designed.

WINCHESTER HANDGUNS?

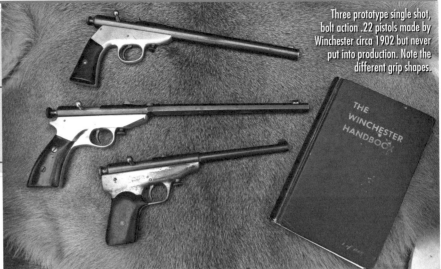

Three prototype single shot, bolt action .22 pistols made by Winchester circa 1902 but never put into production. Note the different grip shapes.

For nearly 150 years the word Winchester was synonymous with long guns. Yet it's a little known fact Winchester Repeating Arms also toyed with the idea of introducing handguns. In 1884 Winchester and Colt met and decided each company should stick with manufacturing the firearms it was best associated with. That meant Colt would drop their Burgess designed lever gun and Winchester would not put their prototype sixguns into production.

Yet the agreement left Winchester free to make other types of handguns. Of course at that time in history the only other handgun mode of operation was single shot. By the early 1900's someone at Winchester decided there was a market for just such a handgun, single shot, bolt action in operation and in .22 Short and Long chambering.

Worthy of note here is firearms designing genius John M. Browning had left Winchester in the 1890's in a dispute over their recalcitrance about moving into more modern firearms designs. By the time someone at Winchester decided a single shot .22 was a good idea, Browning, in collaboration with Colt Patent Firearms, was producing semi-auto Colt Pocket Pistols in .32 Auto.

A DUKE SURPRISE

For well over 50 years I've been unaware of Winchester's bolt-action .22 handguns until a friend dropped by last week. He was packing along three of them obtained after their collecting owner passed away and the inheriting family desired to be rid of them.

All of these single-shot Winchester pistols were based on the company's Model 1902 .22 bolt-action rifle. However, they differed greatly in details. Two had cast bronze grip frames with nickel-plated finish. The third has a lightweight steel grip frame and all had walnut grips.

Interestingly all three grip frames were of different configurations. To me one frame felt most like a semi-auto's. It was rectangular. The second one's grip was a bit akin to the odd-shaped grip frame of a Colt Single Action Bisley. And the third had a sort of saw-handle grip frame as those .44 revolvers bought by the Imperial Russian Government from Smith & Wesson in the 1870's.

Likewise each Winchester .22 pistol had different barrel shapes. Each grip frame at top was semi-circular so a round barrel would bolt right into it. A large thumbscrew directly in front of the trigger guard secured barrel to grip frame. With one pistol, as soon as its 10" barrel cleared the grip frame it was cut into an octagon configuration. For a front sight it had a silver bead type dovetailed to the barrel. Rear sight was open and likewise dovetailed into the barrel. It was made of spring steel so a screw could give it a minor amount of elevation adjustment. The second one had about an 8" heavy round barrel with sights essentially similar to the first mentioned one.

Barrel markings showed the classic Winchester address. Pistols were chambered in .22 Short and .22 Long.

MAYBE A WINNER?

The third one — and the one seeming most practical to me — had about a 7" round barrel stepping down from the part bolted to the grip frame in a rapid taper. I can best describe it as similar to the barrel on the Ruger Mark I Target Pistol I owned in the 1960's. Its sights were a fixed, dovetailed blade front with a fixed, open rear, also dovetailed to the barrel.

The current owner of these Winchester .22 pistols stopped by on his way to the Winchester Museum in Cody, Wyo., so the curator there could examine them. He offered for me to shoot them but I had to decline due to not having any .22 Short or .22 Long ammunition on hand.

Still it was satisfying to have the opportunity to examine such rare items as these Winchester pistols, although their owner and I both agreed on one point. What were the Winchester executives thinking would be the primary purpose for such handguns?

The action of one of the three Winchester .22 pistols shows its Model 1902 .22 bolt-action rifle heritage.

The Greats Of Gunwriting

Photo: John Taffin

Skeeter was famous for his love of 5" S&W. He wrote several books during his short life

Good Friends, Good Guns, Good Whiskey
Selected Works of Skeeter Skelton

According to most every website one visits where gunwriters might be discussed the tone almost universally is, "The great gunwriters are all dead. The ones today are a bunch of no-nothings acting as shills for the big manufacturers." Unfortunately there's some truth to that statement with some writers (none here, mind you, His Editorship won't tolerate it!) but it's not absolute. I know, for I have personally known most of the "greats" of the past half century but I've picked only six because of space — three are still alive and three are deceased.

Who would I rate as the past 50 years' "Greats of Gunwriting?" One of my favorites for over 40 years now is Garry James, who still writes. I've known Garry for at least 30 years, visited his home and spent many hours talking guns and history with him. He likely knows as much about the world's military firearms from the beginning of gunpowder as any person alive. Plus, he's one nice fellow.

Likewise there's Jan Libourel, who is retired now but is past editor of *Handguns* and *GunWorld*. Few readers ever knew he holds a PHD degree from Oxford. We have been friends, visiting nearly weekly on the phone since 1983 and I consider him the most intelligent person of my acquaintance. If I ever voice to Yvonne I'm stumped about some world fact she says, "Call Jan, he will know." His major interest was handguns.

I think Rick Jamison is another of gunwriting's greats who is still alive. I first met Rick in 1974 when stopping by Wolfe Publishing Company in Prescott, Arizona. He worked then as assistant editor. We've visited back and forth to each other's homes and in fact he photographed the covers for three of my books. I think Rick knows more about modern hunting and rifles and understands their cartridges better than anyone. Last time I talked to him he was spending time in Argentina and not writing much anymore.

ELMER

Of course Elmer Keith is the most mentioned of the deceased gunwriters. He perhaps lasted the longest; beginning his writing career in the 1920's and lasting over 50 years. His work was loved by many and hated by some. Regardless he was interesting and even the haters read his work. Back in 1973 I was passing through Salmon, Idaho, where Elmer resided. On a whim I called and was invited to his house where I spent an hour or so in his company.

I left with a copy of his book *Safari*, signed and dated. Please note it was signed to "Duke Venturino." Perhaps that will quiet some of those who think I bestowed that nickname to myself when I signed on with this magazine! I also have one of Elmer's early manuscripts. As might be expected of an old cowboy, he was a lousy typist!

Skeeter Skelton was right up there with Elmer in my estimation as "great." I never visited with Skeeter at his home in New Mexico but did get to spend a bit of time with him at various SHOT Shows and NRA Conventions. One time I heard Skeeter ask someone if western novelists Will Henry and Clay Fisher were one and the same. I spoke up and said, "Yes, they're both pen names for Henry Allen." Skeeter was amazed and asked me "How did you know that? I've been trying to find that out for a long time." My answer was that my sister was a librarian and she researched it for me. If any of you have read Will Henry or Clay Fisher westerns along with much of Skeeter's work you can see the resemblance in styles. Skeeter's career was cut short by illness in January of 1988 at age 59. Skeeter actually wrote a couple of articles for *GUNS* magazine in the early days.

Elmer Keith, the legend himself.

Photo: Keith Family

JOHN WOOTERS

Where Skeeter's primary field of interest was handguns, John Wooters, a lifelong Texan, wrote articles on most any firearm used for hunting. I first met John in 1982 at the very first gun industry seminar I was invited to, and we visited many times afterward at one event or the other. Our most humorous meeting was at the San Antonio airport in January 1998. Yvonne and I were trying a winter out of Montana's cold and at the airport on our way to the SHOT Show in Las Vegas. I was standing at the entrance to baggage check-in when John walked up with a puzzled look on his face. He said, "Mike I know where you are going but I don't understand what you are doing *here*?" John passed away at age 84 in 2013. I never saw an exaggeration or factual mistake in any article he wrote.

You may notice I haven't mentioned any of this magazine's writers. It's because Roy has put together an exemplary team. That's why you're reading this magazine, I hope! We'll have to re-visit this 20 years from now and see where the dust settles then!

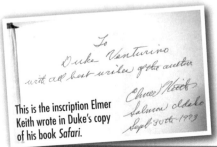

To Duke Venturino with all best wishes of the author
Elmer Keith
Salmon Idaho
Sept 30th 1973

This is the inscription Elmer Keith wrote in Duke's copy of his book *Safari*.

SHOOTINGIRON

THUMB BUSTIN' MUSINGS FROM THE DUKE

MIKE "DUKE" VENTURINO

Photos: Yvonne Venturino

Minor wrinkles and flaws count for nothing in handgun bullets. Shown is Lyman bullet #358430 (195-gr.) loaded in a .38 S&W.

AFTER THE LEAD COOLS

After you have a pile of freshly cast handgun bullets what comes next? For competition cast bullet rifle shooters it's generally inspecting and weighing each one. Except for formal bullseye competition, handgun cast bullet shooters can forget that.

Someone is saying, "What no inspection?" Nope. Here's why. Minute wrinkles and flaws in handgun bullets to be fired say, to 50 yards, are of no importance. And I've checked my notion several times with machine rest testing. We're not talking about bullet bases here. They should be checked when the sprue plate is opened. If rounded they should go back into the lead furnace.

Much more important is bullet size. In days gone by the diameters of handgun bullets made in off-the-shelf molds could be all over the map. Almost always they were oversize on the notion big ones could be sized down but bumping up smaller ones was vastly more difficult. I've bought mass produced molds dropping bullets as large as .004" over their marked size.

Most bullet molds nowadays are darn close to their advertised dimension as long as the alloy used is what the molds were rated for.

Lyman rates their cast bullet weights for their old #2 formula. RCBS rates theirs for a 1-10 tin to lead blend for standard handgun bullets, but for their "cowboy" line the mix is 1-20 tin to lead.

Lubes can be a confusing item for the newbie to choose. There are hard, soft and liquid types to pick from. The shooter needs to judge his choice by his type of shooting.

SIZING THINGS UP

There are certain "suggested" cast bullet sizing diameters. For instance Lyman gives .358 for .38 Special, .429 for .44 Special/Magnum, and .451 for post war .45 Colt SAA's. Don't let "suggested" translate to "mandatory" in your mind. Again relying on a machine rest for more definitive testing, I've gotten better post-war Colt SAA .45 groups with 0.454" bullets but with my Smith & Wesson Model 23 Outdoorsman .38-44, best groups have come with 0.356" bullets. Likewise 0.355" is often recommended for 9mm Luger cast bullets but I have had far better shooting with 0.357" ones. Keep in mind, however, all my 9mm Luger shooting is with military handguns with generously sized chambers. Bullets sized to 0.357" may not chamber in commercial 9mm handguns.

While mentioning Colt, here's another little known dimensional difference. At least until the 1970's Colt's spec for .38 Special/.357 Magnum barrel groove diameters was only 0.354". I didn't believe it at first so I slugged my 1969 vintage Colt SAA .357 Magnum and most certainly it was 0.354". The bottom line is when deciding on cast bullet sizing diameters, do some research, perhaps slug your handguns' barrels or at least get some advice from someone knowledgeable.

A LUBE SMEARED MESS?

Now we come to bullet lubricants and this is a tricky area. If bullets are precise to the size required they can be tumble-lubed with Lee's Alox lube. It works fine. Conversely for use in lube/sizing machines there are two ways to go — hard or soft. I'm a member of the soft lube school because my two lube/sizing machines also lube bullets for black powder use. Soft lubes work better there.

For hard lubes a heater must be adapted under the lube/sizing machine in order to soften it enough to flow. My feeling is hard lubes are best for bullets intended for shipping. Jumble them together in a box and some of the lube will flake off but most will stay in bullet grooves. Ship soft lubed bullets like that and they will be a lube-smeared mess upon arrival.

There's one last step in cast handgun bullet preparation. If your lube/sizing machine causes some lube to adhere to the base of the bullets, wipe it off by rubbing the bullet base

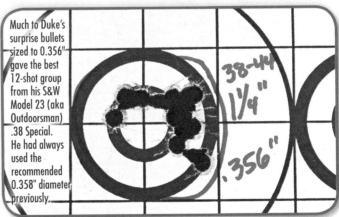

Much to Duke's surprise bullets sized to 0.356" gave the best 12-shot group from his S&W Model 23 (aka Outdoorsman) .38 Special. He had always used the recommended 0.358" diameter previously.

38-44
1¼"
.356"

on a cotton cloth impregnated with a solvent. I use lighter fluid. Otherwise when the loaded rounds are put nose down in storage boxes powder will mix with the lube. That could result in squib loads where the bullet barely makes it out of the barrel, or worse yet — only makes it partway down the barrel or completely misfires. Oops.

DOGS PEOPLE

Duke meeting Brady the first time at his foster home in Texas. Duke says Brady may have saved his life.

Duke in his office with his first collie Brennan. This photo was taken only a couple of hours before Brennan's death.

Since gun people tend to like dogs too, I'm sure you've noticed our pages are regularly graced with smiling dog mugs. Well, this time I was ahead of His Editorship because I'd already started this column before he sent his note asking for pooch pics from us. I've always been more a dog person while Yvonne is more a cat person but there's plenty of cross-over.

Some of the pets I've been closest too have been cats, and Yvonne has been responsible for bringing in five of our current six dogs. Besides being my photographer, Yvonne is also the local animal shelter's photographer and special projects person.

Like most of my generation I grew up with Lassie. I always wanted a collie but for some reason never had one until I was 55. One winter evening as we sat visiting, I happened to mention to Yvonne the two things I wanted most at age 13 was a German army helmet and a tri-color collie. She looked stunned and said, "We have a beautiful one at the shelter and its going up for adoption tomorrow." Briefly common sense intruded and I said, "No, we have too many critters already."

The next day Yvonne worked it so instead of me driving myself she "had" to pick me up after my cardiac rehab exercise class. When we got to the fork in the road where a left turn was needed to go home she drove straight ahead. I said, "Where are you going?" She said, "You need to see that dog."

Bonnie's partner was Clyde and he is more interested in being Yvonne's friend than Duke's.

Duke never expected to have the unreserved love and devotion of another collie but it happened in 2015 when he adopted Bonnie after her owner passed away.

BRENNAN

He was a beauty albeit too skinny. How did he end up at an animal shelter? The city police found him running the streets trying to get into people's cars and brought him to our local Stafford Animal Shelter. I cannot detail what I discovered about him with detective work but suffice it to say it did not reflect well on the human race.

By the second day a bond formed between us, the likes I had never experienced. He stuck to me like glue. I called him Samson but after my detective work I found his given name was Brennan. He answered to it immediately.

He went with me nearly everywhere. At shooting matches I could put him in a stay near my vehicle with water, food and shade and he would be there all day. Then after five wonderful years I was fooling around in the driveway with my pickup and not paying attention. He died there and I held his body until the folks from the animal crematoria arrived. I was devastated.

Yvonne was scared the grief would affect my already damaged heart and kill me too. She knew I needed a mission and found a collie rescue outfit in Texas with a tri-color that had been badly abused and needed a special home. She sent me to get him. Brady is his name. It took a couple of years but he hooked onto me as best as his past would allow. His age is a mystery but he's obviously going blind now and has slowed down considerably in the last year. Heck, I have too. Still he may have saved my life.

ANOTHER ADVENTURE

Yvonne got word through the shelter an elderly gent in town had passed away. He had two collies and no family or friends to take them. We did! They are a merle colored female and a tri-color male of six and five years of age respectively. They were named Bonnie and Clyde. Clyde was friendly when I visited but Bonnie was very stand-offish.

The caretaker said, "Clyde will be your dog but Bonnie is darn near feral. She doesn't like people." I replied, "Well we have a huge fenced back yard where she can live out her years in safety." He was able to get a leash on Bonnie so I could at least get her home.

That first night both dogs were both scared of the new surroundings and the myriad other dogs and cats staring at them. But they responded well to food and warm blankets on the bedroom floor. Then a near miracle happened. The second night I sat down on the couch to watch TV. Bonnie walked in and made eye contact with me for a moment. Then she climbed up on the couch and laid her head on my leg. From then on she has been my constant companion, at home or traveling in the vehicles when it's not too hot. On leash at summer animal shelter functions or even local gun shows, she behaves like a dignified princess. I am a lucky man.

What about Clyde? He's a big friendly fellow but instead of bonding with me he prefers Yvonne and also seems to have adopted Brady as his buddy. He's happy.

We have other dogs but those are my collie stories.

HANDLOADING FOR
RIFLE/HANDGUN COMBOS

Our Editorship, Roy, has a strange affliction in regards to gunzine bosses, as he tries to please readers. This column came about because a fellow shooter (and reader) asked him if there was any difference in reloading when the rounds were meant for both long guns and handguns. This concept of combining long guns and handguns shooting the same ammunition is a firearms institution peculiar to Americans, and we love to exercise that idea.

When Roy first broached this subject I thought, "Well, not really. Nothing is different except some extra thought must go into bullets, primers and powders." I guess that's a bit more than nothing.

Primers first. Many of the cartridges chambered in both rifles/carbines and revolvers take large pistol primers as standard. Take that as fact, for large rifle and large pistol primers differ dimensionally. Rifle primers are "taller." That means they need deeper primer pockets than large pistol primers. Put large rifle primers in pockets in .41 Magnum, .44 WCF, .44 Magnum .45 Colt, etc., and they stick out.

In revolvers this means they won't fit the headspace between recoil shield and chamber, consequently preventing the cylinder from rotating, or at best rotating with difficulty. Additionally when cartridges with high primers are put in lever guns there is the danger of a magazine tube explosion or a slam fire when the bolt is closed. So don't put large rifle primers in cartridges whose primer pockets are intended for large pistol primers.

What about small rifle and pistol primers? Strangely enough they are the same size. However, rifle primer cups are *harder* than pistol primers so a handgun's hammer strike may not set them off reliably. That said, I do use small rifle primers in .30 Carbine when fired in handguns but that is the only cartridge of my combo experience with which rifle primers are used. I've reloaded for most rifle/carbine/pistol/revolver combo cartridges from .32 WCF to .45 Colt.

The idea of rifle/handgun combinations goes back over 150 years.

Here is a Chiappa Model 92 take-down .44 Magnum carbine built especially for Skinner Sights, his "Bush Pilot" model (comes with a rugged bag of survival gear) along with a Ruger Blackhawk .44 Magnum.

BULLET BASICS

Next some deep thought must go into combo cartridge bullets. Of course, in regards to lead alloy bullets the semiwadcutter (SWC) is the Holy-Grail for revolver shooters. They are nigh on useless for most tubular fed rifles/carbines though. The problems are caused by the same sharp edges which make them otherwise popular. Their sharp front driving band tends to hang up on chamber edges. Old time roundnose (RN) bullets used in much factory ammunition in bygone times are likewise taboo in tubular magazines. Not only is it possible for a rounded nosed bullet to set off primers in a tube magazine — I've known several people to whom it has happened.

As early as 1873 the roundnose/flatpoint (RN/FP) shape of bullet was actually introduced for tubular magazine lever guns. It remains the best for tube magazines, and the popularity of cowboy competition these last 30 years have brought many new RN/FP cast designs to mould-makers' catalogs. The new designs have crimping grooves in the proper location so a firm crimp in it will result in cartridge overall length being proper for all the firearms chambered for that particular round.

They won't be a danger in magazines, and most of them have a large flat meplate (front end) which is about as good in the hunting fields as the lauded SWCs.

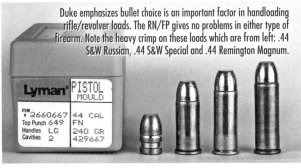
Duke emphasizes bullet choice is an important factor in handloading rifle/revolver loads. The RN/FP gives no problems in either type of firearm. Note the heavy crimp on these loads which are from left: .44 S&W Russian, .44 S&W Special and .44 Remington Magnum.

POWDERS & CRIMPING

Also keep that idea of "proper crimp" in the forefront. The case mouth must be turned *into* the crimping groove. Any edge left at the case mouth is liable to catch on the chamber mouth in lever guns and it also can mean poor powder combustion in handguns — depending on the exact propellant used.

And that brings us to the final factor of powders. Handguns have shorter barrels than rifles. The optimum powders for both are seldom the same. Therefore, it might be best to meet in the middle between fast burning powders and slow burning powders. Such would be Unique, Blue Dot, Accurate #7, etc.

Proper consideration of these factors will net combo shooters good handloads — perfect for use in long and short guns.

SNUB-NOSED S&W'S / *BEFORE* J-FRAMES

Duke found these two Smith & Wesson M&P .38 snub noses at a recent gun show.

When someone says snub-nosed Smith & Wessons to us ancient sorts, my mental image is of a 5-shot, .38 Special J-Frame with a 2" barrel. Prime examples are the Model 36 *Chief's Special*, Model 38 *Bodyguard,* Model 43 *Centennial Airweight* or even the Model 60 *Chief's Special* Stainless.

For nearly 45 years before the J-Frames' debut, Smith & Wesson had other revolvers with 2" barrels. They were 6-shooters, built on the K-Frame; again mostly .38 Specials but some .32's and also some chambered for the ancient .38 S&W. These were the famed Military & Police, a moniker which stuck even after Model 10 was applied to them in 1957.

The K-Frame appeared in 1899 as an introductory vehicle for the new .38 S&W Special but was also chambered as .32-20. It was not until 1905 a 2" barrel was offered. Butt shape could be round or square and finish could be blue or nickel-plated. Both versions had color case hardened triggers and hammers. Perhaps the visual dead giveaway of earlier M&P's/Model 10's of any barrel length was its half-moon shaped front sight. Somewhere in the late 1960's or early 1970's that was changed to a serrated ramp.

On the last afternoon of a recent gun show I finally had a chance to peruse dealer tables. I was about to make the pronouncement — to myself — "Well my money is safe today." That's when I looked into a glass display case and saw two "snub-nosed" M&P .38's. Perhaps it was their contrast setting side by side which caught my attention. One was old, blue-worn and with the half-moon front sight. The other was nickel-plated, pristine and with the serrated ramp front sight. Both were square butt and wore S&W's Magna-style checkered walnut grips with, of course, the older one showing a bit of wear. Both were .38 Specials.

A TWO-FER

Being a willful sort I blurted out to the gent behind the table, "What will you take for both?" His answer was satisfying and now I own them. As close as I can determine the old one was made about the year I was born, 1949, and the newer one circa 1981. It's doubtful anyone knows how many M&P Smith & Wesson revolvers were made with 2" barrels. The percent of total with that length has to be small, which still doesn't compute to rare. The total number of M&P revolvers made to date must be around five or six million at least. Roy Jinks' book *History of Smith & Wesson* says 3,000,000 were made by 1967. They are still listed on Smith & Wesson's website but only with 4" barrels.

Two other variations of K-Frame snub noses are the Airweight version (left) and the Combat Masterpiece (right). Both are .38's.

AIRWEIGHTS AND ACCURACY

Even after the 5-shooter J-Frames made their debut in 1950, Smith & Wesson brought out new 6-shot snubbies. One was the Model 12, which was simply a Military & Police with a 2" barrel but with an aluminum alloy frame instead of steel. Another from the 1950's was the Model 15 Combat Masterpiece, which was short barreled with fully adjustable target sights. Then in 1970 the stainless steel Model 64 was also offered as a snubbie. It was the M&P just made of a different metal.

Practical shooting distance for snub-nosed revolvers is say zero feet to 10 yards or so. I must say, though, in the past I've witnessed some superlative shooting with them out to 60 yards on the old police training course. But I can't do it. Still, my M&P snub noses hit point of aim or just a tad bit high with loads pushing 150/160-gr. bullets at about 750 to 800 fps. And they recoil a lot less than the little J-Frames, even though they wouldn't be so unobtrusive for concealed carry.

Duke's M&P snub nosed .38 fits perfectly with his long-owned M&P .38 with 5" barrel.

IS THE .40 S&W DEAD?

Duke regularly shoots his favorite lead bullet loads in his Kimber .40 S&W 1911 and it's perfectly safe to do so. Yvonne's GLOCK 23, also in .40, warns to not use lead bullets.

An industry rumor I heard recently left me a little distressed. The contention was the .40 S&W is effectively dead as a defensive handgun cartridge. The reasoning was with the FBI's recent return to the 9mm, other LE agencies were following suit. I was also told stocking dealers were cutting back drastically on .40 S&W ammo orders and handguns.

Why would that bother me? Because I think the .40 S&W has been the only well thought out handgun cartridge development in many decades — perhaps since the .44 Magnum came along back in 1956. Some readers with newer cartridges as their favorites at this point must be having conniption fits. Consider these things.

The .41 Magnum was a silly idea, developed to fill an imaginary need — the gap between .357 and .44 Magnum bore sizes. A good portion of the rationalization for its introduction came with its "moderate" lead bullet factory load meant for police use. That consisted of a 210-grain lead alloy SWC moving at about 900/1,000 fps from a 4" revolver barrel. In fact I've heard from those involved in such things, that loading worked very well for its intended purpose.

Here's the "Yeah, but." The .44 Special was already around but hampered because its ballistics only equaled the .44 Russian's. That one was introduced in 1872 and by the early 20th century its load came to be a 246-grain RN bullet at about 750 fps. Load a .44 Special with a 210- to 220-grain lead alloy, SWC bullet at 900 fps and there would have been no need to build all that .41 caliber stuff. Can you imagine the work and expense that went into making tooling for manufacturing .41 caliber items from barrels to cartridge brass?

DUPLICATING EFFORTS

A good example of duplicating something already extant is the .357 SIG; a bottlenecked case using a 0.355" jacketed bullet of about 125 grains at velocities of 1,300 fps or so. It was meant as a semi-auto replacement for .357 Magnum revolvers. Had not anyone heard about the .38 Super? Its factory loads are toned down now but it was introduced as having a 130-grain bullet at about 1,300 fps. Modern handguns could handle that sort of pressure easily.

The 10mm Auto was already on the scene when the .40 S&W was introduced in 1990 and some shooters sneered at the lesser cartridge. The 10mm was just too powerful for proficiently training the huge mass of American law enforcement folks who eventually transitioned to the .40 S&W. There actually was a non-imaginary gap in semi-auto pistol calibers from 9mm's (0.355") up to .45 Auto (0.451"). And it was well filled by the .40 S&W.

Now I'll get personal instead of theoretical. To the best of my memory I've only shot one .40 S&W handgun. That is my Kimber Pro Compact 1911 which I've owned for about 15 years. Yvonne has a GLOCK .40 S&W, but it's hers. I have not fired it and likely never will.

Interestingly enough, the same 0.401" lead bullet used in the classic .38-40 can be used in a modern .40 S&W and that's exactly what Duke does. Ballistics from both calibers can be similar with equal barrel lengths, even when the .38-40 is loaded with black powder!

MOST ACCURATE – EVER

What I like about my Kimber .40 S&W is it is the most accurate centerfire semi-auto pistol I've ever fired from my machine rest. It's also the most accurate semi-auto pistol I've ever fired with cast bullets, either commercial ones or home-made ones. Most of the "New-Age" .40 S&W autoloaders warn shooters not to use lead bullet ammo. My Kimber is an exception.

Some time back I fired hundreds of lead bullet handloads using several powders ranging from Bullseye to Unique in burn rate. Most of those 10-shot groups consisted of ragged holes. As someone who has test-fired tens of thousands of rounds from machine rests, that episode remains one of the most impressive of my experience.

And even better, all the shooting was done with cast bullet designs meant for .38 WCF/.38-40. That's a round for which I have been reloading and casting for since 1975. And yes, the .38-40 and .40 S&W use the same .401" lead alloy bullets. Furthermore, the .38-40's 1880's back powder factory loads duplicated the velocities from modern 21st century autoloaders, considering similar barrel lengths. They're the same, only different.

The only time my Kimber .40 S&W has failed to function was with one particular factory load. Otherwise it's been perfect. I have a plethora of handguns. I could keep most anything near where I sleep. My pick is the Kimber .40 S&W.

GUN-GUYS CAN LIKE CATS TOO

This cat was named Bobbie and she graced Duke's life for over 17 years. She had the comical looking habit of resting with her tongue sticking out.

A few issues back I did a column on dogs and many readers enjoyed it, sending in dozens of "their own stories" about their dogs. This one is about cats and I'll bet in advance fewer readers will comment on it. For some reason many people view cats with a prejudiced eye; mostly men, but some women too. I just read — on a social media site — a man saying, "I got a cat today — but had to swerve into the other lane to get him."

Yvonne and I do not see humor in such stuff. We have both been cat lovers since childhood and agree it doesn't take too much of a man to pick on a 10-pound animal. Oh sure, I know cats kill birds and that gets a lot of peoples' attention, and most assuredly there is a problem with feral cat populations. We get that, but the problem is caused by people, not by cats.

People around here are forever dumping unwanted cats in rural areas despite the fact our town of Livingston, Montana, has the wonderful, non-government owned, no-kill (unless diseased) Stafford Animal Shelter where Yvonne has worked for many years. Cats or dogs, and even mice, guinea pigs and (yuck!) snakes can be surrendered at no cost.

We have a small place in the country here of about 70 acres, and more than a few dumped cats have wandered in over the 30 years we've lived here. Every single one, without exception, we trap and have spayed or neutered as the case might be. Then we turn them out. If truly feral they are free to live in and around our barn. If actually socialized they will gravitate to our house or outbuildings, becoming one of the herd. They are fed and have inoculations. Never, not once, have we allowed kittens to be born here.

Duke and Yvonne's most helpful cat is Fluffy the Terrible. If they are doing something outside he's sure to be in the middle of it.

PANZER & BOBBIE

We have had kittens though. Several times, sick or starved waifs have been brought to the shelter on the very edge of death. Yvonne has an almost uncanny ability to bring them back from the brink so they grow into healthy, beautiful pets. Several I had a hand in naming are Nambu, Spud, Fluffy the Terrible, Lady Star, Stonewall, White Fang, etc. One — named Panzer — is the most responsible dog owner I know. He is my collie Brady's constant companion.

In 1990 Yvonne found a starved, approximately six-month-old female kitten on a city street in mid-winter. Most of its tail and a couple of right hind foot toes had been traumatically amputated. Likely this happened in a car motor when she was seeking warmth. I named her Bobbie due to the short tail. When Yvonne came into the house carrying her the first day, I walked over to look. The kitten reached for me with both front paws, starting a 17-year love affair.

There was never any doubt Bobbie was my cat, or perhaps it could be said I was her person. She usually hung with or near me in the house and at night liked to sleep

White Fang — the kitten that Yvonne brought back to health.

between Yvonne and I. In winter when the sun was coming through our picture window I admit she would abandon me in favor of sleeping in its rays on the back of the couch. One evening when Yvonne's father was visiting for a few days, he saw Bobbie sound asleep draped over my shoulder as I watched TV. His comment was, "That cat sure is stuck on you." It was a mutual thing.

In 2007, exactly 17 years and seven days after Bobbie arrived I had to let her go. She was so ill that last morning she literally crawled across the floor to get to me. I held her in my arms while she got the final injection. No one would have taken me for some macho, kill-crazy gun-guy then. I miss her every day.

Our cats are not just freeloaders. As one photo shows, Fluffy the Terrible is always trying to help with our photo shoots. More practically, I would not have known a rattlesnake was near the house on seven occasions had it not been pointed out by one or more cats. They have enough sense to stay out of its striking range until I arrive with a shot-loaded revolver. They leave then, as if they know they've done their part. I've come to realize a cat or cats sitting staring into the grass means there's a snake there.

I've said before and will likely say again, "You've never truly been loved by an animal until you've been loved by a cat."

Since 1976, 3rd Generation SAA's have had (1st) an "SA" suffix, (2nd) an "SA" prefix and currently an "S" prefix with an "A" suffix.

THE 3RD GEN. COLT SINGLE ACTION ARMY
LOUSY — OR GREAT?

"Colt SAA's of the 3rd Generation are great!" "Colt SAA's of the 3rd Generation are Lousy." It may be a conundrum, but both statements are true. Early 3rd Generation SAA's had some problems in fit and finish. More recent 3rd Generation ones are excellent in those respects. Both of those opinions humbly come from my own experiences.

Back in 1976 Colt reintroduced the SAA after a two-year hiatus for retooling and redesigning. Whereas 2nd Generation SAA's left off in the 74000SA range, 3rd Generation skipped to 80000SA. My first 3rd Generation SAA came in late '76 and was a .45 with a 7½" barrel, blued with case-colored frame. It was in the first few hundred of that 80000SA range.

It was a great disappointment to me, even to my relatively inexperienced eyes. The backstrap and trigger guard did not fit flush with the frame and sharp edges stuck out. Its backstrap came with a small crack and the grip frame's blue did not match the barrel or ejector rod housing. Eventually I actually gave it away.

Among the re-engineered factors was a change in barrel threads, a different ratchet at the rear of the cylinder, with corresponding rotating hand and a pressed-in cylinder pin bushing as opposed to the replaceable one of 1st and 2nd Generation SAA's.

Duke's 3rd Generation .45 Colt SAA's exhibiting many of the options available on them since 1976. The blued and case-colored frame, fully blued and fully nickel-plated version, the three standard barrel lengths and so-called "smokeless powder and black powder frames" showcase available features.

Note all of them wear custom grips.

GOOD ONES TOO

Yet, my most recent 3rd Generation SAA has excellent fit and finish. Nickel-plated with 4¾" barrel, its serial number is in the S48000A range putting it well into 21st century manufacture. A colleague recently told me the highest serial number he has observed was in the S65000A range. Caliber of my newest is .38-40 and its cylinder pin bushing is retro-graded back to the removable version.

Colt SAA serial numbers went to 99999SA in 1978. Then they were switched to SA1001. In 1993 number SA99999 was reached, then Colt split the SA to S2001A. Why they skipped about a thousand numbers when going to the SA prefix and 2,000 when splitting the SA remains a mystery.

One huge boost to 3rd Gen. popularity was the explosive growth of cowboy action competitions. The most popular revolver used being Colt SAA's and replicas. As reintroduced in 1976, 3rd Generation caliber choices were .45 Colt and .357 Magnum. In 1978 .44 Special was added and in 1982 the .44-40 was reintroduced. Prior to my first .44-40 purchased in 1982, I had owned samples of all three chamberings. When the .38-40 was added in 1993 I purchased several.

An interesting sub-variation in 3rd Generation SAA's was the reintroduction of the misnamed black-powder frame. That was the one with a screw angling in from the frame's front to secure the cylinder base pin, instead of the later transverse spring-loaded screw. In 1st Generation SAA's, phasing out the angled screw began in 1892 but Colt didn't warranty the model for smokeless powders until 1900. Hence the misnomer. Also during the 1st Generation, Colt stamped .44-40's, and only .44-40's: "COLT FRONTIER SIX-SHOOTER." Some of the 3rd Generation .44-40's were so marked. I actually have a pair with black-powder frame and consecutive serial numbers.

KNOW THE DETAILS

Normally cataloged 3rd Generation SAA's had 4¾", 5½" and 7½" barrels. However, special runs were made with 3", 3½", 3¾", 4", 6" and 12" barrel lengths. Those are ones I know about, but others could have crept in. I've owned all except the 6" length. Colt also made limited numbers of 3rd Generation .38 Specials and .32-20's.

These days, my shelves hold several 3rd Generation SAA's with 3", 4¾", 5½" and 7½" barrel lengths. They are .38-40's, .44-40's and .45 Colts, while the 3" "Sheriff's Model" .44-40 also has a .44 Special cylinder. It's my all-time favorite rattlesnake handgun around the place here, with .44 Special shot-loads. For regular bullet shooting my favorites are the .44-40 and .38-40 with .45 Colt a distant third.

Standard finishes for Colt SAA's since 1873 have been fully nickel-plated or blued, with case-colored frame. They sometimes case-colored the hammer, too. Occasionally, on special order, fully blued SAA's have been available. Back in the 1990's Hank Williams Jr. presented me with a full-blued 3rd Generation .45 with 4¾" barrel and my name inscribed on the back-strap. It's one of my most treasured possessions.

Being more of a shooter than a collector, I've sold off all my 1st Generation SAA's and many of my 2nd Generation ones. I've kept samples of the 3rd Generation in various calibers, barrel lengths and finishes. That's because they're fine shooters and, well, once they get under your skin, you can't live without some in the safe!

GO FANCY—LIFE IS SHORT

My dreams — good or bad — are vivid. Late in 2015 I had to undergo open heart surgery. Still under the effects of anesthesia a night or two after the successful surgery I dreamed I was shooting a Colt SAA revolver. Not just any Colt. Specifically it was with a 4¾" barrel and fully nickel-plated. That dream was powerful enough I mentioned it to Yvonne shortly thereafter.

While in the early stages of healing I did contact a friend to whom I'd sold a nickeled 4¾" .45 about 20 years ago. It even had factory ivory stocks with Rampant Colt medallions. He did not want to sell it. Full recovery from the operation seemed to take forever and in fact I didn't fire a single round from any sort of firearm for almost six months.

By the time I did feel like shooting, the Black Powder Cartridge Rifle Silhouette competition season was upon us. So our warm months were filled with casting, handloading and traveling to state, regional and national championships. I placed well at several after about a five-year slump. I attribute this to my improved heart function! With so much going on I put my nickel-plated Colt fantasy on the back burner.

For most of his shooting career Duke has eschewed ostentation. Now he seeks it, as evidenced by this shiny Colt .38 Super and its El Paso Saddlery carved holster.

NO FIRST-TIMER HERE

After all it wasn't like I had never owned a nickel-plated Colt SAA with 4¾" barrel before. My first was a 2nd Generation .38 Special bought in 1971. A 3rd Generation .44 Special came along in 1980. In 1983 I got dirt cheap a 2nd Generation .45 with ruined barrel because some tourist-town, street actor/gunfighter used black powder blanks in it. Cleaning it afterward evidently was not part of his act. That barrel was 5½" but — you guessed it — I replaced it with a 4¾" one. Circa 1996 I bought the 3rd Generation ivory stocked .45 mentioned above. And lastly, in the late 1990's I bought a .44 WCF 3rd Generation Colt for use in cowboy action competition.

Why did I sell or trade all those nickeled, 4¾" barreled Colt SAA's? That is a good question. I think my personality has a tiny core of showmanship but it's been hidden by a thick veneer shunning ostentation. In my youth I ordered my handmade saddle with plain leather, sans any decoration. Early on, the only holsters I would buy were also plain leather. Slowly as I grew older things began to change. From the famous S.D. Meyers holster maker in El Paso I ordered several holsters and belts with no ornamentation except my MLV initials. Nowadays I plaster them everywhere.

The core of my being yearned for fancy but my exterior said, "No. Go plain. Don't be noticed." That dream, after a life-threatening heart problem, was my core shouting out. "Go fancy. Life is short."

As you may have noticed Colt SAA's of any sort are not exactly lying around every dealer's display cases. Ones with 4¾" barrels are rare. Nickeled ones in that length are even more so. Nor are they inexpensive. Colt's own website lists nickeled finish at $300 more than standard versions.

DUKE'S OUTTA' CONTROL

Come autumn when life slowed down, that nickeled Colt dream came back into my consciousness so I turned to Internet sites. However, there was one quandary — my dream had no mention of caliber. Personally, I don't care for SAA's in small bore sizes such as .32-20 or .357 Magnum. Their heft is just off. So my hunt was for .38-40's and up.

And this is exactly what I located in a Texas gun shop. It was made circa 2004 or so because it has the removable cylinder bushing and it was new-in-the-box. As such its action was rougher than sandpaper so it was turned over to my friend Tom Sargis at Bozeman Trail Arms. Now it's slick as the ice in my driveway. I wasn't done, though. Spotted next was a .44-40 made about 2002. Located in Florida, it also was new-in-box. It is now waiting its turn for Tom's attention.

Still, I was not satisfied. Even though I'm not the greatest .45 Colt fan, I did spot a used one fitting my criteria. It was over in Oregon. Perhaps if it had not had bison thigh bone grips I wouldn't have bought it — but it did. So I did. A bonus discovered on arrival was it had previously been slicked up by someone who knew their craft. I'm also not a big .44 Special fan as certain some gun'riters (You listening, Taffin?) but now my obsessed brain is pulling me toward nickeled ones with 4¾" barrels. It seems John has corrupted me at least a little bit.

There is a cliché saying, "Follow your dreams." Pardon me while I do.

Duke's "dream guns."

LITTLE BIGHORN COLT SAAs

Duke's US Firearms Company's Custer Battlefield single action .45 was patterned after the one residing in the Little Bighorn Battlefield Museum.

His Editorship, Roy, emailed me concerning a forthcoming auction item he had seen advertised. It is listed as the only completely intact Colt SAA .45 documented to have been at the Battle of the Little Bighorn. If some genie popped out of a bottle and told me I could have any one gun in existence, it would be *that* Colt .45.

How exactly can a firearm be verified positively as having been at a battle? There are two methods. It can be listed by serial number on official documents or it can be tested forensically by firing pin marks. In the 1980's archaeologists performed three digs at the Little Bighorn Battlefield recovering thousands of battle-related artifacts. Using firing pin evidence on recovered cartridge cases it has been proven no fewer than 29 Colt .45 revolvers were fired during the fight.

Here's some heavily researched material from the book *Colt Cavalry & Artillery Revolvers* by Kopec and Finn. When the 7th Cavalry's 12 companies rode into that valley, 632 Colt .45 government-owned handguns were with them. When the remnants of the 7th left a few days later, 302 of those revolvers were absent. Kopec and Finn feel perhaps 252 were captured by Sioux or Cheyenne warriors or were lost on the field. Another 50 were destroyed by the soldiers. They were disassembled and the parts strewn to the four winds. Why? They had been carried by troopers killed or wounded. The surviving 7th's troopers were already over-burdened horse soldiers. There was no way to pack extra equipment and they certainly didn't want operable weapons falling into Indian hands.

BATTLEFIELD VISIT

Duke has accumulated these four 7½" .45 caliber single actions. The two at left are a 1984 vintage Colt and a 2005 vintage US Firearms. The two at right are Colt Peacemaker Centennials.

For over 50 years I've been an avid student of that US Cavalry trooper versus Indian warrior fight in June, 1876. Interest in it consumed me to the point at age 19 I drove from my native West Virginia to Montana in order to walk the battlefield. In the process I discovered the state where I would live almost all of my adult life. Naturally, the museum there contained artifacts pertaining to the battle, with my interest focusing on the weapons. The enlisted troopers were all armed with Colt SAA .45's with 7½" barrels and US Model 1873 "trapdoor" .45 Gov't carbines.

It became my quest to own such guns. That happened a few years later with a late 1870's vintage "trapdoor" carbine. I still have it. It never did happen with a US Colt .45, and counts as perhaps my lifetime's only gun quest failure.

I never was able to collect a sufficient amount of bucks to pay for one. Trapdoor rifles and carbines were made to the tune of over 600,000. Conversely, the US Government only bought 37,000 Colt SAAs and then around the turn of the 19th/20th centuries they refurbished most still in stock, numbering about 20,000. The process included cutting their 7½" barrels to 5½".

Where did the other 17,000 or so go? Some were surely worn out. Many others were stolen. If memory serves me correctly soldiers were charged the government's price for "losing" their issue revolver. That figure was $13.50. In the early days of Colt's SAA civilians were willing to pay $50 to get one. With a private soldier's pay at $13 a month it's easy to see what happened to many.

MAKING DO

The Colt .45 Roy informed me about evidently was not forensically tested for having been fired at the Little Bighorn but was documented in a report by Capt. Frederick Benteen as having been with his Company D. It was one of three reported as damaged in the fight and eventually just disappeared from government hands. The authors of "Colt Cavalry & Artillery Revolvers" were privileged to examine this specific Colt in preparation for their book. They report it as being serviceable mechanically but with deep areas of corrosion likely caused by blood.

Not finding original US Colts affordable, I hunted up substitutes. The first was in 1975 with a beat-up 1880's .38-40 rebarreled and recylindered to .45. The hunt ended in 2005 with a US Firearms Company (now defunct) Custer Battlefield model aged to look just like the one in the battle museum. It even has 1876 for a serial number.

In between I ordered one in 1984 directly from Colt with the so-called black powder frame and wore it on the 1986 horseback re-ride of the 7th Cavalry's trail the day of their fight. In 1975 Colt released 2,002 Peacemaker Centennial .45's as commemoratives. They exactly duplicated US Colts. One of those eluded me until in the 1990's when I landed two. I've shot them all extensively.

By the time you read this the auction will have been long over. Did I bid on the Colt? With the predicted selling price being between $175,000 and $275,000 no gun'riter of my acquaintance bought it. *(Editor's note: It sold for $460,000! RH)*

SHOOTINGIRON

THUMB BUSTIN' MUSINGS FROM THE DUKE

Photos: Yvonne Venturino

MIKE "DUKE" VENTURINO

Duke's Enfield No. 2 Mk I .38 was manufactured in 1936 and is marked "R.A.F." Did it fly in a Spitfire?

ALMOST RIGHT:

Starting in 1932, the Enfield No. 2 Mk I .38 at right was adopted as a replacement for the huge Webley Mk VI .455.

THE ENFIELD NO. 2 MK I .38

I n regards to handguns, the British often don't get things right. Well, they *usually* don't get things right. Oh, heck, they almost *never* get things right. One example will suffice. They adopted the Webley Mk VI .455 in 1916. It's a huge honker of a sixgun but chambered for a little quack of a cartridge. That's a 260-grain bullet at 650 fps!

But one time with one handgun the Brits *almost* got things right. That's the Enfield No. 2 Mk I .38. It's a delightful little revolver with break-open function and a double-action trigger mechanism. A

variant — the No2 Mk I* — is double action only because it was issued to tank crewmen who didn't want hammer spurs hanging up in emergencies such as bailing out of their burning Sherman after tangling with a German Tiger.

The Enfield No. 2 Mk I in my collection weighs a mere 28 ounces with a 5" barrel and checkered walnut grips. Its double-action trigger pull is one of the shortest I've ever encountered during 50+ years of shooting. Its single-action trigger is reasonable at five pounds. The grip's backstrap is serrated, and the hammer and break-open lever are nicely checkered. The whole thing is finished dull blue. Interestingly, its barrel is oddly shaped: flat on the sides, rounded beneath and with a full-length rib on top.

The muzzle end of the rib ends in an integral ramp into which various heights of sight blades can be affixed for zeroing elevation. Rear sight is a large blade with square notch as part of the break-open lever. Those sights beat anything on American fighting handguns of the same era. And the era ran from adoption in 1932 to replacement by the FN Hi Power (P35) 9mm in 1957 although it continued to serve in British holsters into the early 1960's.

Here's three variations of the same cartridge. At left is a Winchester factory round called Colt New Police. Middle is a Remington factory round called the .38 S&W and at right is a British military load named the .380 Revolver Mk II.

SPITFIRE GUN?

S ometimes my impetuous nature gets me into trouble at gun shows when I quickly buy something catching my attention — without proper consideration. Buying this little .38 wasn't one of those times. It was made by Enfield (some were made by Birmingham Small Arms) and dated 1936. It carries all the little British proof marks they customarily scratch up guns with and best of all, is stamped R.A.F. on its right side. In my mind then it just had to have ridden inside a Spitfire, circa 1940.

Why I say the British almost got my sixgun right is its little .38 cartridge. They named it the .380 Revolver Mk 1 but it's nothing more than the .38 S&W introduced in Smith & Wesson's Baby Russian circa 1875. First off, the Brits loaded it with 200-gr. lead-alloy bullets at a miserable 630 fps. This was a duplication of Winchester's .38 S&W Super Police load from the early 19th century. Germany rightly squawked about Britain's use of lead bullets in World War II so the load was changed to a 178-gr. FMJ (.380 Revolver Mk II) to make them happy. Winchester factory ammo for .38 S&W is still factory loaded with 145-gr. lead alloy roundnoses rated at a nominal speed of 685 fps. From my little Enfield they clocked at 667 fps.

Better yet, Starline makes .38 S&W brass and Lyman's bullet mold #358430 is nominally for a 195-gr. roundnose. My 1-20 tin to lead alloy makes them drop right at 200 grains so it's easy to duplicate the Brits' initial .38/200 lead bullet load with a charge of 2.0 grains of Bullseye or Titegroup.

My Enfield must have been sighted for the .38/200 Mk I load because it hits to point of aim with the above handload. Once for fun I set a surplus US army helmet on a fence post and popped it with one of those 200-grain loads. The old steel pot wobbled, wasn't dented and didn't even fall off the post.

Shame the British couldn't come up with a better cartridge for such a nice little handgun.

THE ODD COUPLE

One perk of being a gun'riter is there's a never-ending array of things to write about. While many choose to be on the "cutting edge," I look backwards. That's exactly what I did last winter at two Montana gun shows. By happenstance I encountered two vastly different handguns. Neither were models I had ever laid a hand on previously and both date from the early 1900's. I was intrigued.

The first one's a dainty little thing. It's a Smith & Wesson Hand Ejector: Model of 1903 according to Roy G. Jinks' *History of Smith & Wesson*. According to the book, the gun is known to collectors as the "First Change" because its serial number puts it under 51,126. Chambering is .32 S&W Long. These tiny revolvers were based on an I-Frame, manufactured until 1960, with some time out for World War II. They were made to the tune of more than 700,000.

Think about it for a moment. More than 700,000 translates to twice as many I-Frame .32's being made than all Colt SAA's in all calibers up to 1941. The SAA is famous worldwide and yet I'd never held an S&W I-Frame .32 until then.

Anyway, S&W offered several options with them. Full blue or full nickel-plate; fixed or target sights; and barrel lengths of 3¼", 4¼" or 6". My find had the latter. While grips were supposed to be black hard rubber with the S&W monogram, the one I bought was fitted with later J-Frame wood grips. The little thing is so beautifully made I considered hunting down a proper set of grips but it's also so tiny my big paws can hardly hold it.

This said I have shot it a bit — mostly at chunks of firewood out in the yard, but a 98-gr. bullet at about 700 fps just doesn't have what it takes to knock 'em over. It's hard to believe police departments ever issued such things.

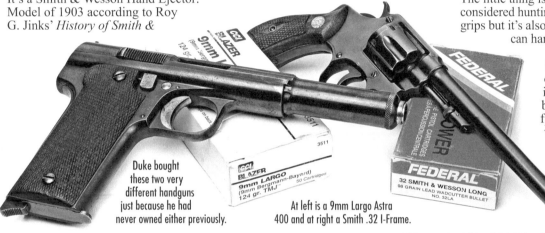

Duke bought these two very different handguns just because he had never owned either previously.

At left is a 9mm Largo Astra 400 and at right a Smith .32 I-Frame.

A 9MM WHAT?

My second gun show find wasn't so odd 50 years ago. Back in the '60's I saw them advertised in gun magazines at ridiculously low prices. Now Astra Model 400's — also known as Model 1921's — are not common. These were made by *Unceta y Compania* of Guernica, Spain. The caliber is stamped *Pistola de 9m/m (38)*. According to the *Standard Catalog of Military Firearms* by Ned Swing, this particular Astra is chambered for the 9x23mm, aka 9mm Bergmann, aka 9mm Bergmann-Bayard, aka 9mm Largo. *Military Small Arms of the 20th Century, 7th Edition* by Ian Hogg and John Weeks states the Model 400 will also accept 9mm Steyr, 9mm Parabellum, 9mm Browning Long, 9mm Glisenti and .38 Colt Auto — although the authors do caution reliability might be suspect with some of the variations.

Also relatively unusual is the fact the mode of function is blowback, like what's used with .22 rimfire autoloaders and submachine guns. Being a centerfire auto-loading pistol, this necessitates a stiff recoil spring. This in turn makes the slide more difficult to pull back than most 9mm pistols. To address this, prominent grasping handles are machined as part of the slide.

From left to right: 9mm Largo (aka Bergmann-Bayard), 9mm Parabellum and for contrast a .380 ACP.

SURPRISINGLY HIGH QUALITY

Magazine capacity of the Spaniard is eight rounds. Sights are a notched rear and small blade front integral with the slide. They are actually more visible than my military 1911/1911A1's, but certainly don't lend themselves to any sort of sighting-in. Grips are checkered wood and the safety is a striated lever just above the left grip panel. Also incorporated into the design is a grip safety. Generally speaking, while vintage Spanish handguns don't have great reputations this Astra's manufacturing quality is quite good. In my opinion some American makers could take lessons from it. Yep, you read that right.

A box of CCI-Blazer labeled 9mm Largo came with the pistol. I shot only a few and the Astra functioned perfectly. Then I fired some standard 9mm Parabellums and, to my surprise, they functioned perfectly.

I must admit, I found both handguns to be interesting, fun to learn about and to shoot. However, I'm probably going to put them both back on the block here in the near future. How else will I fund my gun show habit and find the next oddity to try out?

PICK YOUR POISON

These are a selection of representative bullet shapes. Those on the left work well collectively in semi autos while those on the right are all good choices for revolvers.

WHAT'S THE BEST HANDGUN BULLET TYPE?

I like bullets. I'm speaking of actual bullets and not loaded ammunition, which the idiots in the news media continually and mistakenly call "bullets." Bullets can be hollowpoint (HP), jacketed soft point (JSP), full-metal jacketed (FMJ), wadcutter (WC), semi-wadcutter (SWC), roundnose (RN), roundnose/flatpoint (RN/FP) and many other types. My favorite bullet style is the RN/FP.

My preference is for lead alloy bullets, which I have been casting for myself since 1966. The exact temper of the alloy depends on the bullet's purpose. For example, in .38 Spl. my alloy is 1-20. This means one part tin to 20 parts lead, with a Brinell Hardness Number (BHN) of about 12. But for semi autos I use Linotype alloy because it's very hard with a BHN of about 22. That extra hardness is needed because semi-auto pistol bullets are rather violently slammed from magazines up feed ramps and into chambers. Hard bullets are "slick," so this helps the function in autoloaders.

The most accurate bullet I've ever tried, as in machine rest testing of pistols and revolvers, is the full WC. It is not uncommon for WC's to cut a ragged hole at 25 yards from a good handgun. Here I'm speaking of both home cast WC's and swaged lead WC's as offered by the major bullet manufacturers. Going a step further, the swaged lead hollow-base WC's (WC-HB) are usually more accurate than flat-base WC's.

WHEN IT REALLY MATTERS

Hollowpoint bullets, either JHP's or home cast HP's, can be very wicked on live tissue. Of course, jacketed ones have very soft cores to enhance their expansion properties. Home-cast ones can be about any alloy mixture, but hard-cast HP's tend to fragment on impact instead of mushrooming and very soft ones tend to lead foul revolver barrels badly. This is where the gas check enters our bullet picture. Plain-base cast bullets of 1-20 alloy work well for me at revolver velocities up to about 900 fps. Using a gas check design ups their good performance to about 1,200 fps.

Next to HP bullets, the most effective on tissue are lead alloy SWC's. Again these can be swaged or home cast. In my experience my home-cast SWC's are just as accurate as full WC's. For decades SWC's have generally been considered the best all-around revolver bullet.

In earlier, less affluent years I cast all my handgun bullets, from .32 Auto all the way up to .45 Colt. The only caliber I've had trouble achieving acceptable results with has been 9mm Parabellum. This is not the same as saying I've never had decent results, it's just not a cut-and-dried thing. Some 9mm handguns have handled them adequately, some have handled them to a mediocre level, and others have just tumbled them out the barrel.

Recently, I got two surprises in regards to 9mm bullets. A batch of bullets from Missouri Bullet Company arrived. Surprise one was they were RED! This was because they were "coated" bullets. Giving a detailed description of coated bullets is too lengthy to delve into here, but suffice it to say the coating keeps lead alloy from touching the barrel and also serves as a lubricant. I tried both 124-gr. RN's and 147-gr. tapered flatpoints (TFP) in a World War II German P-38 and they shot into two 2½" groups at 25 yards. This pistol doesn't do any better with jacketed bullets.

Duke's favorite bullet style for all handgun shooting is the roundnose/flatpoint (RN/FP).

WHAT'S MY PICK?

In the first paragraph I said the RN/FP was my favorite bullet style. Why? Because it functions just as well from lever-action rifles and carbines and semi-auto pistols as it does from revolvers. And with a wide-flat-nose, it rivals SWC's as game bullets.

My shelves, cabinets and reloading benches are always stuffed full of the types of bullets mentioned here to the tune of tens of thousands. Like I said in the beginning: I like bullets.

After firing 35, 5-shot groups through his early S&W M&P, all Duke learned was it shot Remington 148-gr. wadcutter loads pretty good. On average and with that particular lot of ammo!

"LOAD/ACCURACY CHARTS ARE A WASTE OF TIME!"

HUH? WHAT?

At times readers ask me, "Why doesn't *Handgunner* have many load or group charts?" My response is, "Because we think they are next to worthless." That always brings a frown because many readers think those figures encompassed in a chart are carved in stone.

A load/accuracy chart shows what *one* gun did in the hands of *one* person in *one* weather condition, with *specific* lots of ammunition. Variables abound! For any chart I put together, the firing here on my Montana property will be at 5,000 feet, will likely be at sub-30 percent humidity, temperature under 70 degrees and almost assuredly in at least 10 mph winds. Give another writer the same handgun to fire at sea level in 90 percent humidity at 90 degrees, in dead calm and our results are not going to be the same.

Even different lots of powder, primers and factory bullets are variables. Factory ammo lots certainly vary. I've had factory 250 grain .45 Colts clocking near the advertised 860 fps and other lots of the same brand averaged about 750 fps. All were fired from the same .45 revolver. All a chart might give you is a rough idea — but even that just applies to *that* one situation.

And the biggest variable of all is that a single handgun drawn from a manufacturing run of thousands may be the best one made. Or it may be the worst one. Yours may be in the middle. Many readers think we writers get hand-picked samples. Maybe some do. I don't think the industry in general values 'ole Duke's opinion enough to care because I've received test samples with serious problems. One single-action revolver arrived with no rifling in its barrel. A 5-shot, double-action revolver loaned to me would not fire a cylinder full without a misfire.

A BIG GRAIN OF SALT?

At a Montana gun show one time a reader debated the idea of load charts with me, saying, "But a load chart proves the writer test-fired the gun. It contains velocities and often group sizes." All it proves, to me, is *those* figures are in the chart.

Once I asked another writer, whose veracity I consider 100 percent, what he thought of a particular writer's extensive load chart. To me the group sizes seemed far too consistent. He told me to look at a certain reloading manual, then add "7" to its velocity figures for the same loads that guy had listed. Sure enough, the fellow I doubted had simply copied velocity numbers from a manual and added seven fps to each. Rest easy though, as His Editorship would fire us

instantly if we ever tried to pull anything like that! Which we wouldn't, regardless!

For the group sizes in a load chart to mean anything, there must be many shots with each factory load or handload combination. One time, I put my late 1940s vintage Smith & Wesson Military & Police .38 Special in a machine rest for an experiment. Remington generously furnished me a quantity of their excellent 148-grain wadcutter load. I fired five, 5-shot groups at 25 yards from each chamber loading one round

BE A SKEPTIC

What to beware of when reading load charts is amazing consistency. Before I entered the business I'd look at test results in *The American Rifleman* magazine. They would shoot a string of five 5-shot groups from handguns, with several loads and list smallest group, largest group and the average. Often their largest group was several times larger than their smallest. I'd think, "What's wrong with those guys? Why are their groups so inconsistent?" It was because their staffers were telling the truth. I learned that after buying machine rests and doing my own testing. If you're looking at a wide range of loads, then groups are likely going to often be significantly

at a time. Then five, 5-shot groups using all chambers. One at random wasn't used each time the revolver was loaded.

At the end I had 35, 5-shot groups from *one* revolver with *one* factory load. The total average was only about 1.2". My point was to determine if one chamber was significantly capable of better precision than the others. It didn't happen! What all that work proved to me was my old .38 was a superb shooter and Remington's 148-grain factory ammo was excellent. At least *that* lot was.

different. If they're not, I'd be suspicious of the results.

So what I do when getting a new fixed sight handgun is try it for point of aim versus point of impact with a small variety of factory loads or favored handloads. If it's adjustable-sighted, then I shoot it enough to get it zeroed. Both autoloaders and revolvers are checked for reliability with a couple hundred rounds. Then I try to spend enough time with it to actually hit something with it instead of just trying to make miniscule groups.

Read all the charts you want, but keep in mind the info may not apply to you or to the real world at all. The only chart to really trust is one in a legitimate loading manual. But even then, only use current loading info, not something from a 50-year-old manual!

Two revolvers, two different chamber mouth measurements.

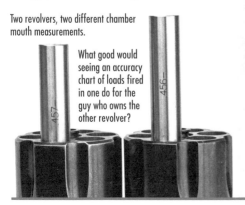

What good would seeing an accuracy chart of loads fired in one do for the guy who owns the other revolver?

WORLD WAR I HANDGUNS

THE U.S. MODEL 1911 .45

When the United States entered World War I on April 6, 1917, the standard sidearm for the US Army, Navy and Marine Corps was the Model 1911 .45 Auto. The Colt Patent Firearms' contract allowed these pistols to be made in government facilities after Colt had delivered the first 50,000. Incidentally, those first 1911s cost the government $14.25 each with two magazines. After that, magazines were 25 cents each.

The first ones arrived in government hands by April 1912 and within three years Colt had supplied over 72,500, so the government facility, Springfield Armory, tooled up to also manufacture them. That was a short-lived project, stopped in its tracks with the declaration of war. Logically the government felt Springfield Armory's manufacturing potential should be devoted to making Model 1903 rifles instead of handguns so only about 26,000 Model 1911s were finished at the government facility. Colt received a $2 royalty for each of those.

Almost simultaneous with the United States' declaration of war, Colt received a contract to supply another 500,000 1911s, and Remington-UMC got one for 150,000, with another 350,000 added to it shortly after. Military planners felt by the time World War I could be brought to a victorious conclusion American armed forces would need at least 2.5 million 1911s. To that end contracts were let out far and wide. Winchester Repeating Arms received one, as did Savage Arms, along with a newly formed outfit in Quebec, Canada named North American Arms. No one expected Germany's army would collapse completely as it did in November 1918. No Model 1911s reached the completion stage except for Colt and Remington-UMC. And the latter factory's total was a mere 22,000.

In the mid 1920s ordnance officers changed some original Model 1911 (below) design elements, creating the 1911A1 (above). Note the dished out frame area behind the trigger. Can you spot any other changes? Duke will cover the A1 later.

COLTS ONLY

According to most research sources, if a Model 1911 .45 saw combat in World War I, it almost assuredly was made by Colt. The company's manufacturing feat was astonishing. By the armistice on the 11th day of November 1918 Colt was finishing about 2,000 pistols *each day*. My gun collection holds two Model 1911s. The one made in 1917 has a serial number of 179XXX, while the other was made in 1918 and its number is 375XXX.

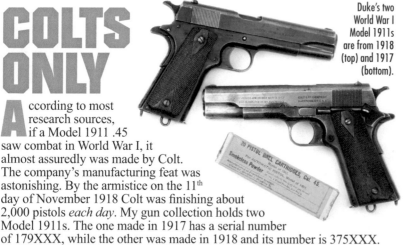

Duke's two World War I Model 1911s are from 1918 (top) and 1917 (bottom).

They were each alike in form if not in their exact markings. Barrels were 5" in length, weight was 2½ lbs. and grips were checked walnut panels. The sights were a tiny notch in a sight bar dovetailed to the slide's rear and a tiny nub staked into the slide's front. Zero was at 50 yards from the factory, and windage could be adjusted slightly with the rear sight. There was no manner in which elevation could be changed.

Magazine capacity was seven rounds and American military doctrine was the pistol be carried with an empty chamber until immediately before entering combat. Model 1911s had three safeties built into the design, including a grip safety, a small up/down lever on the frame's left side and a half-cock notch in the hammer.

830 FPS?

Nowadays the common word is .45 Auto factory loads with 230-gr. FMJ "ball" bullets have a muzzle velocity of 830 fps. I've managed to land a couple of unopened boxes of US military loads dated 1915. Their boxes have velocity rated at 800 fps with a plus/minus of 25 fps. Canvas pouches holding two magazines were issued with each 1911 and its leather holster. Counting one magazine in the pistol a combat load was 21 rounds.

So who was issued 1911s? They went to officers, non-commissioned officers, enlisted men who were members of crew-served weapons teams, and every man in the still-active horse cavalry was issued one to go with his Model 1903 "Springfield." Of course most historically minded readers already know the shortage of 1911s caused the government to purchase over 300,000 .45 ACP revolvers from Colt and S&W between 1917 and 1919. We'll cover those later.

By the mid-1920s with the war emergency long over ordnance officers had enough changes dreamed up for the Model 1911 basic design. It became the Model 1911A1 (A1 = Alteration One). The military made it easy on themselves to discern between the two versions. If serial numbers were under 700,000 the pistol was a Model 1911. Over that and it was a Model 1911A1.

I'll bet nobody back then ever dreamed those pistols would still be in at least some US military holsters even today!

Duke's Artillery Luger with replica holster set and shoulder board along with a 1916 German helmet. Note the rare "red-9" grip.

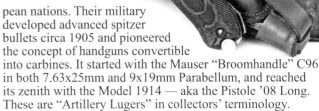

WWI HANDGUNS
THE ARTILLERY LUGER

Being as how we're around the centennial of America's involvement in World War I, his Editorship Roy gave me the go ahead to cover some combat handguns used in *The Great War*.

First off let me say the word "combat" deserves emphasis. I'll say up front it's likely handguns saw much more combat in World War I than any significant conflict since. That's because so much fighting in the intervals between huge battles involved close quarters such as trench raids for prisoners. Oral histories sometimes mention going on such endeavors armed with only handguns and grenades.

Germany often led firearms innovations among European nations. Their military developed advanced spitzer bullets circa 1905 and pioneered the concept of handguns convertible into carbines. It started with the Mauser "Broomhandle" C96 in both 7.63x25mm and 9x19mm Parabellum, and reached its zenith with the Model 1914 — aka the Pistole '08 Long. These are "Artillery Lugers" in collectors' terminology.

GOING LONG

The name "Luger" is almost as much a household word in this country as is Colt, so it's interesting to note there never was a *Luger* factory. During World War I P'08s were made by the *Koniglich Gewehrfabrik Erfurt* and *Deutsche Waffen-und-Munitionsfabriken.* Usually, P'08s made by these firms are simply referred to as Erfurts and DWMs.

P'08 Longs/Model 1914s were originally developed for protecting artillery emplacements. Consider this: Artillery emplacements were usually far behind frontline trenches, but in World War I massive attacks sometimes resulted in breakthroughs. Instead of using desperately needed infantry troops to guard artillery, the Germans issued these long-barreled, fast-firing pistols to artillery troops to defend the

emplacements. However, they were not intended for use as ordinary handguns.

Instead of the 4" barrel of the standard P'08, Artillery Lugers wore 8" barrels chambered for the same 9mm Parabellum. Also, the rear sight was a folding tangent type with graduations all the way to 800 meters. Some optimistic thinking there, huh? Front sights were the same as normal P'08s — a blade dovetailed to a stud machined integral with the barrel.

As issued, P'08/M1914s came with a full clam-shell style of holster carried diagonally across one's body by a strap over one shoulder. The

The 32-round drum gave the little carbine a lot of "trench-sweeping" firepower.

Shown with an original World War I box of 9mm Parabellum.

holster was backed by a hardwood board of about 1/2" thickness with a metal latch to mate with the machined lug found on the backstrap of all P'08s. This holster/shoulder stock turned a handgun into a fairly effective semi-auto carbine.

But, that's not all. While standard P'08 magazines hold 8 rounds of 9mm Parabellum and the issue holster rig came with a dual magazine pouch, Artillery Lugers became much more effective when a 32-round drum — collectors call them "snail drums" — became available. A special tool was needed in order to stuff them to the brim with cartridges.

Besides guarding artillery emplacements, the Long P'08s soon became a stalwart of *Sturmtruppen* (Storm Troops) for trench raids. Jumping into an enemy trench with 32 rounds available with 32 trigger pulls, even of 9mm, would quickly clear it of troops. The only weapon Allied forces could use to combat such an effective trench-raiding weapon was the 12-gauge Winchester Model 1897 "trench" shotgun.

HANDS ON

A few years back while confined indoors recovering from an illness, I spent way too much time on my iPad checking out Internet firearms auctions. Long story short: I ended up with a DWM, 1917-dated Artillery Luger. While not in pristine condition, it's still a fine shooter and even has one of the rare "red-9" grip panels. Sadly, the left-side grip is a replacement. Along the way I acquired a very fine replica holster set complete with magazine pouches, and in 2017 a friend even

presented me with a snail drum. Now I'm searching for the special drum magazine loading tool. A good problem to have, right?

After attaching the shoulder board, inserting the 32-round drum and popping away with this P'08, I began to understand why the victorious Allies decreed Germany get rid of their Artillery Lugers. France, Great Britain and the United States had no weapon that could compare with it. Boy, am I glad I have one!

WORLD WAR I HANDGUNS

British .455 factory ammo is still made by Fiocchi in Italy (far left) and some were recently made by Hornady (2nd from left).

WEBLEY MKVI .455

Webley MKVI .455 as adopted by the British in 1916. Gun in background is the 12 gauge also used in World War I. Canvas holster and ammo pouch made by World War Supply.

The Webley MKVI certainly fits the criteria British ordnance people evidently set for their service revolvers: big, ugly, underpowered and top break. I recently read the opinion of a now deceased gun'riter saying he thought the Webley MKVI .455 was the best combat revolver of its day. To that I enthusiastically disagree. The only place it could better either Colt's or S&W's Model 1917 .45 ACPs is it has a replaceable front sight whereas theirs are silver-soldered (Colt) or forged integral with the barrel (S&W). That made it easier to zero if a taller or shorter sight was needed for zeroing.

US Model 1917s were chambered for a more powerful cartridge, a 230-gr. bullet at 830 fps versus a 262-gr. bullet at 650 fps. The '17s could be quickly reloaded with a pair of three-round "half-moon" clips. In fact the U.S. supplied .45 ACP pre-loaded in those clips. The Webley's rounds had to be replenished one at a time. In my collection, the Colt Model 1917 and Webley MKVI match weight at 39 oz. but my S&W Model 1917 only weighs 35 oz.

Webley began their series of top break revolvers circa 1887 with the MKI and continued revamping it until the MKVI appeared in 1916 midway through World War I. Most of the earlier "marks" came with 4" barrels although some were available with the 6" length. As far as I can tell the MKVI came only with a 6".

The Brits dropped the Webley MKVI in 1928 in favor of the smaller .38 Enfield No. 2.

.455 TO .45 ACP

The top-break Webley is opened by pushing down on a rather large lever positioned to the left side of the hammer. Simultaneously the barrel is pushed down while the extractor is pushed up popping all empties free of the chambers. After each chamber is loaded, the barrel's then pushed up to lock in place. Firing is the same as any other double action, by pulling the trigger or by cocking the hammer first and then pulling the trigger. Grips are made of some sort of checkered synthetic material.

Webley MKVIs stayed the official British military sidearm from 1916 until 1928 when the smaller and equally underpowered Enfield MkII .380 was adopted. However, along with all other armaments when the British declared war on Germany in 1939, they were woefully short of the Enfields so thousands of MKVIs were kept in service.

Starting in the 1950s most of the remaining MKVIs were sold off to the American market. Over here .455 Webley factory ammunition was not common. To make the MKVIs sell better many had their chambers faced off to handle .45 Autos in half moon clips. I knew this 15 years ago when searching for an MKVI to use when writing my book *Shooting World War II Small Arms*. Regardless, in an initial fit of enthusiasm I bought the first MKVI I encountered without looking to see if it was altered or not — it was. Luckily a friend was looking for just such a Webley and took it off my hands. The next one I checked thoroughly and still own. Let that be a lesson to you if you're looking!

AMMO TODAY?

The ammunition maker Fiocchi of Italy still produces .455 Webley with a 262-gr. lead alloy bullet. For a time Hornady made some for a distributor with 265-gr. lead alloy bullets. To American eyes these bullets look strange, with long cone-shaped noses, but they actually duplicate the original FMJ .455 military bullets. RCBS even offers a hollowbase bullet mold of that configuration in their special order section. I have that mold, but looking for a less time-consuming alternate found Hornady's 255-gr. RN/FP *Cowboy* bullet shoots nicely in the .455 Webley. A charge of 4.0 grains of Bullseye propels it to about 700 fps.

While my opinion is the Webley MKVI .455 was not the best combat handgun of its day, it's not the worst either. The prize must go to Russia's Model 1895 Nagant 7.62mm. More on that another time.

SHOOTINGIRON
THUMB BUSTIN' MUSINGS FROM THE DUKE

MIKE "DUKE" VENTURINO Photos: Yvonne Venturino

WORLD WAR I HANDGUNS:
THE U.S. MODEL 1917
COLT & S&W

Duke's U.S. Model 1917 .45's: S&W is at left, Colt at right.

When Woodrow Wilson's administration declared war on Germany on April 6, 1917, the American military was woefully unprepared. Regarding handguns, American manufacturing might have helped fill a significant gap. This was when both Colt and S&W factories adapted their large frame, DA revolvers to fire the government's .45 Auto cartridge. The official issue American handgun at the time was the U.S. Model 1911 of which there were too few to equip an army of the size envisioned by the U.S. Department of War.

Most of you already know autoloading handguns are usually chambered for rimless case designs. There are exceptions such as .22 Long Rifle, .32 Auto and .38 Super — the first being rimmed and the latter two being semi-rimmed. Rimless cases were not considered feasible for DA revolvers because there's no rim their extractors can push against to eject rounds from the chambers. Some employee at S&W, whose name seems to be lost to history, worked out a method so revolvers could use .45 Auto cartridges. They were simple, stamped steel clips fitting in .45 Auto extractor grooves. They quickly gained the moniker of "half-moon clips." In more modern times firearms engineers succeeded in developing a few revolver models capable of functioning with rimless cases sans any sort of clip.

U.S. Model 1917's by Colt and S&W were stamped identically on their butts — "U.S. Model 1917."

SAME NAME?

Colt's and S&W's big .45 Auto revolvers hold a special spot in American military history. They are the only firearms to get the same model designation but without any parts interchangeability. The name given them was US Model 1917. Both companies were already making the basic revolver becoming the 1917's; Colt from 1899 and S&W from 1915. Colt called theirs the New Service and S&W's name was Hand Ejector, 2nd Model.

As ordered by the government both firms' revolvers had 5½" barrels, plain walnut grips and lanyard rings on the butt. Also on the butts of both brands is the stamp "U.S. Army Model 1917." And on the underside of both company's barrels is the marking "United States

Property." Finish on S&W's version was their usual bright blue but Colt turned theirs out with a less polished blue finish. My personally owned samples weigh 36 oz. for the S&W and 39 oz. for the Colt.

During World War I both versions of U.S. Model 1917's were issued with Model 1909, flap style, leather holsters. Intended originally for cavalrymen these holsters were worn on the soldiers' right side with gun butt forward. A canvas pouch with three pockets holding two half-moon clips each was also standard issue. Therefore, a combat load for U.S. Model 1917 .45 revolvers was 24 rounds. By 1919 when production ceased for the government the two firms had produced well over 300,000 U.S. Model 1917's.

TOSS THE CLIPS

Back in 1968 I shelled out $35 for my first S&W Model 1917. Its bore was a little rough and being in college I could not afford jacketed bullets for handloading. At the time I was already loading Lyman's cast bullet mold #452374 (220-gr. RN) in .45 Auto so those rounds were put in my new revolver. That was a joke. No matter how I tried, no sort of crimp locked the smooth sides of the bullet into cases. By the time about three were fired recoil caused bullets to pull forward in cases to the point cylinder rotation was blocked.

Ammo was issued pre-loaded in half moon clips and packed 24 rounds per box.

So that's my first advice to modern handloaders. Get a bullet with a crimping groove and roll-crimp the case mouth into it. My second tip is to forget half-moon clips. They're a pain to get loaded cartridges into or empty cases out of. The Army recognized this trait and made life easier for 1917 revolver-packing soldiers by issuing .45 Auto preloaded in clips in 24-round boxes. My personal U.S. Model 1917's get fired with handloads in .45 Auto-Rim brass. It's simply the .45 Auto case with a thick rim. Auto-rim cases are reloaded with the same dies as .45 Auto, only a different shell-holder is needed.

Several U.S. Model 1917 .45 revolvers by both makers have passed through my hands over the past 50 years. Right now I have nice samples by Colt and S&W, and a near miracle is both shoot to their sights at about 20 yards. U.S. Model 1917's are a significant bit of American military history and my current ones will be keepers 'til the end.

THE .45 COLT'S IDENTITY CRISIS

With the Colt Model 1909 the U.S. Army adopted the .45 Colt the second time.

I t seems to me the .45 Colt is having an identity crisis, especially among handloaders. Some want it to perform as a magnum — heavier than factory bullet weights at higher velocities. Others want it to behave like a .38 of some sort — lightweight bullets going so slow as to be almost visible in flight. It's neither — it's a .45 Colt.

Consider this: handgun hunters or outdoorsmen can have truly powerful handguns from .454 Casull to .50 S&W. Why try making the .45 Colt into something it was never meant to be? Also consider this: Cowboy action shooters can buy almost any style .45 Colt revolver also chambered for .38/.357 Magnum for lighter recoil and noise. Again, why try making the .45 Colt into something it was never meant to be?

And what was it meant to be? It was developed specifically as a combat weapon for horse-mounted troops. There's a myth the .45 Colt in 1873 was introduced with a 40-gr. charge of black powder. The myths also state its bullet weighed 255 grains. Both of those myths are wrong. The .45 Colt was adopted by the U.S. Army the first time with a 30-gr. powder charge and 250-gr. bullets in a case 1.29" long.

THE "NEW" NEW .45

W hat did I mean about the "first time?" The .45 Colt's first term of service was 1873 to 1892. The revolvers had 7½" barrels and the issue loads as described above, or sometimes the .45 S&W load commonly nicknamed "Schofield" was given to troops. That one had a 230-gr. bullet with 28-gr. powder charge in a case 1.10" long. About the turn of the 19th/20th centuries the U.S. Army had all remaining Colt .45's in inventory sent back to the factory for refurbishing and barrel shortening from 7½" to 5½". They were reissued for use during the Philippine Insurrection and most likely their ammunition was left over black powder .45 Colt/.45 S&W from the Indian Wars era.

Then the U.S. Army adopted the .45 Colt again with the U.S. Model 1909. However, the revolver was now Colt's double action New Service with 5½" barrel. This second term of service was officially only two years when finally the Model 1911 .45 Auto was accepted. By 1909 smokeless powder was the norm in military ammunition. Bullets were still 250 grains, but on my unopened box of 1909 ammo powder was listed as R.S.Q.

Here's an interesting twist. Early copper cased .45 Colt military loads measured 0.502" for rim diameter

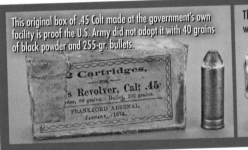

This original box of .45 Colt made at the government's own facility is proof the U.S. Army did not adopt it with 40 grains of black powder and 255-gr. bullets.

2 Cartridges, FOR s Revolver, Cal; .45' der, 20 grains. Bullet 200 grains. FRANKFORD ARSENAL. JANUARY, 1874.

This box of Model 1909 .45 Colt loads is rated at only 725 fps. Note how much wider its rim is than the .45 Colts made in 1874.

20 CALIBER .45 REVOLVER BALL CARTRIDGES, Model of 1909. For COLT'S DOUBLE ACTION REVOLVER, Model of 1909. Smokeless Powder Muzzle velocity 725 ± 25 feet per second. R. S. Q. Lot No. 4, of 1913. Manufac ed at FRANKFORD ARSENAL. Class 47, Division 1, Drawing 8.

but the 1909 loads had 0.530" rim diameters. Measurements were taken from rounds in my collection. The reason was the double-action Colt Model 1909s needed wider case rims for their star-type extractors to eject cases properly.

According to my own chronograph testing with .45 Colt revolvers, 30 grains of black powder and 250-gr. bullets gives about 850-875 fps from a 7½" Colt barrel. Figure about 800 to 825 fps from 5½" barrels. Add about 100 fps if you can figure out how to cram a full 40-gr. charge in modern brass. I've also test fired .45 S&W black powder handloads. With 230-gr. bullets and 28 grains of black powder they hit right at 730 fps. The military saves us from guessing about 1909 ammunition. The box label rates them at 725 fps, plus or minus 25 fps.

RELIVING HISTORY

T his following might be a strange concept to some readers. How about loading for .45 Colt revolvers so the ballistics equal originals? Proper powder charges and other loading info is in any manual containing lead alloy bullet data. Right this instant, someone is thinking, "But my Ruger Blackhawk/Vaquero/ Bisley is far stronger than ordinary .45 Colt revolvers!" So what? That doesn't necessitate hot-rodding them up to ridiculous levels. There must be about a million .45 Colt sixguns of lesser strength on the planet. I'd hate for some of them to get hot handloads meant for Rugers. It's bound to happen — and it has.

Sometimes it's interesting and enjoyable to just experience historic cartridges as they were intended.

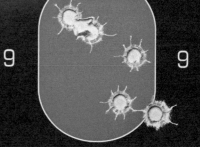
If your handgun will group like this at say 20 to 25 yards, and hit to its sights like this one does, then forget bench shooting and begin practicing with one hand.

HOW WE SHOOT:

IS ONE-HANDED SHOOTING DEAD?

To become a proficient handgun shot Duke says to shoot slowly, use small targets and a good trigger press. It's also very satisfying to see the hits doing it "the hard way"!

The vast majority of handgun shooting competitions nowadays are geared to speed. That's understandable. It's fun to do and fun to watch. There's movement, steel targets ringing from hits, and/or reactive targets. With perhaps hundreds of people wishing to participate, a match must keep rolling. Each competitor's allotment of shooting time is limited if the event is going to finish up by day's end. Also there must be a way to quantify matters for scoring. Usually that's actual time the shooter used for the string of shots minus penalties for missing, etc.

Speed shooting events necessitate targets are mostly steel, large in size and placed close to the firing line. The problem I see is a hit on a two foot square piece of steel say in the lower left hand corner at 10 paces counts just as much as a dead-center strike. In other words speed shooting negates precision shooting. And that's too bad because the primary focus on shooting a handgun should be to direct the first shot dead center on target.

Don't get me wrong at this point. I've done a bit of speed shooting in competition in my 50-plus years as a handgunner and I've loved it. However, when I began at age 17 I'd never heard of competitions based on speed. The elderly gents — they were much younger than I am now, by the way — at the local gun club were bullseye target shooters. They were aiming at about 6" black circles on white paper at 25 and 50 yards. The idea was each shot was an individual one. Reacquiring only the front sight for fast follow up shots because the targets were mere yards away was unknown. In fact those older guys who let me participate with them sometimes set their handguns down between shots.

SLOW WAS GOOD

Back in those days my only centerfire was an S&W K38. Even after becoming a handloader and bullet caster I couldn't afford a great deal of shooting with it. Often for practice I only had 25 or 50 rounds of .38 Special wadcutter handloads available. In order to stretch my shooting enjoyment my method was to load and fire one shot at a black bullseye. Then I would set the revolver down and take note of where my bullet hit. Every shot was made one-handed. This was repeated until my supply of .38's was depleted. In this manner I managed to become a reasonably good handgun shot.

As time passed, I grew more affluent and acquired many other handguns; .357's, .44's, .45 revolvers and semi-autos. With most of them I used the same technique: load one round, shoot one round and concentrate on keeping the shots close to one another on the target. I hardly ever blasted away an entire cylinder-full or magazine quickly.

Then things began to change. I began my writing career so most handguns were fired from a bench rest, or even better from a mechanical pistol machine rest. The shooting wasn't so much for enjoyment but for gathering information to present in articles. Next came action shooting. Instead of one-handed shooting for precision, two hands steadied the handgun better. In cowboy competition one hand held and fired the revolver while the other one manipulated the hammer.

ERODING SKILLS

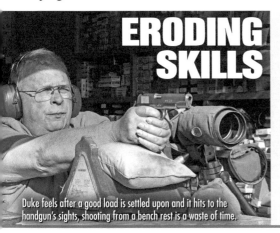
Duke feels after a good load is settled upon and it hits to the handgun's sights, shooting from a bench rest is a waste of time.

It was great fun but the ability I had built to shoot precisely began to disappear. Yvonne proved this to me. Firing our single action .44's quickly at dueling trees or falling plates she couldn't come close to my speed. Shooting slowly as in seeking center hits on paper or steel she was able to easily beat me. Why? How? Because in teaching her to shoot handguns I stressed each shot was a separate feat and she took that to heart.

So, what I think is this. Shooting a handgun from a bench rest is just to ascertain a good load and determine if it hits reasonably close to point of aim. What's a good load? With factory load or handload all that's needed is a load grouping tighter from a bench rest than you can group standing. Then teach yourself to shoot slowly, perhaps only using one hand seeking precision instead of speed. If you become a good one-handed shot, adding the other for support will only make you an even better shot. Use small targets, not so close — and always strive to hit them center.

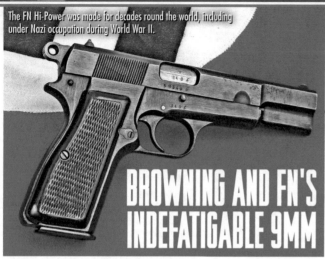

The FN Hi-Power was made for decades round the world, including under Nazi occupation during World War II.

A HIGHER POWER

BROWNING AND FN'S INDEFATIGABLE 9MM

I was saddened to hear Browning discontinued the Hi-Power in 2018. It was ahead of its time when introduced in 1935, and still as practical an autoloading pistol as you can get at its demise 83 years later. Beyond being a great design, it was also a trendsetter with its 13-round magazine making it one of the first, if not the actual first, double-column 9mm pistols.

The Hi-Power was John M. Browning's last design. He passed away in 1926 while residing in Belgium and working with the *Fabrique Nationale* firm. At his death, another talented firearms designer at FN named Dieudonne Saive took over.

FN's Hi-Power was introduced almost a decade later.

A WORLD-WIDE WEB

A little-known fact among modern handgunners is the Hi-Power was truly international in both manufacture and usage. FN had Hi-Powers in full production for only five years when the German Wehrmacht invaded Belgium. When the dust settled, the Germans instructed FN to continue production of it under the name 640b. Less formally, it was called the P35, short for *Pistole 1935*. Tens of thousands served in both *Heer* (army) and *SS* hands.

Around the same time, a Canadian firm with firearms manufacturing capability was tasked with duplicating them for issuance to the armed forces of Great Britain, China and Canada. This was the John Inglis Company Ltd., of Toronto. However, there was a problem. The engineering drawings were in Nazi-occupied Belgium. It's believed some FN-made Hi-Powers were reverse engineering by Inglis' draftsmen.

The Hi-Powers ordered by the Chinese from both FN before the war and Inglis during the war are very interesting. They have tangent rear sights graduated to 500 meters and were issued with wooden shoulder stocks also serving as holsters. Logically, the British and Canadian ordnance officers who placed orders for Inglis Hi-Powers considered the shoulder stocks and tangent sights as ridiculous. Their Hi-Powers had a simple notched rear with dovetailed front blade.

Post-World War II, FN continued to make Hi-Powers, and according to

Three versions of Browning Hi-Powers. At left is an FN and middle is a Canadian Inglis version made for a Chinese contract. Both are World War II production. At right is a modern Hi-Power.

the book *Military Small Arms of the 20th Century* by Ian Hogg and Charles Weeks, no fewer than 55 nations adopted the pistol for their armies. If Hi-Powers are not still in some military organizations' holsters today, I'll eat John Taffin's hat.

COMING AROUND

The Browning Hi-Power's use extended well past military service. They've been popular in this country for decades for defense and target competition. I fired my first one in 1971 and was duly impressed with its fit and finish. However, I never actually owned a Hi-Power until about 2006 when I was putting together my World War II firearms collection. Then I purchased a Chinese-style Inglis, one complete with shoulder stock and an FN variant with Nazi stamps.

During my shooting of World War II Lugers and P38 9mms, there were occasional stoppages. The ammunition

While a shoulder stock and tangent sight on a 9mm might seem silly, Duke's Chinese contract Inglis Hi-Power is certainly an eye-catcher!

was both factory and handloads with various bullet types such as FMJs, JSPs and cast bullet RNs. Neither of my Hi-Powers hesitated with any ammunition fed to them.

In 2015 I found myself in need of a "modern" 9mm for an article, so I turned to Browning for a Hi-Power. Interestingly, its parts were produced in Belgium but assembled in Portugal. It was a fine quality pistol and, like its older military brethren, it gave nary a bobble with any sort of ammunition. If I'd known it was going to be dropped in 2018 I might have purchased it instead of sending it back when the loan time was up.

My guess is the new, curveless, blocky, soulless, synthetic pistols spelled the demise of Browning's all-steel Hi-Power. I find this to be a true shame for a gun with its pedigree that's soldiered on for so long.

Duke practicing double taps with his S&W Model 442 .38 from about seven paces. Many people carry small guns like this, but never practice. Don't be that person.

Duke's hot weather handguns are these two 5-shooters — an S&W Model 360 and S&W Model 442 loaded with .38 Special ammo.

ALMOST... A DQ STOP TURNS UGLY

Last summer for the first time in my life I thought I might have to use a gun to defend myself. I did not, but the episode rattled me that day, and six months later I still wonder about it. The encounter was very strange.

It was a hot July evening. Yvonne had some sort of meeting for horse lovers, so a visiting friend and I decided we needed ice cream. We duly drove into town to the nearest Dairy Queen and each got chocolate sundaes. For some reason my friend was driving, but we were in my mini-van. The evening was decidedly warm so we parked under a shade tree in a parking lot behind the DQ. It belonged to them, was paved, I'd say about 50 yards long and perhaps 20 yards wide. It could be entered from both the front of the DQ and an exit at the rear onto another city street. There were a few picnic tables but we had the place to ourselves — briefly.

While we sat there enjoying our treat, I happened to notice a fellow in the next lot about 20 yards away behind an electrician's or plumber's business. He was unloading tools from a work truck. I'm fairly situationally aware and pointed out to my buddy, "The guy over there is packing." That's perfectly fine here in Montana, openly or concealed with a CCW license. The fellow appeared to have a 1911 on his right hip and a spare mag on his left side.

Now hold that thought for a moment.

About then what I call a "bubba-mobile" roared in from the front parking lot entrance. It was painted primer gray, had rusted-out fenders and a muffler so loud we could barely hear one another. The driver had on a straw hat and at least a three or four day's beard stubble. He backed into a parking space about 20 feet to my right, parallel with us, but only stayed a moment. Then he roared away, screeching his tires, out the back entrance to the street. We shrugged and continued minding our own business.

Mere minutes later Mr. Bubba again roared into the lot from the front passing close behind our parked mini-van. He then stopped with his truck situated so we would be perfectly T-boned if he backed up. And that's exactly what he did, again screeching his tires — but stopping a mere foot or two from the driver's side door of our vehicle. Then he roared away out the back entrance again making his tires squeal. My friend said, "Heck if he had kept going he would have hit me dead center."

That's when I double checked my S&W Model 442 .38 to make sure it was loaded.

BUT WAIT

Minutes later, for a third time the guy roared into the lot from the front. This time, without slowing, he tried to turn beside my van's driver's side. In doing so he whacked the van's bumper taking it and the tail light out. Sitting inside we got a severe jolt. At this point I exited the van's passenger side and went around behind it. The .38 was in my right hand shoved out of sight into my pocket. I could see Mr. Bubba jumping out of his truck and running around the front of it. My decision then was made. He had acted aggressively for no reason and if he had been armed even with so much as a tire iron I was going to shoot.

Instead he was unarmed and immediately started blubbering, "I'm sorry, oh God, I'm sorry! I'll make this right. I've got insurance. I didn't mean to hit you." This was being shouted at me with whiskey breath. And by his manic behavior I figured drugs were involved also.

At this point seeing there was no danger I happened to glance past Mr. Bubba to where the workman had been unloading tools. Bless his heart; he had his 1911 out and was braced against his work truck covering me. I raised my left hand palm out to show him we were okay and he holstered and went on about his business. You've got to love Montana!

POST THOUGHTS

I took the fellow's insurance information, never dreaming for a moment it would be valid but it turned out to be good. Still, because of the damage I had to call the city police. When I started dialing the cops Mr. Bubba took off on foot like a scared rabbit and I never saw him again. The cop asked his whereabouts and I told him. He said, "Never mind. His address is right here on his insurance information. I'll get him later." That was the end of it.

The guy's behavior was completely erratic. Why keep coming back to this parking lot? Why peel rubber? Why pull so close to us in a completely empty lot? I'll guess I'll never know. What I did learn is a peaceful situation can go to hell instantly. My hot weather handguns are S&W 5-shooters — a Model 360 and a Model 442. High capacity autoloader packers might sneer at my choice but the first rule of self-defense is to have a gun, and I did.

I'm also glad someone I didn't even know was prepared to help me. And finally to critique myself, being right handed I stepped into the open between our vehicles to confront the guy. I should have remained behind cover, for I had no idea if he was armed or not.

A REMINGTON RESURFACES

This is the near forgotten Hartford Armory replica of the Remington Model 1875 .44-40 Duke landed recently.

Back in the first years of this century a fellow contacted me saying he was putting a replica of the Remington Model 1875 revolver into production and he would like to visit and show me his prototypes. Definitely! Especially because in my opinion the Remington '75s were about the most unheralded sixguns of the black powder era.

He showed up with a satchel full of revolvers, even including a prototype of the very rare Model 1890 Remington.

We spent an afternoon shooting his revolvers and as I remember they were in .44-40 and .45 Colt calibers. They were beautifully crafted pieces of machinery. The best way I could describe them was they were reminiscent of the fit and finish of 1960s vintage Ruger Super Blackhawks. The new manufacturing company was called "Hartford Armory" and of course located in that Connecticut city. The revolvers were all going to be purely "Made in USA."

I was impressed with the samples and told the fellow once he had them in production, to send me a sample or two. I'd write them up fairly and probably buy one or both. The fellow left and I never heard another word from him. I did learn a replica importer back east was going to be sole source for the Hartford Armory revolvers. Then, at least in my life, they faded into obscurity.

THE ORIGINAL

Remington's Model 1875 was intended as a competitor with Colt's new "Strap Pistol" of 1873 that eventually gained the moniker of Colt Single Action Army. In some ways the Remington was superior to Colt's design. Whereas the Colt's grip frame consisted of two pieces bolted to each other and then to the main frame by six screws, the Remington's grip frame was forged integral with the main frame, with the single piece trigger guard held in its recess by a single screw.

Obviously, Remington borrowed heavily on the SAA's basic design, as the 1875's mechanical function was the same. Anyone familiar with a Colt SAA could pick a Remington Model 1875 up and go right to work with it. Of course both revolvers were single action only.

There was a half-cock notch allowing the cylinder to rotate freely for loading. Cartridges were inserted into chambers by means of a loading gate on the frame's right side. After firing, empty cases were punched out of chambers by means of an ejector rod mounted on the barrel's right side. The Colt's ejector was housed in a steel tube but Remington's version was exposed. Sights were similar, grooves down the frames' top straps for the rear, and blades (Colt) or tapered posts (Remington) for front sights. The two single actions are so close in size holsters for them are interchangeable.

The '75 had one feature the Colt did not. Running from the frame to near the end of the 7½" barrels were what some collectors call the "sail." It's a sturdy piece of steel serving to brace the barrel when the revolver was used as a club in combat. I've actually encountered Colt SAAs with barrels bent upward from striking something or somebody with a downward blow.

As this photo shows the Colt SAA (bottom) and Remington Model 1875 (top) are similar in size and function exactly the same.

REMINGTON'S BIG MISTAKE

Except for a few specimens made as .45's for government trials, the Remington '75's were all .44's. One chambering was proprietary, the .44 Remington. The other was the great .44-40, and this might be where Remington made a grave mistake. Their .44 round used a heel type bullet actually about 0.451" in diameter. I've had the opportunity to check chamber mouths on two vintage Remington '75 .44-40's and both had 0.446" chamber mouths. At that time .44-40's were factory loaded with .425" bullets. So you can guess how badly those guns shot with this arrangement.

Duke has only owned one original Model 1875 .44 Remington chambered for its proprietary caliber. He had it refinished along the way.

I only got to fire one of those original Remington .44-40's and it keyholed every bullet. The only original Remington Model 1875 I've owned was pretty much a gray relic. However, it was in .44 Remington caliber and its chamber mouths likewise measured 0.446". Recently a correspondent told me his Remington Model 1890 .44-40 had 0.457" chamber mouths!

Now back to the Hartford Army revolvers. Recently on a website I saw an HA Model 1875 .44-40 listed for sale. Duke's luck again! I spoke for it without hesitation. It appeared brand-new/unfired on arrival with serial number HA0010. How does it shoot? That's going to be a topic for a future column after I get a variety of factory loads and handloads through it. I'm just happy as heck to land one after all those years!

Photos: Yvonne Venturino

Besides shortening their Super Blackhawk's barrels Duke and his friend had them fitted with more hand-filling grips — one of fancy walnut and one of rosewood.

REUNITED

Back in 1973 a friend and I got it in our heads we should take a couple saddle horses and my trusty steed "Duke" as a pack horse and head south. As in south from our normal stomping grounds around the Livingston/Bozeman area of southern Montana. We didn't have a specific goal; we would ride until our money or our enthusiasm ran out. Coincidentally, both happened a little past Jackson, Wyoming. We won't go into detail about a couple of blondes met along the way of whom we didn't want to lose track.

For people who live in the area under discussion, it will be no surprise to hear the weather in this high country can be fierce in June. So, rather stupidly, we started our adventure on the first day of June. It rained and snowed much of the trip, and then the sky cleared. Temperatures rose instantly into the comfort zone for mosquitoes, which was another factor in our quitting.

People living in this area also are aware it's the best grizzly bear habitat left in the continental United States. Admittedly much of our journey was poorly planned, but one factor given considerable thought was the handguns we would pack. Up front we decided they should be chambered for the same cartridge. We figured robust Ruger Super Blackhawk .44 Magnums would be best except for the long 7½" barrel which can be uncomfortable in a belt holster while riding. Thus we got the idea of having our Rugers' barrels shortened to 5½". Although those two handgun barrels were cut by different gunsmiths far apart they both came out nicely. His got a matte blue in the process but mine got a less attractive but functional touch up around where the front sight was silver-soldered in place.

HORSE SENSE?

One factor about the Rugers we both disliked was their factory grips. They were homely and too thin. On a side trip before our trail excursion started we roamed through Twin Falls, Idaho, where we had heard of a small custom grip maker named Cloyce's Gun Stocks. Anyway they fitted us up with fancy walnut for my buddy and rosewood for me. They were more hand-filling than factory stocks and far more attractive.

We also needed leather gear for the big Rugers. My friend was a talented leather worker and made his own beautiful belt and holster. I turned to S.D. Myres of El Paso for a Threepersons style single-action holster with my initials "MLV" hand carved, and a matching belt with only 10 cartridge loops. We figured 10 on belts and five in .44's was enough.

Only once on the trip was one of the Rugers unholstered. Our packhorse, Duke, was big and intelligent, which was why I was nicknamed after him — or at least it's what I say about it. Unfortunately his smarts sometimes got him in trouble, just like me. Toward the end of the ride he learned he could pull his lead rope free just by laying back on it. I remember my palm sizzling as the rope burned through.

I'm ashamed to admit it but in my fatigued, irritable state, the sixth time this happened I dismounted and gave him a good whack up the side of his head. Not so smart on my part; after the seventh time when I dismounted he ran from me. As he rounded a curve in the trail I pulled my .44 and put a bullet in the ground about 10 feet ahead of him. When the plume of dust rose he froze in his tracks until I walked up and retrieved the lead rope. Like I said he was smart.

LOST PARTNERS

My riding partner on that trip and I have now been friends for 48 years. Although he's been living "Down Under" for the last 24 we have always kept in touch. These last five years he has come to Montana for summers. A few years ago we were reminiscing about that ride and our .44's.

He said his Ruger and holster had been stolen from his mother's home in California where he left it when going abroad. I had no memory whatsoever of where my Ruger had gone.

Then *surprise, surprise.* My friend found his Ruger (sans belt and holster) in storage along with some of his other property. About the same time another long-time friend mentioned in passing, "For 12 years in Alaska I had that Ruger .44 I bought from you back in the '70s. I never fired it."

For this column I borrowed it from him for photography. Those two fine old Ruger .44's were reunited after almost 50 years.

Duke and a friend had these Ruger Super Blackhawk .44 Magnum barrels shortened to 5½" for comfortable carrying in the saddle. After being separated and thought lost, Duke was able to reunite them briefly after almost 50 years.

ACCOUTERMENTS

Duke ended up paying more for his Artillery Luger accouterments than he did for the pistol itself — stocks, loaders, holsters and more abound for it.

My dictionary says "accouterments" are military accessories. I love the word because to me it seems like a combination of accumulate and collect, both endeavors I do very well. Let's apply accouterments to handguns: What do they need in the way of accouterments? The first two in my mind are the most common. They are holsters and nice grips (stocks). Make mine leather in the first and some sort of organic material in the second.

Then there are accouterments specific to certain types of handguns. Speed loaders for DA revolvers or even half- or full-moon clips for .45

Because Yvonne is around horses daily Duke insists she carry a small knife in case of tangled ropes, etc. Maybe you should too?

Auto revolvers come to mind. And don't forget lots of spare magazines and magazine pouches for semi-autos. Most young shooters need more accouterments. Laser-dot sights, flashlights and whatnot to fill up the rails placed all over many semi-autos nowadays fill the bill.

What about single action revolvers? Since they are not commonly considered fighting handguns nowadays they usually (hopefully) don't have rails. What could possibly be necessary accouterments for them? From my 51 years of experience as a single-action shooter there are two. A screwdriver is essential! By my count Ruger Old Model SAs have 10, New Models have nine and Colt SAAs (and replicas) have 11 external screws that are forever

working loose. A properly fitting screwdriver is a necessity. I've ruined more SA screws than most people will ever see by using poor screwdrivers!

Then there's the problem of stuck cylinder base pins. Anyone who has owned and fired Colt SAA type revolvers knows about this problem. I've driven out many after dismantling the sixgun and punching them out from the rear. Peacemaker Specialists markets both proper fitting screwdrivers for single actions and a special prong-shaped steel tool to pry those recalcitrant base pins out.

Single-Action revolvers sometimes need specialized accouterments such as this stuck base pin puller. Duke reminds you to use proper fitting screwdrivers too.

LUXURY LUGER GOODIES

If you really want to get involved with a firearm — the accouterments for which could properly be termed "money pit" — then buy a German P08 *Lange* (meaning long). American collector types refer to them as Artillery Lugers. They actually were first intended for troops protecting World War I artillery and machine gun positions. I know the "money pit" deal because I bought one.

Germany's P08 *Lange* pistols came in sets with plenty of accouterments. Included were standard 8-round magazines, snail drum 32-round magazines, a special lever-actuated loading tool for the latter, a take-down tool also used for helping load the 8-round magazines and a special tiny spanner wrench for zeroing rear sight for elevation. Sound like a lot? I'm not finished!

Also issued with them were a leather

holster, straps and magazine pouches. The holster had a slot especially for storing the special long cleaning rod needed for a P08 *Lange's* 8" barrel and a pocket for the take down tool. The holster was secured to a wooden "shoulder board" that, when attached to the Luger, turned it into a carbine. It took me several years but I finally added all those accouterments to my Luger P08 *Lange*. Only the leather gear is reproduction; all the rest are original. The accouterment cost was above and beyond what I paid for the pistol itself. I just couldn't stop myself from searching out and buying it all.

For the more practical sort, a knife is a good accouterment for handgun-packing folks. Fighting men and outdoors types need them for all sorts of reasons. Folders and sheath knives abound in pockets and on belts here in

Montana. Back in my horse-riding days I wouldn't be without a knife, and since Yvonne is still around horses nearly every day, she packs a small sheath knife. You might be surprised even here in Montana she is sometimes told she cannot enter an establishment wearing that petite knife.

And finally we get to the ultimate handgun accouterment — a carbine in the same caliber. I've been working with a couple of modern ones. The idea started in the 1870s and is far from dying today.

SLIP-UPS AND BLUNDERS

Duke has written the .38-40 caliber stamp (bottom) was never put on 1st Generation Colt SAAs. It was always .38 WCF (above). He was wrong.

Duke was wrong that Model 1875 Remingtons were never chambered as .45's — he stands corrected.

Duke felt logically, the .44 S&W Special (right) was never loaded with black powder as was the .44 S&W Russian (left). He was wrong again.

With my writing career nearing 50 years (full time since 1981) with over 2,000 printed features and columns I'm bound to have made mistakes. I'm talking not of mistakes in opinions. Those can modify or change entirely with age and experience. I'm talking about mistakes of facts.

There was a pretty good one in my column in the Nov/Dec 2019 *Handgunner*. I stated Remington's Model 1875 revolver had not been chambered as a .45 except for a "few for government trials." I was wrong on two points. The more minor one was saying "few" without double checking my sources. Actually there was only one .45 sent to the U.S. Army. It was chambered for the then-standard .45 Government, aka .45 S&W, aka .45 Schofield. However, its chambers were bored straight through so longer .45 Colt rounds would also chamber. The Army officers testing that .45 sample liked it, but no orders to Remington followed. My bigger mistake was saying Model 1875 .45's had not been made otherwise. Mostly my statement was based on an original Remington catalog dated 1877 and my own observations at dozens of antique gun shows.

Thanks to reader Daniel Pozerak of Michigan I've been hereby corrected. He sent me documentation that Remington actually did make .45's to the tune of hundreds (exact number unknown). These had mostly been ordered by the Mexican Government, chambered for .45 U.S. Government and fitted with 7½" barrels. He also enclosed a copy of a Remington advertisement dated 1882 saying the Model 1875 was available in chamberings of .44 Remington, .44 Winchester and .45 Government. Thanks for this info, Dan!

MISTAKES GALORE!

Here's another boo-boo of mine. Several times over the decades I've written, although Colt's 3rd Generation Single Action Army revolvers have mostly been caliber-stamped, .38-40 originals never were marked so. I said they were all marked ".38 W.C.F." I discovered this was wrong when a friend handed me his late 1st Generation SAA marked .38-40 exactly like the new 3rd Generation ones. I'm not sure when the caliber stamping was changed. I have one with a factory letter saying it was shipped in 1926. It's marked ".38 W.C.F." on its barrel's left side. An original Colt catalog I have dated 1935 says the SAA is available in "38-40 (.38 Winchester)". So the change probably came somewhere in those nine years.

Here's another example of a mistake you can enjoy celebrating with me. In his book *History Of Smith & Wesson,* author and S&W historian Roy Jinks said their .44 Special was developed in 1907 so it would hold 26 grains of black powder compared to 23 grains used in their 1872-introduced .44 Russian. As .44 Special fans know it was the introductory cartridge for the S&W Hand Ejector, 1st Model (Triplelock). Several times, I doubted in print the .44 Special had ever been loaded with black powder because its heavy fouling would have quickly tied up those Triplelocks' finely fitted mechanisms.

I was proved wrong when another writer found black powder .44 Special factory cartridges listed in a 1916 Winchester catalog. And on this note I did more searching and found in the *Ideal Handbook No. 28* dated 1926, Remington's black powder .44 Special factory loads with 246-gr. lead bullets were rated at having 820 fps velocity from a 6" barrel. I still think black powder would have tied up a triplelock in only a few rounds, but .44 Specials factory loaded with black powder indeed existed.

ONE MORE OOPSIE

That was in copying previous writers in saying .45 Colt SAAs had 0.454" barrel groove diameters in the 1st Generation and the dimension was changed to 0.451" simultaneously with the introduction of the 2nd Generation in 1956. Nope. Not so. Never happened. Back in the 1990s I was given a 1922 factory spec sheet from the Colt factory. It said all their .45 barrels — .45 Auto and .45 Colt — were to measure 0.451" minimum and 0.452" maximum across their grooves. I have an SAA from 1926 and its barrel slugged 0.451". Also, the 1926 *Ideal Handbook No. 28* lists .45 Colt groove diameter as 0.452" and .45 Auto as 0.451".

So here's my advice to future gun'riters. Don't discount everything you read from us current ones. But check our facts for documentation. We might not know what we're talking about!

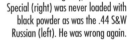

A COLT BUNTLINE SPECIAL FIND

Upon entering the door of a recent Montana gun show, I thought, "My money is safe. There will be nothing in here that trips my trigger." Having walked no more than 10 feet and inside of five minutes, I was nigh on broke.

What got my wallet was a pristine 2nd Generation Colt Buntline Special .45 still in its dilapidated original box along with instruction pamphlet. For younger readers who might read this and not understand; a Buntline Special is a standard Colt Single Action Army except it wears a 12" barrel. I am no great fan of Buntlines having owned a 3rd Generation one back in the 1990s. I purchased this one because Colt Buntlines are moderately rare — especially 2nd Generation models. And this one was in *like new* condition. Truthfully, I couldn't tell for sure if it had ever been fired. It will have been by the time you read this.

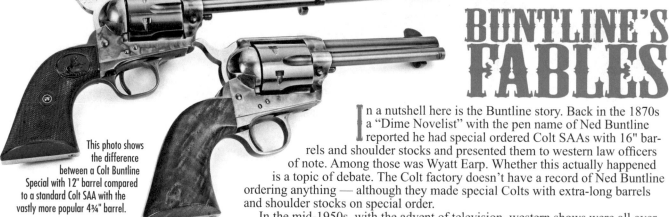

This photo shows the difference between a Colt Buntline Special with 12" barrel compared to a standard Colt SAA with the vastly more popular 4¾" barrel.

Colt also gave the 12" barreled SAAs their own name of Buntline Special.

BUNTLINE'S FABLES

In a nutshell here is the Buntline story. Back in the 1870s a "Dime Novelist" with the pen name of Ned Buntline reported he had special ordered Colt SAAs with 16" barrels and shoulder stocks and presented them to western law officers of note. Among those was Wyatt Earp. Whether this actually happened is a topic of debate. The Colt factory doesn't have a record of Ned Buntline ordering anything — although they made special Colts with extra-long barrels and shoulder stocks on special order.

In the mid-1950s, with the advent of television, western shows were all over prime time. I for one loved them. *Cheyenne* was my favorite but *Have Gun Will Travel* was another good one, *Maverick* was entertaining and gave James Garner his start. Another one well remembered was about Wyatt Earp as portrayed by Hugh O'Brian. His Colt Buntline also got plenty of airtime.

It was the popularity of those TV westerns that nudged Colt back into reintroducing the SAA in 1956. Naturally, the company capitalized on the popularity of the Wyatt Earp TV show by introducing their "Buntline Special" in 1957. The one I found at a Montana gun show was made during that first year judging by its serial number.

Early 2nd Generation Buntline Specials had a separate serial number for their barrels.

This is Duke's number BB318. Colt started the numbering with BB100.

BUNTLINES BY THE NUMBERS

Colt did something unique, at least with their early Buntline Specials — they added serial numbers to barrels that weren't matched to numbers on the frames. These numbers had a BB prefix for "Buntline Barrel" and then numbers starting with 100. Those numbers are stamped on barrel bottoms just in front of the cylinder's base pin. Mine is BB318. According to the book *Colt SAA Post War Model* by George Garton, Colt produced 595 Buntline Specials with blue/case colored finish in 1957. There's more proof mine was first year production.

Also in Garton's informative book are basic Buntline Special production numbers for both blue/case color finish and nickel-plating. Colt made 3,994 blue/case colored Buntlines between 1957 and 1974 when 2nd Generation SAA production ended. During the same time frame the company only manufactured 65 nickel-plated Buntline Specials. All were chambered as .45 Colt.

Sales of Buntline Specials followed TV western trends. They sold best in their first three years: 595, 1644 and 277 of blue/case color. Figures didn't reach triple digits again until 1970.

Did the extra-long Buntline barrel give super velocity to .45 Colts? Some comparative testing I did with my old 12" barrel Buntline Special and a 7.5" standard SAA says no. A charge of 8.0 grains of Unique with 255-gr. lead alloy bullet gave 999 fps from my 7.5" barreled SAA and 10 fps less from the Buntline Special. Next I tried a charge of 7.2 grains of W231 with the same bullet. The 7.5" barrel gave 937 fps and the Buntline Special beat that by only eight fps.

Obviously, the Buntline Special was a novelty sold by Colt without actual practical purpose. I've never been especially attracted to them but finding one from first year production still with its original albeit nearly destroyed box definitely tripped my trigger. Next I'd like to stumble on a 2nd Generation .45 with a 3" barrel. Only 503 of those were made.

.44 RUSSIAN, SPECIAL & MAGNUM

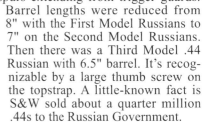

It amazes me how many shooters — young and old — talk about their .44 Specials or .44 Magnums without having a clue as to their ancestry. Neither arrived on the revolver scene as full-blown innovations. They were derived in a stair step fashion. Their story started in 1872 in what might be called *an instance of Russian collusion*. S&W introduced their first metallic cartridge-firing revolver in 1870. Named Model #3, it was chambered for the .44 Henry, same as used in Winchester's Model 1866 rifles and carbines. Hoping for army contracts S&W submitted the new Model #3 to the U.S. Government for testing. It was almost immediately rejected because .44 Henry was rimfire — the government wanted only centerfires. So, S&W remodeled the .44 Henry cartridge to centerfire ignition and called it .44/100.

Above: Samples of revolvers chambered for all three .44s. On the left is a Navy Arms replica of a 3rd Model S&W .44 Russian. Below, from left to right: .44 S&W Russian, .44 S&W Special and .44 Remington Magnum.

COLLUDING FOR GOLD

A Russian general serving as a diplomat in America took note of the Model #3 and thought it would be an excellent sidearm for the Czar's cavalry. Except he disliked the two-diameter heel-type bullet used in .44/100. The general *had this crazy idea a bullet's body should be the same diameter* and fit inside a cartridge case. Since the Russians promised to pay for their S&W Model #3 in gold, the company was happy to accept their idea. Thus was born the S&W .44 Russian, and henceforth the .44/100 was called .44 American.

Early on factory .44 Russian loads contained roundnose bullets as heavy as 275 grains. Winchester's 1899 catalog listed them at 255 gr., still roundnose. Some of these early factory loads had lube grooves exposed. Later all lube grooves were covered as would be right and proper with lead alloy bullets. Case length was 0.97" and velocity was likely a bit over 700 fps. The black powder charge was 23 grains.

As matters progressed, the Russians wanted changes in the Model #3 and the allure of gold was incentive for S&W to make them. First model .44 Russian Model #3s looked identical to the company's .44 Americans, but soon the Russians wanted some changes. Most notable were humps at the top of Model #3's grips and odd-looking spurs extending from trigger guards. Barrel lengths were reduced from 8" with the First Model Russians to 7" on the Second Model Russians. Then there was a Third Model .44 Russian with 6.5" barrel. It's recognizable by a large thumb screw on the topstrap. A little-known fact is S&W sold about a quarter million .44s to the Russian Government.

ALL-AMERICAN .44 SPECIAL

Now jump to 1907. S&W wanted to enter the large frame, swing-out cylinder market. As a cartridge for the Hand Ejector, First Model .44 (nicknamed triplelock) they introduced a wild and crazy idea. They lengthened .44 Russian's case to 1.16", using the exact same 246-gr. bullet at a similar velocity of about 750 fps. It was named .44 S&W Special. Factory loads carried either smokeless or black powder. S&W carried the .44 Special through four remodels stopping in 1966. In the 1980s they reintroduced Model 24s (Hand Ejector, Fourth Model) and Model 624s (stainless steel) and in the 21st century there have been some .44 Special limited editions.

Then in 1956 S&W knocked the

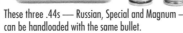

These three .44s — Russian, Special and Magnum — can be handloaded with the same bullet.

gun world on its ear by introducing the .44 Remington Magnum with its introductory vehicle being a strengthened N-Frame. In 1957 the company went to model numbers with .44 Mags getting Model 29. Again, the new cartridge was *a wonder of innovation* (sarcasm intended). The new magnum case was the .44 Special stretched to 1.29". However, bullets changed from 246-gr. RN to 240-gr. SWC with a gas check. Velocity changed also to nominal 1,470

fps. Those factory loads leaded like the dickens! I know — 18 such rounds came with my first S&W .44 Magnum in 1968.

Personally speaking, I've owned and handloaded for a multitude of revolvers for all three of these .44s. Of course, Russian and Special .44s can be safely fired in .44 Magnum revolvers, but I freely admit nowadays I'm far fonder of shooting the Russian version from Navy Arms replica 3rd Model No. 3.

Like me, it's big but gentle.

BBQ COLT

R ecently on an Internet website a fellow asked me, "Do you have a bar-beque Colt?" I replied, "Um, No, I don't think so." Then another fellow, sensing my ignorance, added the term arose from fancied-up handguns Texas Rangers reserved for backyard BBQs. A third fellow added, "Mike, you just showed a picture of an engraved Colt SAA, so you definitely have a BBQ Colt." All this got me to thinking, "What if I was invited to a BBQ requiring a fancy handgun?"

Most of my life I could have been named Mister Ordinary. My hats, saddles, boots and clothes were all plain. At age 24 I surrendered to just a mite of ostentation. Throughout my high school years, I used laundry markers to put my MLV initials in brand, so when I ordered my first S.D. Myres holsters I had them hand-carved accordingly. Since then, I've plastered my "brand" on just about everything. Over the years two readers had branding irons made as presents for me. Once when heating one of those branding irons Yvonne said she saw *a strange gleam in my eyes* and vacated the premises. I deny that!

One of Duke's BBQ guns could be this polished stainless-steel Colt .38 Super with floral carved holster by El Paso Saddlery.

CANDIDATE EVALUATION

A fter this Internet chat and weeks of lockdown boredom, I sat in my gun vault and considered my candidates for BBQ guns. One would be a Colt 1911 of the ELCEN serial number range. These were ordered by a major distributor supposedly for sale "south of the border." For this reason, they were all .38 Supers. Made of stainless steel (except for the sights) they were given such a high polish I thought at first it was nickel-plating. Grips on mine are checkered rosewood. Then I turned to El Paso Saddlery for a floral carved holster for packing it.

However, my most gussied-up handguns are single actions. In fact, I could attend BBQs every weekend for months without feeling underdressed toting a fine SAA. Two of mine are engraved Colts. The .38 WCF/.38-40 was made up expressly for the Colt Collector's Association. It's numbered 79 of 150. It has 4.75" barrel with tasteful engraving, but as yet I've not equipped it with

fancy grips. I can't make up my mind as to what material they should be crafted from — fancy walnut, checkered rosewood, bison bone, ivory, or something else.

My other fancy Colt SAA was engraved here in Montana by Brian Gouse. It's also 4.75" barreled with the factory issue grips — for now. What takes it a notch up is the two cylinders are fitted. The original one is .44 WCF/.44-40. With considerable searching I located an unfired .44 Special cylinder and had it engraved also by Brian. If attending a backyard BBQ *where I might be charged by a raging bull or hungry panther* I'd fit the .44 Special cylinder and load it with the special run of Black Hills .44 Special factory loads with 250-gr. SWCs.

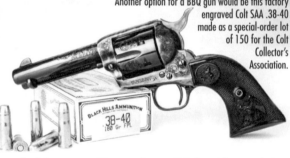

Another option for a BBQ gun would be this factory engraved Colt SAA .38-40 made as a special-order lot of 150 for the Colt Collector's Association.

If attending a BBQ with prestigious guests where I might have to resort to name dropping in order to get my proper quota of attention, I'd wear a very special Colt SAA. This one is a .45 with 4.75" barrel and full blue finish. Its stocks are exquisitely relief carved ivory with MLV on one side and steer head on the other. They are the work of Paul Persinger of El Paso. This Colt bears name dropping because it was ordered from Colt by country/western musician Hank Williams, Jr. with my name engraved on the backstrap.

A very special Colt SAA of Duke's is this gift from Hank Williams, Jr. It is a full blued .45 with relief carved ivory grips by Paul Persinger of El Paso. Note Duke's MLV initials.

DON'T FORGET YOUR BETTER HALF

S o far, I've left Yvonne out of this imagining game. I couldn't attend such a BBQ so finely adorned with her looking plain. If we were attending a BBQ together, we have a perfect, yet not identical pair. Back in the early 21st century when U.S. Firearms was making beautiful quality single actions, I ordered two with engraving. Yvonne already had a Colt SAA .44 WCF/.44-40 with a 5.5" barrel, so she asked for her USFA to have the same length. Obviously, my preference for barrel lengths is 4.75". Hers has serial number YMV1 and mine is stamped MLV3.

Truth be told, the backyard BBQs I've attended in my lifetime could probably be counted on the fingers of one hand. But who knows? It could happen.

HANDGUN MILESTONES

Strangely enough Duke's first handgun was a French Model 1935A 7.65 Long given to him by his father circa 1961.

The year 1968 was a banner one for Duke for acquiring handguns. The first one was a Smith & Wesson .44 Magnum pre-Model 29 which he kept until 2010.

Duke's third 1968 handgun was a Remington Rand U.S. Model 1911A1 .45 which he shot very poorly.

Recently a fellow asked me when I became interested in guns. My reply was … I was born with it. My older sister chimed in and said by age three the first thing I did every morning was buckle on my gun belt with its toy cap gun. This wasn't TV influence; we didn't have one.

From the beginning, I've hand jotted a list of every firearm I've owned. So, I have a timeline of handguns purchased, traded for or otherwise acquired.

MY FIRST... WHAT?

About 1961 Dad came home with my first real handgun. Neither of us had any idea what it actually was. I was allowed to keep it in my room but not show it off to other kids or take it out of the house. Dad felt safe because he somehow knew ammunition for it wasn't readily available.

I eventually learned the pistol was a French Model 1935A chambered for an odd 7.65mm Long round. Dad and the local police chief were both born of Italian immigrant parents and the police chief "gave" the pistol to my father. As my father was a bill collector, I have an idea why he was given it. Some French military surplus 7.65mm Long ammo did become available, so I finally did shoot the Model 1935A. In an ironic twist, I later sold the pistol to the police chief's son.

Following my inborn interest in cowboy handguns I received for my 17th birthday in 1966 a Colt Frontier Scout .22 LR. It was a short-lived treasure. The little single action was enjoyable to shoot, but hitting anything with it past about 10 yards was a matter of chance. In frustration I traded it back to the store with a few bucks extra for a Ruger Mark I .22LR. With its 6⅞" barrel and target sights, I could at last direct bullets to a target. I became enamored with bullseye shooting, which led to my next handgun milestone.

That same summer and by shenanigans too lengthy to detail here, I raised enough cash to buy a slightly used Smith & Wesson K38 with a 6" barrel. Cost: $50. However, factory ammo cost was a shock to my system. This led to me soon becoming a handloader.

A BANNER YEAR

The next year passed with no milestones, but 1968 was a banner year. During the winter a retiring West Virginia's Mingo County deputy sheriff had his S&W pre-Model 29 .44 Magnum for sale. He was asking $100. My soon-to-come income tax refund was nearly this much, so Dad floated me a loan to nab the big .44. I kept it 42 years; packing it up and down Montana mountains until deciding to let it go when I got too old for such pursuits.

By June 1968, my first year of college was finished. I was making $1.60 an hour hustling freight on the docks of a trucking company. A friend, the aforementioned chief of police's son, also worked there. One day he pointed out a truck driver and said, "He owns one of those SA Colt .45s you're always talking about." Long story made short: I aggravated the truck driver till he sold me the Colt. Cost again was $100. The .45 was of the second generation made in 1964.

A few evenings later Dad came home from work, reached into his hip pocket and handed me a WWII Remington Rand 1911A1 .45 Auto. He said, "I took this for a bill today. Do you want it?" I did! In just a few days, two .45s had been added to my growing assortment of handguns.

By the start of West Virginia's Marshall University's 1968 fall semester, I had saved enough money to buy reloading dies and bullet molds for my new handguns. After some shooting, I was happy with them except for the Remington Rand. I couldn't have hit one of John Taffin's hats with it at 25 yards. I sold it for $35, redirecting the cash to powder and primers.

Before classes started in September 1968, I conned a friend to share expenses for a camping trip to Montana. My idea was to visit the then-named Custer Battlefield. I fell in love with Montana and have been a full time Montana resident for nearly 50 years. In that half century I've owned hundreds of handguns including about 100 Colt SAAs, a passel of U.S. Model 1911A1s and even another French Model 1935A.

Still, the excitement of those first handgun milestones remains most vivid in my mind.

GENEROSITY OR STUPIDITY?

Back in the 1970s, during the years I lived in and around Yellowstone National Park, I became friends with a Mississippian named Jim Shumaker. For several years we lived in that area having lots of good times as single men in their 20s are apt to do. Jim was the sort of friend who stepped up when I busted my knee in 1976. Until I got back on my feet, he stopped by my place every afternoon after work to see to it my dog and I were cared for.

Duke sold this 2nd Generation Colt SAA .357 Magnum to Jim Schumaker in 1977 and bought it back from him in 1996.

I WANT THAT

Not long into our friendship, we discovered a shared interest in single action revolvers. His was a Ruger Blackhawk (Old Model) .357 Magnum. Mine were Colt SAAs (2nd Generation) in calibers .357 Magnum and .45 Colt. As soon as he laid eyes on my Colts, he became covetous. Many times he said, "Sell me one of your Colts: either one." Of course, my answer was always, "Nope, ain't gonna happen."

One fine spring day while I was still on crutches he came by and said, "Put on your boots. You need to get out in the sunlight. And get both your Colts out too." He had permission to shoot "gophers" (actually ground squirrels) on a nearby ranch. The place was truly infested with the little varmints, and we shot away lots of my .357 and .45 handloads that afternoon. Jim intermittently pleaded, "Sell me one of these." And I always said, "Never." In those years between the end

of 2nd Generation production and beginning of 3rd Generation production, you couldn't just walk into a gun store and buy a Colt SAA off the shelf.

One Saturday in 1976 Jim and I drove to Bozeman, Montana, and as usual perused gun stores. In the Powder Horn on Bozeman's main street, we were looking over the used gun racks for anything of interest. A fellow walked past us and I, ever being observant, noticed the grip of a Colt SAA sticking out of the fellow's front trouser pocket. So, I sort of followed him and eavesdropped as he spoke to the store owner behind the new handgun counter. He wanted to trade his Colt SAA .45 for a S&W .357 Magnum. The store owner said he wasn't interested.

ART OF THE DEAL

At that point I intruded and asked the gent if we could look at the Colt. It about made me speechless — a condition my friends think is nigh impossible. It was an early 1900s 1st Generation .45 with 4¾" barrel in very nice condition. I asked, "How much?" He said, "That .357 S&W I want is about $250. I'll take that much." Now this is where the question about me being generous or stupid arises. I turned to Jim and said, "Well there's your Colt, right there." The deal was consummated, and we walked out of the store with what turned out to be a 1914 vintage SAA. The .45's seller was happy to get his .357 Magnum, and the store owner was happy to make a sale.

Walking down Bozeman's main street we both were enveloped in the pleasant aura of a job well done when suddenly the thought hit me, "I could have sold Jim one of my Colts and bought that .45 for myself." Almost simultaneously, Jim turned to me and

Jim Schumaker's 1914 vintage Colt SAA .45 — a happenstance find in 1976.

said, "Why didn't you buy this one for yourself?" The question remains unanswered to this day. Was it generosity or stupidity? I'll let you readers decide for yourselves.

Jim got set up to reload .45 Colts and we did lots of SAA shooting. In fact, we both bought 3rd Generation SAAs after they came out. His was a 7½" barreled .44 Special and mine was the same barrel length .45. Ironically, Jim did end up with my .357 SAA, after I became involved in varmint shooting and needed some bucks for a new scope. Nineteen years later Jim visited, and I bought it

back from him and still have it.

As always, time changes things. We both got married and began careers. Jim was hired by a nationwide hotelier and managed establishments from coast to coast. And of course, I became a gun'riter and stayed in Montana. We kept in touch over the years and Yvonne and I were pleased he and his wonderful wife Karen decided to return to this area upon retirement. He still has that Colt .45 and once in a while we get together and I get to shoot it again. Always we reminisce about those great old bygone days.

SINGLE-ACTION

These are Duke's 3rd Generation Colt SAA .44-40s for which he searched out .44 Special cylinders, turning them into "convertibles."

This Ruger New Model Blackhawk Convertible has 9mm and .357 Magnum cylinders.

VERSATILITY

It's odd how some things stick in your mind and others fly away as in a stiff wind. For instance, I can't remember to whom about 40 years ago I sold a 6"-barreled S&W Model 19 .357 Magnum. (I'd like to have it back.) However, I clearly remember a magazine article Skeeter Skelton wrote over 50 years gone by. In it he related in his youth he somehow got his hands on a Colt SAA Bisley Model stamped .41 Colt. But it was minus its cylinder. He took it to the local gun expert who put a .38-40 cylinder in it and said, "There, now you have a .38-40 because .41 Colts and .38-40s use the same barrel bore/groove dimensions." (Or something like that. Remember it was over 50 years ago.) The young Skeeter was confused then as was I being a young reader.

CYLINDER SWAP MEET

Right now on my desk is a 1904 vintage Colt SAA .38-40. With it is a .41 Colt cylinder that fits and times perfectly. What's more the old sixgun shoots fine with proper ammo from either cylinder. According to a factory spec sheet dated 1922, Colt used 0.401/0.402" for groove diameter for all their .41s and .38-40s. Factory loads for .41 Colt at that time had 0.386" soft lead bullets with deep hollowbases, so they would expand to grip rifling. Factory .38-40 loads used 0.400" bullets.

Such a capability is one of the single action genre of handguns' best benefits. As long as barrel bore specs are the same, switching cylinders to a different cartridge is a cinch. All that must be done with traditional SAs is half cock the hammer, open the loading gate, pull the base pin and drop out the current cylinder. To install another just reverse the process. With Ruger New Model single actions just start with opening the loading gate.

Ruger still catalogs their .357 Magnum/9mm Luger and .45 Colt/.45 Auto New Model Blackhawk Convertibles, along with their .22 Single Six Convertible with .22 LR and .22 WMR cylinders. I've owned or used them all. Once I was loaned a rare New Model Blackhawk .38-40/40 S&W convertible that shot superbly. However, I totally missed the .30 Carbine/.32-20 New Model Blackhawk Convertible.

Colt made a small run of their 4" barreled "Storekeeper" Models with both .45 Colt and .45 Auto cylinders and sold many more 3" barreled "Sheriff's Models" with both .44 Special and .44-40 cylinders. I had one of the former. With the .44 Special cylinder in place, I still use one of the latter with shot loads as my primary rattlesnake revolver during warm months.

Perhaps the most unusual dual cylindered single action I've ever owned was from the now defunct United States Firearms Company. They called it their Battle of Britain Single-Action. It was full blued, beautifully crafted with 5½" barrel, lanyard looped in the butt and caliber stamped .45 Automatic. Of course, it also came with a .45 Colt cylinder.

Duke once owned this rare U.S. Firearms "Battle of Britain" single action. It was caliber stamped .45 Automatic but also came with a .45 Colt cylinder.

VERSATILITY PAYS OFF

These last few years I've been picking up good Colt SAAs if the price is reasonable and inevitably my storage area was getting crowded. Then one day I got a brainstorm, "Why keep my two 3rd Generation .44 Specials? Why not sell them and let the money raised finance .44 Special cylinders for my 3rd Generation .44-40s?" I did just that but must say the search wasn't quick or simple for I needed one nickel-plated and the other blued. I spent months searching classified ads on websites or gunbroker.com auctions, but eventually my persistence paid off. The blued one had to be engraved with a gold line inlaid around it. This wasn't a problem as I knew the SAA's original engraver. It just added time and money to the project.

Now some very intelligent reader is thinking, "But, your .44-40s are factory sighted for 200-grain bullets and will shoot high with the 240/250-grain bullets normal for .44 Specials. Correct! But it just so happens I have a nice four-cavity bullet mold for 200-grain round nose .44 bullets of 0.430". So, my self-made convertibles are easy to hit with using either cylinder.

In a time when handguns are becoming increasingly utilitarian, I appreciate single actions for their gracefulness and versatility.

An array of Duke's black powder handloads for Frontier cartridges. From left: .38 Long Colt, .44 S&W American, .44 S&W Russian, .44 American, .44 WCF (.44-40), .45 S&W Schofield and .45 Colt.

FRONTIER FIREPOWER

irepower of Old West revolvers is one of the most mis-represented historical aspects of that era. No doubt most of the nonsense comes from Hollywood or, to a lesser degree, western novels. Bad guys get thrown about when struck by good guys' revolver bullets. Even horses take dramatic spills.

Truth is, it just wasn't so — at least not with holster size revolvers. In the beginning of the revolver era, sixguns were huge. The fabled 1847 Walker Colt at 4½ lbs. weighed about as much as the famous American M1 .30 Carbine. It was never meant for belt carry by troops — horses bore the weight in saddle holsters. However, Walkers with their .44 pure lead 148-grain balls over 60 grains of black powder did approach the power of a modern .357 Magnum.

THE "BELT PISTOL" ERA

By 1850 Colt finally brought out a revolver actually called a "belt pistol" meaning it was supposed to be worn on one's person. Today, that one is known as the Model 1851 or the Navy Colt. Its caliber was called .36 but ball size was 0.375" because back then a weapon's caliber was rated by the barrel's bore, not its groove diameter. A 0.375" round ball weighs about 80 grains and a 25-grain blackpowder charge from a '51 Navy or its successor, the Model 1861 could push it to about 900 to 1,000 fps. Black powder quality varied immensely in those days. That's about equal to one of today's .380 autos. Jesse James took a body hit from a .36 caliber revolver fighting as a guerilla in the Civil War and carried the ball until his death in 1882.

Even the hidebound U.S. Army thought .36 revolvers were a bit weak and therefore decided to switch to .44s when Colt managed to make one light enough for belt carry. That was the Model 1860, which was rivaled by Remington's Model 1858 in popularity during Civil War combat. Their 148-grain 0.457" round balls might hit 800 fps, which would give them just a mite more striking power than one of today's 148-grain .38 Special wadcutter target loads.

Duke shooting a Colt Model 1861 .36 cap and ball. A mere 25-grain powder charge made that much smoke.

Duke has handloaded black powder cartridges for these reproductions.

Model 1861 "converted" to .38 Colt.

Navy Arms Model # 3 .44 Russian.

Colt 1873-1973 .45 duplicate of a U.S. Cavalry SAA.

CARTRIDGE POWER

The above cap and ball revolvers reigned supreme among fighting men in the Old West until the advent of metallic cartridge revolvers circa 1870. Did the new self-contained cartridges dramatically increase revolver firepower? They did in regard to speedy reloading, but not so much in terms of knockdown power.

Take, for instance, the .36 caliber Colts. Many of those were "converted" to fire .38 Colt rimfire and centerfire cartridges. In the 1990s I had one of Colt's 2nd Generation Model 1861s converted to duplicate the very valuable originals. With a 130-grain heel-type bullet over 18 grains of black powder, it would barely break 700 fps. When the "long" .38 Colt version came along with a 145-grain bullet, it did break 700 fps by just a bit. When I fired those loads into a fence post on my property, the bullets' bases were sticking out.

Handgun power did begin to progress. S&W developed .44 American and .44 Russian in 1871 and 1872, respectively. Colt's .44 Colt also came in 1871. These rounds collectively carried bullets from about 210 to 255 grains, but none of them exceeded 750 fps from the 7½" to 8" barrels of their various sixguns. In other words, they about equaled the hitting power of a modern .44 Special round with the traditional loading of a 246-grain round nose bullet at about 750 fps.

Many six-gunny folks today think Colt and the U.S. Government finally got on the ball in 1873 with the new Colt "Strap Pistol" (topstrap) and .45 Colt cartridge. It's often touted about its load was 40 grains of black powder and 255-grain bullets. No. Not really. In January 1874 the .45 Colt was loaded by Frankford Arsenal with 250-grain bullets and 30 grains of powder. This load hit about 775 fps from the SAA's 7½" barrel. By 1875, the U.S. Army also accepted S&W's Model #3 Schofield .45 revolver. Its shorter cartridge only carried 28 grains of black powder with 230-grain bullets for 725 fps.

Finally, in 1878, Colt adapted their big single action to .44 WCF (.44-40) and got real power from a sixgun. The rounds did carry 40-grain powder charges with 200-grain bullets and velocity from 7½" barrels most certainly broke 900 fps.

Think about this: At the famous fight at the OK Corral most everyone had either a .45 Colt, .44-40 or perhaps even an S&W .44 Russian revolver. Not one combatant was put out of action with a single hit, except from Doc Holliday's shotgun.

CONSIDER CASTING

This was the very first machine rest group from this USFA .44-40 with Duke's home cast bullets.

T he purpose of guns and cartridges is to direct a bullet into a target. In other words, without bullets, guns are useless. Shooters in this COVID-19 era of almost non-existent components are learning this the hard way. Since 1966, I've never been without bullets for my handguns and plan to never be without them. In just the first three months of 2021, I've cast over 3,000 handgun bullets for various writing projects in calibers .32, .38/357, .38-40, .41 Long Colt, .44 Special, .44-40 and .45 Colt. I enjoyed every minute of it.

Back when I became a .38 Special reloader, in my locale there were no handgun bullets to buy. None! Nada! Some older gents in the local gun club told me if I was going to shoot, I would have to cast. One guy sold me a cast iron lead pot for use on gas stoves for $10, and another for $7.50 sold me a Lyman single-cavity bullet mold with handles. I've owned literally hundreds of handgun bullet molds since, but don't want any more single-cavity molds for handgun bullets. I may enjoy my casting sessions, but there's a limit to my patience.

Duke discovered MP Molds when their innovative sliding base plugs for hollow-base (and hollow-point) bullets allowed use in multiple cavity molds.

UNIVERSE OF CASTING

I n terms of cast bullets for repeating handguns (excluding single shot pistols) we have a bewildering array of designs to choose from. They include shapes of full wadcutter (WC), semi-wadcutter (SWC), roundnose (RN), roundnose/flatpoint (RN/FP), hollowpoint (HP), hollowbase HB, plain base and gas-checked base.

So, what's best? That's an impossible question, but any of them is better than no bullets. Personally speaking, on my reloading bench I have dies for .32 Auto, 7.65 French Long, 8mm Nambu, 9mm Parabellum, .38 Super, .40 S&W and .45 Auto. Also on my loading bench are dies for 16 revolver cartridges. They range from .32-20 to .455 Webley. Some of those cartridges are loaded rarely, such as 8mm Japanese Nambu and .41 Magnum, but I still acquired molds for them. The flip side is I load .38-40 and .44-40 by the hundreds and thousands.

The most accurate shooting Duke ever experienced with cast bullets in semi-autos came with this Kimber Pro Compact .40 S&W.

A FOR EFFORT?

T he only handgun caliber with which I consider myself a failure with cast bullet shooting is 9mm Parabellum. My cast bullet luck with my current five World War II 9mm pistols and two submachine guns has ranged from barely okay to downright dismal. Groups are large, bullets sometimes tumble in flight and barrel leading is bad. Some manufacturers such as GLOCK recommend not shooting lead alloy bullets in their barrels. Fine. Drop in, aftermarket barrels are offered for lead bullet shooting in GLOCKs. If I had a GLOCK, I'd buy one of those barrels. Get this: The same poorly performing 9mm cast bullets when fired in my single Colt .38 Super of 1990s vintage shoot nicely. Go figure.

SUCCESSES

T he best cast bullet accuracy I've ever gotten with semi-autos was with a Kimber Pro Compact 1911 .40 S&W. From machine rest using cast SWCs and RN/FPs it usually shot ragged clusters at 25 yards. *I always use a hard alloy for semi-auto pistol bullets.* They get slammed about a bunch going from magazine to chamber. Revolvers are a cinch. *I always use a softer alloy for revolvers.* Used to be .45 Colt gave me fits until I discovered Colt SAAs

have 0.451"-barrel groove diameters but 0.456" chamber mouths. Load 0.454" bullets of soft 1:20 tin to lead alloy and .45 Colt SAAs become tack drivers. For cast bullet revolver loads over 1,250 fps I often use a gas check design.

A softer bullet often will compensate for mismatched revolver barrel/cylinder dimensions. I've come to favor the RN/FP design of bullet for most of those revolver cartridges. Used to be I'd avoid HP or HB cast bullet designs because they were only available in single cavity molds. Now I've discovered MP Molds where one can obtain multiple cavity

HP and HB molds. I've used their four-cavity convertible .32-20 mold for both HPs and FPs and their two cavity .41 Long Colt mold for HBs.

If this column inspires you to run out and get a casting setup, save your gasoline. Along with everything else involved in reloading, casting stuff is in short supply. Hopefully by the time you read this the ammo, component and reloading equipment drought will be over. Just beware! It could happen again!

TWO FOR ONE: CREATIVE RELOADING

This is the Astra Model 1921 (aka Model 400) 9mm Largo Duke bought on a whim.

Duke's shiny stainless-steel Colt 1911 .38 Super

I'm nothing if not impetuous. A few years back I got it in my head a shiny nickel-plated Colt 1911 would suit me, so I bought the first one encountered. I would have preferred .45 ACP but this one was 38 Super. It sufficed anyway because all the necessary .38 Super cases, bullets and reloading dies were on hand.

Imagine my surprise after getting the 1911 home when I discovered it was actually brightly polished stainless steel. No matter, shiny is shiny. Right? My new handgun turned out to be one of the "ELCEN" series Colt had produced in the 1990s for a large distributor to sell south of the border. It actually had the flat mainspring housing of earlier 1911s, but sights were modern, high-profile front and rear with white dots. It is a fine example of quality pistol manufacture.

9MM... SOMETHING

Fast forward a few years to a Montana gun show when I spotted a pistol with which I was familiar without having ever held one. On its slide was stamped "Modelo 1921 (400)." It is an Astra made in Spain. Naturally, I had to nab it too. I say it was familiar to me because back in my teens (1960s) they were offered for sale dirt cheap by modern standards in many gun magazine advertisements. Converse from the flat-side Model 1911, these Astras are rounded in shape but crudely made compared to the Colt ELCEN 1911. Crude but certainly robust as befits a pistol designed for military use.

Remembering from those old ads that Modelo 1921s were 9mm I

Starline's rimless "comp" .38 Super brass works perfectly in both his .38 Super and 9mm Largo pistols.

wouldn't have known exactly which 9mm this one was chambered for except it also came with a box of CCI Blazer ammo labeled 9mm Largo. In Spanish "largo" means long. This cartridge started as the 9mm Bergman Bayard, dating from the early 1900s. The Spanish military adopted it circa 1913 and renamed it 9mm Largo. Its case is 0.905" in length as opposed to 0.754" of 9mm Parabellum or 23mm compared to 19mm. However, both 9mms fire bullets nominally of 0.355".

NOT ENTIRELY DISTANT RELATIVES

My original plan was to shoot up the now discontinued box of Blazer 9mm Largo and then sell the Astra. Then I noticed in the instruction sheet accompanying the pistol that shooting .38 Colt Auto in it was acceptable. *Please note: the .38 Colt Auto cartridge is not the same as the .38 Super!* The .38 Colt Auto and .38 Super Auto are the same dimensionally, but the latter version develops much higher pressures which would be dangerous in the old Astra or any other .38 Colt Auto. The .38 Colt Auto's and .38 Super's case length is 0.900" and a 0.005" difference in semi-auto pistol case length is negligible. New cases will vary that much in the same lot.

However, I wondered about the following. Case design for the 9mm Largo is rimless but .38 Colt Auto is semi-rimmed. I had some old .38 Colt Auto factory loads on hand and they sure enough wouldn't chamber in my 9mm Largo. But Starline's .38 Super Competition cases are rimless and most certainly they chambered perfectly in the Astra. So, I was set. No new brass or dies were needed. *One handload could be assembled that would*

function perfectly in both pistols — at least I hoped.

However, there is one caveat. Reloading data for .38 Largo is limited. The only current manual in which I could find data is Speer's *Reloading Manual #14*. Starting loads listed for .38 Super are at or near maximum for the old Astra 9mm Largo. Of course, 0.355" bullets are proper for both rounds.

I settled on 5.0 grains of Unique with Zero Bullet Company's 124-grain, 0.355" RN and also with Oregon Trail's 0.356" 124-grain commercially cast RN. Both bullet and powder combinations chamber, function and fire fine through either semi-auto. Velocities run about 1,100 fps. Somebody has to be mentally asking, "Duke, what size are the groups each pistol delivers?" I say, "Who cares? I hit what I'm aiming at more often than not." Incidentally I chronographed the CCI Blazer 9mm Largo factory loads through both pistols and got about 1,200 fps.

With this two-for-one situation, I'm not as keen to sell off the Astra as I formerly intended. It's a neat historical handgun, albeit in an odd clunky way. And the shiny 1911 gives me some "bling!"

MIKE "DUKE" VENTURINO Photos: Yvonne Venturino

COLT'S MOST POPULAR CHAMBERINGS ARE ... WINCHESTER?

As odd as it may seem, some of the Colt SAA's most popular chamberings have been developed by Winchester; as in Winchester Center Fire or as we know them today .32-20, .38-40 and .44-40. Why? Because in the infancy of repeating rifles such cartridges were as long as Winchester's Model 1873 could handle, which in turn made them ideal revolver cartridges. All three have maximum overall cartridge length limits of 1.592".

Adding those rounds as options in what was quickly becoming America's most popular revolver was a brilliant move by someone at Colt Patent Firearms. It enabled anyone packing guns for serious purposes to stock only one type of ammunition for their rifles/carbines and revolvers. (There's a story of at least one Texas Ranger who packed a .44-40 '73 Winchester with his .45 Colt revolver. In a gun battle with outlaws, he managed to get a .45 cartridge into his lever action. With bullets incoming he had to remove the Winchester's side plates to get the .45 round out.)

Duke's trifecta of Colt SAAs chambered for WCF cartridges. All are 3rd Generation with 7½" barrels. From left, the .32-20, .44-40 and .38-40. Note the one-piece style grips Duke favors.

These are original factory loads. From left, the .32 WCF (.32-20), .38 WCF (.38-40) and .44 WCF (.44-40).

SLOW TO MARKET

What surprises me is Colt was so slow in adapting their new sixgun to the pistol-size WCFs. Perhaps it was because in its early years of manufacture Colt's factory was busy getting the new revolvers into the U.S. Army's hands. Regardless, by my research, the soon-to-become world famous SAA was introduced in 1873, yet it took nearly five years for the .44 WCF to be a caliber choice. The same was true with the .38 WCF. Winchester added it as a '73 option in 1879: not 1874, as often mistakenly written. Colt didn't bring out SAAs for it till 1884. Naturally the .32-20 came last with Winchester adding it in 1882 and Colt in 1887. (These dates of introduction are taken from several sources. Other sources may vary.)

The primary appeal of WCFs in Colt SAAs was the ability to have matching repeating rifles and handguns.

Even Colt has been confused about naming the WCFs. Top is a 1904 marked .38 WCF. Below is a 2004 marked .38-40.

HALF WCF?

Colt's First Generation of SAA production lasted from 1873 to 1941. In that time period, and including standard SAAs, Bisley SAAs and target models of both, 71,292 .44-40s were made, 50,402 38-40s and 43,102 .32-20s. That was of 357,859 made in total. (Figures quoted from *The 36 Calibers of the Colt Single Action Army* by David M. Brown, ©1965.) During the Second Generation of SAA production from 1956 to 1974, none were made for the WCFs as standard. That's discounting 2,002 .44-40s made as part of the special run Peacemaker Centennial Commemorative. My figuring says the WCFs counted for a bit over 46% of SAA production between 1873 and 1941.

People's desire for SAA chamberings changed after the Third Generation of production began in 1976. I was at the NRA Convention in Philadelphia in 1982, where Colt announced the .44-40 was being introduced. I ordered one right on the spot. Also around that time was the advent of cowboy type competition, which opened up an entirely new market for Colt's SAAs. By 1993, the .38-40 was returned and in 2002, so did .32-20. My understanding now is while the Third Generation of SAA production is still ongoing only .357 Magnum and .45 Colt are caliber options. That's truly a shame.

Be that as it may, there are plenty of Third Generation .44-40s, .38-40s and .32-20s floating about, albeit admittedly the latter one is the most difficult to obtain. As my eyes age, it seems to help to shoot the SAAs with 7½" barrels. So, while I've owned many dozens of Colt SAAs — from both First Generation and Third Generation production — it wasn't till 2021 I had a "trifecta." That's all three Third Generation WCFs with 7½" barrel lengths.

And brothers, let me tell you, they are all winners. Just recently I put the 7½" .44-40 in my Ransom Pistol Machine Rest and shot 20 handloads through it. Those loads contained four different cast bullets I made and five different powders. The total average of 20 groups was a mere 1.79" at 25 yards. I'll give details someday.

When talking about this subject, I'm often asked, "Which of the three is your favorite?" My usual answer is, "On what day?" Over the years, I didn't feel the need for a .32-20. Nowadays, its mild noise and recoil make it very attractive. As for which is in first and second place, I bounce around. Honestly, I cannot make a choice.

MORE HANDGUNS HERE

americanhandgunner.com

SHOOTINGIRON
MIKE "DUKE" VENTURINO   Photos: Yvonne Venturino

THE WORST MILITARY HANDGUN?

Duke's Japanese Type 26 9mm (rimmed) revolver with its clamshell style holster.

Anyone who has studied the history of military handguns must wonder how some ordnance officers formed their concepts of ideal handguns. For instance, consider the Russian Model 1895 Nagant revolver with its odd 7.62mm cartridge wherein the bullet is seated fully inside the cartridge case. That was because when the hammer is cocked, its cylinder is pushed forward over the butt end of its barrel. The idea with such a system is gas cannot leak upon firing. Never mind the gas leakage between barrel/cylinder gap has been of no importance with successful revolver designs for a half century!

American ordnance officers were not exempt from mistakes. In 1892, they chose to drop .45 Colt as the U.S. Army's handgun cartridge in favor of .38 Colt (aka .38 Long Colt). It was a piddling little round pushing a 150-grain bullet at only about 750 fps. Its lack of power resulted in it being replaced by .45s again in only a few years. The abovementioned 7.62mm Nagant used a 108-grain bullet at a mere 900 fps.

The sideplates of Type 26 revolvers are hinged, revealing their innards. Great for cleaning, but perhaps an attraction for tinkerers.

Bottom: From left: original Japanese 9mm rimmed cartridge, Duke's handload with Buffalo Arms brass and Oregon Trail 147-grain bullets, U.S. .38 Long Colt military round, and a U.S. .38 Special military round. Note the FMJ bullet.

THE WORST EVER?

But personally, I think the biggest joke among military handguns is Japan's 9mm Type 26 revolver introduced in 1893. Don't let the 9mm moniker fool you as it has nothing to do with the famous rimless 9mm Parabellum (9mm Luger) that pushes 115/124-grain bullets in the 1,200/1,300 fps range. Nope. The 9mm Japanese revolver cartridge is rimmed and fired a 149-grain bullet at approximately 750 fps. (Did the Japanese ordnance officers copy American's .38 Long Colt?)

A weak chambering isn't enough to consign a military cartridge into the silly category. After all, three decades later, the Brits thought a 200-grain .38 at 650 fps was sufficient for combat. It's just that the Type 96 incorporated several other poorly thought-out features. One is it fires in double-action mode only (otherwise known as self-cocking). Again, a few decades later, the Brits followed with a variation of their little Enfield Mk. 2 No. 1 .38s. They removed the hammer spur, so only double-action shooting was feasible. Supposedly, this was done for tank crewmen because hammer spurs entangled on things inside a crowded turret.

A worse idea with Japan's Type 26s is that locking bolts only hold chambers aligned with barrels when triggers are pulled. Otherwise, the cylinder is free to rotate. This feature might have back-fired on "Dirty Harry" when he asked, "Did I fire five or six?" With the Type 26, who would bet their life the next round coming up in a free-wheeling cylinder was live? Any sort of strenuous activity might have rotated it.

MODEL #3 INSPIRATION GONE BAD

Type 26s are of top break design, obviously leaning on S&W's Model #3s from the late 1800s. Lifting the barrel hinge allows it to pivot downwards, which then cams its extractor up simultaneously emptying all six chambers. (Japan had purchased thousands of S&W Model #3s for the .44 Russian cartridge. I recently read of a U.S. Marine on Iwo Jima finding six pristine condition S&W .44s in a cave while the battle was still raging.) Type 26s had 4.7" barrels and weighed 2 lbs. Sights were a simple groove in top strap for rear and a half moon front. One good feature is the front sight blade is pinned

to a stud machined integral with the barrel. Therefore, front sight blades can be changed to help zeroing for elevation. Grips are checkered wood, round in shape and obviously meant for smaller hands than my big American mitts.

Pulling down on Type 26 trigger guards frees side plates so they swing away, revealing the revolver's inner workings. That would be great for cleaning, but I'm sure Japanese soldiers were instructed not to mess with their revolvers' innards without supervision. For Americans, with their penchant for figuring out how things work, such instructions would have been considered suggestions or challenges. By

World War II, Type 26s were obsolete and mostly were issued to NCOs.

My Type 26 showed up at a Montana gun show, complete with its clamshell holster and carrying strap. It has a minor amount of pitting on it indicating it saw service but still its excellent manufacturing quality is evident. It's not a hunk of junk; just poorly thought out. Cases can be made from .38 Specials, but I just bought mine from Buffalo Arms of Idaho. My handloads consist of 2.0 grains of Hodgdon's Titegroup under 147-grain Oregon Trail 0.356" bullets. Assembling the rounds can be done with .38 Super or .38 Long Colt dies. I have shot it enough to know I cannot hit much with it past about 50 feet.

It's my pick for the all-time worst military handgun.

TWIN

.32-20s

Duke's twin .32-20 Colt SAAs. The top one is from 1899 and the bottom is from 2010. Both have 7½" barrels.

This is why Duke's .45 Colt SAA weighs 9 oz. less than his .32-20. More metal is removed by boring the barrel and cylinder's chambers.

Duke's 3rd Generation .32-20 SAA had its case hardening colors removed by a previous owner. Mike later had the re-coloring done by Clear Creek Armory of Ten Sleep, Wyo.

My love affair with Colt Single Action Army sixguns started in 1968. Thus far, I've owned over 100 of the graceful revolvers. Until recently, only one has been chambered for .32-20 (aka .32 WCF), which might sound odd because the caliber was the fourth best-selling between 1873 and 1941 during the 1st Generation of SAA production.

My aversion to .32-20 formed over 40 years ago with my very first SAA of that caliber. It was most contrary — when machine rest mounted, it would only group into about 4" at 25 yards. Eventually, I measured its bore and chamber mouths by driving soft lead slugs through them. Cylinder chamber mouths were universally 0.310" but barrel groove diameter measured 0.314". This combination is a certain situation for poor accuracy from any revolver. Thusly I became soured about SAA .32-20s.

Fast forward to SHOT Show 2004. I was on the staff of a different magazine when my boss heard Colt was reintroducing SAA .32-20s in 3rd Generation (1976 to present). He asked me to obtain one for a feature article. I approached some of the three-piece suited reps standing idle at the Colt booth, presented my business card and asked about a consignment .32-20 when available. One fellow looked at my card, and then me, and said, "I've never heard of you, and we're not sending you anything." Yvonne was with me, and as we walked away, she commented, "Aren't you mad?" I replied, "No, that guy was too stupid to care about. He's an example of why Colt is on a downhill slide."

TA DA! A REVELATION!

Now move on to 2021. That summer, much of my free time was spent shooting and handloading for .38-40, .41 Long Colt and .44-40 WCFs. On an Internet website's classified section, I spotted a 3rd Generation SAA .32-20 with a 7½" barrel for sale at an attractive price. The owner was honest; the price was low because he'd chemically removed the frame's case hardening colors. He did so because surface rust on the frame would deepen into pitting if left be. Since I had previous positive dealings with the seller, I bought that .32-20, figuring to use it for gathering load data for my ongoing SAA project. Its serial number dated it as manufactured in 2010.

Shooting the .32-20 was like having a window opened in a stuffy room. Its accuracy and lack of recoil felt like a breath of fresh air. No need for tedious handload development. This .32-20 shot every load combination well and others outstandingly. There was no need to check, but from curiosity, I found barrel groove diameter, and all six chamber mouths measured 0.310". My only complaint — a minor one — is that smaller bore and chambers weigh much more than a similarly configured big bore. I compared a .45 and this .32-20 alike in every way down to fancy walnut grips. The .45 weighs 39 oz., and the .32-20 is 48 oz.

A NEW PASSION

My new Colt so pleased me I soon sent it to my friend Bill Fuchs at Clearwater Armory in Ten Sleep, Wyo., for re-color case hardening and a set of presentation grade walnut one-piece style grips. While it was there, I instructed Bill to color case harden its hammer as that was standard at one time in SAA manufacture.

People who know me well say I'm impetuous. I say I just make decisions fast. Either way, with such positive .32-20 experience, I began a hunt for another. This time my quest was for a 1st Generation SAA with a 7½" barrel. Such are hard to find, but one is here now, and I'm more than pleased with it. Made in 1899, its condition is about 75%. The newer .32-20's grips are all that keep it from being 100% original. In its website photos, the grips seemed white plastic on which someone had doodled with a felt marker. Showing the Colt to Yvonne, she exclaimed, "Wow, these are real mother of pearl." Looking closely, it was evident someone had carved lines and curlicues then traced them with ink. There are also a set of stylized initials. Also prominent are checkered finger grooves even carved in the left side grip panel. While not a beautiful set of grips, someone went to great effort to make them personal, so they will stay on the Colt as long as I have it.

How does it shoot? Just like my 3rd Generation .32-20 bullets go right where aimed at 25 yards. Like someone separated from a loved one for a long time, I have renewed my acquaintance with SAA .32-20s with enthusiasm.

THE MOST PRACTICAL REVOLVER

In its 122-year history, S&W M&P/Model 10 .38 Specials have been made with blue and nickel-plated finishes.

For starters, let me say I've never been a certified firearms instructor, never been trained as a law enforcement officer, never served in the military and never been involved in a firearms altercation. I have been an avid handgun shooter since 1966, having owned hundreds of revolvers and pistols, and fired untold thousands, maybe over 100,000 factory loads and handloads through them during the 55 years. And I've written a couple of thousand magazine articles.

With the above in mind, I'm not keen to give opinions on defensive firearms. Regardless, I'm sometimes asked for advice by non-shooters who somehow become aware of what I do for a living. The conversations go like this, "Mike, what do you recommend I (or my wife) get for a handgun?" My reply, "To what end?" They usually say, "Uh, to get one to keep in my home." Again, I question, "Do you intend to get involved in recreational shooting, competition or at least attend a training class?" Vague reply, "Uh, maybe someday, but I'm awfully busy right now."

That's when I stop and say, "Find yourself a .38 Special double-action revolver, preferably with a 4" barrel. Other brands exist, but my favorites are S&W Model 10 M&P .38 Specials. My answer generally takes the questioner by surprise, and they respond, "I thought you would say GLOCK or SIG or some sort of semi-auto."

SEMI-AUTOS FOR BEGINNERS?

No, I wouldn't recommend a semi-auto for a novice: Not now, not ever, never! Semi-autos require training and experience. Have you ever watched a novice fumble about loading magazines and getting them seated in pistols properly? Some pistols have safeties that need mastering. Also, they will have either a single-action or double-action trigger mechanism. And how about the following: malfunctions caused by ammunition, malfunctions caused by limp-wristing, or malfunctions caused by dirty gun and/or ammo? And perhaps above all, the matter of whether one should keep a semi-auto's chamber loaded or unloaded.

Now consider this. A Model 10 M&P has no safety, but it won't fire unless the trigger is pulled. In a double-action with the trigger's long pull, firing must be intentional. Model 10 M&P sights are fixed and duly (hopefully) factory regulated for ammo with about 150- to 160-grain bullets at about 800 to 850 fps. There are oodles of factory loads that fit those parameters.

Time Tested

S&W unveiled the K-Frame Military & Police in 1899, and the revolver, in turn, was the introductory vehicle for the .38 Special. It is one of the finest all-around revolver cartridges ever developed. Until 1957 the S&W factory assigned names to their handguns. This new one became Military & Police, but after 1957 it officially became Model 10. M&P/Model 10s have been made in blue finish, nickel-plated finish and even stainless steel. The SS ones were named Model 64 and Modelv65. There is also a variation called Model 12. It is nothing more than the Model 10 but with a frame of aluminum alloy. Barrel lengths have been 2", 3", 4", 5", 6" and 6½". Maybe there are some others of which I'm not aware. Model 10/M&P barrels were almost pencil-thin, but the company offered a heavy barrel option in later years.

In his excellent book *The K-Frame Revolver*, author Timothy J. Mullin relates that over 8,000,000 K-Frame S&W revolvers had been made by the time of his writing (Copyright 2013). Of course, many of those were .22s, .32s, .38 S&Ws and .357 Magnums. I'd bet cold, hard cash the most significant number were chambered for .38 Special. They are still available, newly made by

S&W, albeit only with 4" barrels. Used ones are not rare.

After my comment to advice seekers, some get snarky and say, "So you'd have us rank and file buy obsolete old revolvers, but I bet you keep modern pistols for yourself." As a rule, I wouldn't say I like to give advice preferring only to relate what I do personally. So, my answer to such a comment is, "I won't tell you where I keep them, but in my home are stashed away two S&W Model 10/M&P .38 Specials. One has a 2" barrel and the other a five incher. Also, there is a Model 12 with a 2" barrel." And I don't keep them loaded with the newest types of ammo: just ordinary factory loads with lead semi-wadcutter or semi-wadcutter hollowpoint bullets.

S&W Model 10 Military & Police .38 Specials are point-and-shoot home guns. No more practical, down-to-earth, no-nonsense handgun has ever existed.

Two of Duke's S&W M&P (pre-Model 10) .38 Specials with 2" and 5" barrels.

This assortment of cartridges illustrates a small part of .38 Special factory loads past and present. From left: 158-gr. "Police" RN, 148-gr. WC, 200-gr. "Super Police" RN, U.S. military 130-gr. FMJ tracer, 158-gr. SWC-HP in an aluminum case, 125-gr. +P JHP and 158-gr. "Cowboy" load.

Photos: Yvonne Venturino

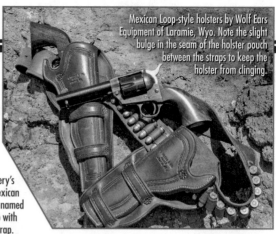

Mexican Loop-style holsters by Wolf Ears Equipment of Laramie, Wyo. Note the slight bulge in the seam of the holster pouch between the straps to keep the holster from clinging.

MEXICAN LOOP HOLSTERS

This El Paso Saddlery's variation of a Mexican Loop holster is named Mexican Loop with Texas Jockstrap.

WESTERN HOLSTER FASHIONS

In my teens, my ignorance caused me to buy a low-slung Buscadero rig for my very first Colt Peacemaker. Later I found out Buscadero-type rigs were mostly Hollywood's fantasy, so it was discarded. Not until getting involved in cowboy action competition in the mid-1980s did I begin learning about authentic Old West holsters.

Instead of trying to cover all the myriad types for this column, I'm only going to write of the style I have come to favor. Naturally, that's the Mexican Loop. By the mid-1870s to early 1880s Mexican Loop holsters became the fashion. They could have one, two or even three loops. The most colorful name given to one variation was the Mexican Loop with Texas Jockstrap. As the photo shows, it had a strap from the muzzle end and then spreads crosswise to hold the pouch to the back flap. Mine is from El Paso Saddlery.

Not being a collector, most of my Mexican Loop holsters are modern replicas, although one that came with a 1915 vintage S&W .44 Special "triplelock" was found in a small Montana town. It's a classic example of a double Mexican Loop holster made by F.O.K. Company with no location given.

My eight-year-older sister told me that by about age four, my warm-weather routine every morning was to put on my cowboy boots first and then strap on my gun belt. I should probably have been called "The Tighty-Whitey Kid" because, in the heat of West Virginia summers, that's all I wore. It's true, for I have seen old family photos. Where that cowboy fascination came from is a mystery — we didn't have television.

The reason I tell this story is because I still have my holster from then. It is real, not a toy. Actually, so was my sixgun. My father got an old revolver, cut or ground off its firing pin and plugged its chambers with lead so it couldn't be fired. That's all the family, or I, remember about it. Somehow, through the decades, it just disappeared.

Its holster stuck. Many years passed before I knew the name for its style. It's a modified Mexican Loop. As such, it was cut from one piece of leather. The holster pouch is sewed together with a back flap doubled over to make a belt slot. Instead of the back being split like traditional Mexican Loop holsters, mine has a strap with a buckle holding the back flap and holster pouch together. It is heavy duty leather carved in a floral pattern and made for a small frame revolver. Although stiff with age, it still holds a Colt Model 1877 DA with a 4½" barrel.

FLAWS

Over the years, I've found two flaws with Mexican Loop holsters.

First, the leather can be "grabby" when the revolver is pulled. The holster clings and tries to rise with the revolver. There is a leather craftsman in Laramie, Wyo., named Stan Dolega. His business name is Wolf Ears Equipment. He cured the "grabby" holster problem by giving his Mexican Loop holsters a curve in the pouch seam. It fits between the two straps, locking the holster in place as the gun is withdrawn.

The second flaw I've experienced is most Mexican Loop holsters have no hammer thong. That's simply a piece of bootlace threaded through two holes punched in the leather where the hammer sets. The thong is wrapped around the hammer so the revolver doesn't also take a spill if the wearer does.

One beneficial attribute of most Mexican Loop holsters is they will fit many different revolver models. For instance, my Wolf Ears Mexican Loop holster for 7½" Colt SAAs also accommodates a 7" barreled Navy Arms 3rd Model .44 Russian and a 7½" Remington Model 1875 .44-40.

Age has taken its toll on me. Now I only pack a Colt SAA on my property instead of shooting events or riding horses in Montana's mountains. But when I decide to have an afternoon's fun with some of my single-action revolvers, they're stuck in one of my Mexican Loop holsters.

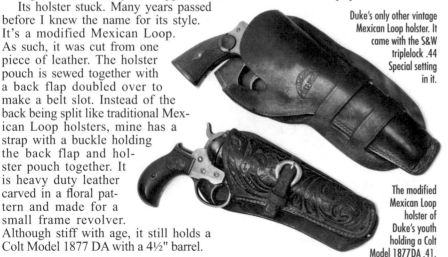

Duke's only other vintage Mexican Loop holster. It came with the S&W triplelock .44 Special setting in it.

The modified Mexican Loop holster of Duke's youth holding a Colt Model 1877DA .41.

Photos: Yvonne Venturino

A problem commonly encountered with .45 Colt revolver cylinders is that chamber mouths are too large and often vary in size.

REVOLVER DIMENSIONS

Not long into my shooting career, I realized not all revolvers were equal in terms of closely putting bullets near one another on paper targets. Many years passed before experience began to reveal why that was. It is because almost all problems in revolver accuracy could be laid on mismatching dimensions. That's not a blanket statement because poor barrel quality can contribute, as can damaged crowns at barrels' muzzles or weak firing pin strikes.

Think about it this way; a revolver is a precision instrument. The cylinder must rotate precisely, so chambers are perfectly aligned with the barrel forcing cone. That forcing cone must be minutely funnel-shaped so bullets don't just slam into its sharp edges. If they do, the shooter will certainly notice it by small particles of lead or bullet jackets along with unburned powder stinging hands and face. The common name for that is "spitting lead." There is actually an implement sold named the "range rod." Its purpose is to slide down a revolver's barrel and into cylinder chambers. If it hangs up even a tad, then cylinders are not aligning properly.

Duke doubted Colt .38/357 barrels measured a nominal 0.354" in their grooves ... ... until he measured a few and found that to be true.

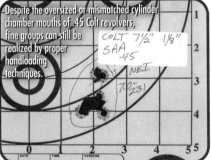

Despite the oversized or mismatched cylinder chamber mouths of .45 Colt revolvers, fine groups can still be realized by proper handloading techniques.

MATCHY MATCHY

Next is the notion that cylinder chamber mouths and barrel bore diameters should match, at least to an acceptable degree. If chamber mouths are tighter than a barrel's grooves, bullets are swaged down upon firing. Then they will be smaller than the barrel's grooves. As a rule, this does nothing for revolver precision. However, I've occasionally experienced an exception to that rule. It may be if the revolver's cartridge generates enough pressure and bullets are soft enough, they will expand in the barrel's forcing cone to still grip rifling suitably.

Here's an example. My first .32-20 Colt SAA had a 0.314" barrel groove diameter but 0.310" chamber mouths. Mild loads would not group better than about 4" at 25 yards. However, heavy charges of 2400, as given in old reloading manuals, would deliver groups down around 2".

The flip side of that coin is if chamber mouths are significantly larger than barrel groove diameter. Bullets can then enter the barrel, forcing cones slightly tilted off-center. Colt SAA .45 revolvers are especially bad offenders in this respect. I've used plug gauges to check many SAA chamber mouths. They have almost all ranged from 0.455" to 0.457". However, since early in this century, Colt specs called for all .45 barrels nominally 0.451"/0.452". (Source: factory spec sheet dated 1922.) That's why Colt SAA .45s have no great reputation for precision shooting.

CASTING SOLUTION

My solution to this problem was to size .45 Colt cast bullets to 0.45" — close to the chamber mouth dimensions — and to use relatively soft cast bullets. They will swell to fill chamber mouths but also swage down easily in forcing cones. For example, regardless of the powder used, my .45 Colt bullets are cast from soft 1-20 tin to lead alloy. And I have no complaints about how well my Colt SAAs shoot.

In my early years, I always took gun'riters' advice and shot hard cast bullets in my Colt .45s, sized no larger than 0.452". With decades of experience behind me, the idea finally dawned on me that softer bullets would obturate (yes, that is the proper word!) to fill chamber mouths. Regardless of the exact powder charge, bullets fired through my dozen .45 Colt SAAs cluster into acceptable sizes. This method also

works with the fairly common problem of Colt SAA cylinders not being the same in all six chamber mouths.

I've often been asked, "Isn't it harmful to shoot 0.454" bullets down 0.451" barrels?" No. Soft bullets will harm nothing. Again, referring back to my beginning years, manuals advised sizing .38 Special cast bullets to 0.358" or 0.001" over my S&W K38's nominal 0.357" barrel groove diameter. Upon buying Colt SAA .38 Special and .357 Magnum revolvers, nothing changed in my reloading habits. Many years later, I discovered Colt SA and DA barrels were all nominally 0.354" in their grooves. I didn't believe it until I slugged those barrels myself. They indeed were 0.354"! Did I change my load recipes? Nope, I kept shooting the same handloads as prepared for S&W .38s and .357s and have suffered nary a problem.

For over 50 years, I've strived to understand all the ins and outs of revolver accuracy. Much has been learned, but there is a ways to go yet.

Duke's favorite 7.65mm Long handload uses 81-grain cast bullets from Lyman mold #313249 in newly manufactured Starline brass.

THE .30 SUPER CARRY
BACKSTORY

There is much hoopla in the firearms press about the new .30 Super Carry and the handguns being built for it. I don't own one of the pistols, have never seen one of the cartridges and doubt I ever will shoot a .30 Super Carry. This isn't being ugly; it's just the *Way of the Dinosaur.* (That's me.)

This is an original box of the U.S. .30 Auto Pistol Model of 1918 ammunition. The cartridge at the left is a round from the box. At right is a round of French 7.65mm Long.

40-CAL. 30 AUTO. PISTOL
BALL CARTRIDGES
MODEL OF 1918
THE REMINGTON ARMS
UNION METALLIC CARTRIDGE COMPANY,
BRIDGEPORT, CONN.

THE PEDERSEN DEVICE

But I can give you some interesting backstory. Let's return to 1917/1918. The U.S. Army was embroiled in World War I's trench warfare. Invading German trenches with five-round capacity Model 1903 Springfield rifles battle-zeroed for 547 yards and fighting at off-the-muzzle ranges just wasn't an optimal situation. Especially considering the Germans had thousands of their 8"-barreled P08 "Artillery" 9mm Lugers with 32-round drum magazines with which to shoot back. Of course, the reverse was true when German Sturm Truppen landed in Doughboy trenches.

Therefore, a solution to the U.S Army's dilemma was envisioned in 1917 by noted arms designer J.D. Pedersen. On his own, he developed a device that could be fitted to M1903 .30-06 Springfield rifles converting them from bolt

action, five-round shooters to semi-auto, 40-round shooters. U.S. Army officials were wild about the idea.

However, the Pedersen Device necessitated a new cartridge. Mr. Pedersen had developed it too. It used a rimless case, 0.78" long with a 0.308", 80-grain bullet giving nominal velocity from an M1903's 24" barrel of 1,300 fps. The U.S. government christened it with the lengthy name of U.S .30 Auto Pistol Model of 1918. (The words "Auto Pistol" were used to fool German spies.)

The Pedersen Device fed those rounds from an awkward-looking magazine angled from the top right of special Mark I M1903s and ejected fired cartridges through a port on the action's left side. Pedersen Devices and its ".30 Auto Pistol" ammunition made it to France but hostilities ended before them seeing action.

THE FRENCH GO .30

Now we're into the mid-1930s. A French engineer named Charles Petter, working for *Societe Alsacienne de Constructions Mechaniques* (SACM), designed a new pistol for the French Army. Although it vaguely resembled the American U.S. Model 1911, it was petite in comparison. Barrel length was 4.30" with a weight of only 26 oz. Chambering was for a likewise petite cartridge called 7.65mm Longue (Long). Have you figured out where I'm heading here? That's right, the "new" French cartridge had a rimless case of 0.78" length, with an 85-grain bullet at a nominal velocity of about 1,100 fps. Evidently, the French had obtained some of the U.S. .30 Auto Pistol Model of 1918 ammunition and liked it, except they increased the bullet diameter to 0.310/0.311".

France's new military pistol was designated Model 1935A. It is a delight to handle with a slightly curved grip frame that fits hands better than most straight grips. Also, its checkered black plastic grips are

At right is a French Model 1935A. At left is a U.S. Model 1911.

comfortable. Safety is a hammer block type. Flip it up and solid steel blocks the hammer from hitting its firing pin. A magazine disconnect doesn't allow the pistol to fire if its magazine is absent. Sights are simple: a small blade front dovetailed to the slide and notched rear machined integral with the slide. What ruins its aesthetics is a baked-on, black paint finish.

Are you wondering why I'm so familiar with the French Model 1935A? The story is too long to detail here, but I got my first while in my teens and sold it long ago. I bought another in 2010. I managed to purchase some original French ammo with the newest one. In sealed boxes and looking pristine, not one round of it would fire. My shooting has been chiefly with cast bullets from Lyman mold #313249, sized

to 0.313" and weighing 81 grains. Brass is brand-new from Starline. In fact, I use properly adjusted .32 Auto reloading dies. My velocities are running around 1,100 fps, depending on the exact handload.

WHAT COMES AROUND, GOES AROUND

So how does this connect to the new .30 Super Carry? Well, the new case is rimless, 0.827" long and loaded with 100- to 115-grain, 0.313" jacketed bullets. The velocity quotes I see mention 1,250 fps but with stupendous pressures of 45,000 psi. By comparison, the maximum 9mm Luger pressures are 35,000 psi. Is the .30 Super Carry just a copy of the old U.S. .30 Auto Pistol Model 1918 round but made a mite longer for safety's sake? Supposedly not. Regardless, there is definitely a backstory worth considering.

Duke considered himself very lucky to get 1876 for the serial number of his USFA Custer Battlefield .45.

Duke's USFA Custer Battle .45. This is not one of the actual headstones from the LBH Battlefield — it's a plaster movie prop left over from some local filming.

A MILESTONE SINGLE ACTION

Mostly, I don't get sentimentally involved with my firearms. When I sell or trade one, it goes with no, or at the most, minor regrets.

There is one handgun in my racks, however, that gives me a warm fuzzy feeling every time it's in my hands. It was made by the now-defunct United States Firearms Company (USFA) and labeled as their Custer Battlefield .45 single action. I first discovered this special run of revolvers at USFA's booth at the 2004 SHOT Show in Las Vegas.

It stunned me, not because it was a thing of beauty. It was just a brown finished (antiqued) .45 with plain walnut, one-piece grips. What stopped me in my tracks was that it was a nigh-on perfect reproduction of the very first 7½" barreled Colt Single Action Army .45 I had ever seen.

That USFA revolver on display took me back to August 1968 when I entered the National Park Service museum at the then-named Custer Battlefield in southeast Montana. It's since been renamed Little Bighorn Battlefield. There in a display case was a worn Colt single action .45 with a 7½" barrel, patina finish and walnut grips. It was representative of the nearly 700 or so revolvers that were carried onto the battlefields that June day of 1876. From that first moment, I wanted one like it.

Duke's path to the USFA. From left: 1984 Colt with misnamed black powder frame, USFA Custer Battlefield .45 and the two mid-1970s vintage Peacemaker Centennials.

ROAD TRIP

That August, my summer job ended, leaving a break before college began. Many readers know the said battle happened when 12 companies of the U.S. 7th Cavalry rode into the Little Bighorn Valley, where five companies were killed to a man, and the other seven were severely handled by Sioux and Cheyenne warriors. I am not alone in my fascination with that fracas; people still come from all over the world to visit the battle site.

Anyway, on a whim, I said to a friend. "Let's go to Montana so I can see the Custer Battlefield." Take note we were in West Virginia, and neither of us had been farther west than the Ohio River. Even though he had little idea where Montana or the Custer Battlefield was, my friend said, "Sure." We loaded up my sister's VW "Bug" with camping gear, and after a rather erratic 2,000 miles, we arrived. That trip was a milestone. From the first day in Montana, I knew I would spend my life in this state.

THE REAL DEAL COLT

Afterward, finding myself a suitable 7th Cavalry type .45 Colt took a while — a long while. In 1984, Colt again offered the misnamed black powder frame as was typical for their SAAs from 1873 to the mid-1890s. I ordered one, had it fitted with one-piece walnut grips, and carried it on the 1985 battlefield re-ride. That was a horseback trip retracing the 7th Cavalry's path from the morning of June 25 to where the battle happened that afternoon. Still, something was missing about that Colt. Eventually, I gave it to a friend.

In the mid-1970s, Colt made 2,002 Peacemaker Centennial .45s, almost identical to the ones issued to the 7th Cavalry in the summer of 1874. Sadly, Colt had stamped those two words on the PC's left sides. By the year 2000, I had rounded up two of those fine revolvers. I considered my 1968 craving satisfied, happily blazing away with my pair of .45s in cowboy action shoots and here on my range.

Then came SHOT Show 2004, and I was standing there near stupefied, looking at USFA's display Custer Battlefield .45 single action. That revolver was precisely what I had wanted for so many years. As matters turned out, Doug Donnelly, founder of USFA, had visited the Little Bighorn Battlefield himself and was also smitten with the .45 still on display in their museum. To honor the LBH Battlefield, he decided to offer the special version. In placing my order with Mr. Donnelly, he asked what serial number I wanted, as he was allowing buyers to choose. I said, "I suppose 1876 is taken?" As a matter of fact, it was not. Mine wears it now.

USFA no longer exists as a manufacturer and having traveled nearly around the world, I'm no longer the inexperienced 19-year-old that drove so far to see the LBH Battlefield. Hundreds of handguns have passed through my hands, but there is only one that takes my mind back to a memorable trip that changed my life. And yes, I shoot it whenever I can make time!

PISTOL POWDERS

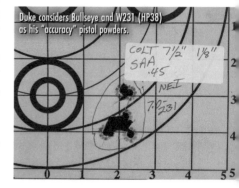

One of Duke's most used pistol powders is the relatively new Trail Boss by Hodgdon because he favors many cartridges dating from the black powder era.

Left: It is virtually impossible to double charge with Trail Boss powder, even in voluminous cases like these .44-40s. The case at right has the proper charge of Trail Boss. The case at left has a double charge plus some that spilled over.

Fifty-six years ago, I embarked on my career as a handloader focused solely on the .38 Special for an S&W K38. Today, I'm loading for handguns chambered for 25 different cartridges ranging from .32 Auto to .45 Colt.

My very first reloading manual, *Lyman Reloading Handbook #44* (1967), is still on my desk. Along with it is their new one, *#51* (2022). *Handbook #44* lists 34 choices for *all smokeless powders*, of which pistol powders amounted to 13. *Handbook #51* lists 152 smokeless powders. At least 55 could be termed "pistol powders." By "pistol powders," I'm referring to those usable in repeating handguns like revolvers and semi-autos, not the single-shot hand cannons, many of which are chambered for full-power rifle cartridges.

Surely all of you readers have heard the modern cliché, "Too much

information!" Well, I paraphrase that to mean "too many pistol powders." Life was simple back in 1966. The older gents who helped me get started in reloading said, "Just get a can of Bullseye and use 2.7 to 3.0 grains with 148- to 158-grain cast bullets." What to start with today? I would be hopelessly lost. Also, powders cost enough now that most of us can't just buy pound after pound of different types for experimentation. That's where we few gun 'riters enter the picture. We're supposed to try powders and report the results. Still, it's virtually impossible to try all 55 of today's smokeless "pistol powders," even with the companies helping us out with supplies to work with as long as we don't get greedy.

So, here's my take on pistol powders after 56 years of using them to load several hundred thousand rounds. (I stopped keeping track in 1980 after exceeding 80,000.)

For accuracy at velocities up to about 750 to 850 fps, Bullseye and W231, aka HP38, are winners. That's speaking of most handgun cartridges from .32 Auto to .45 Colt. My experience with Red

Dot is more limited, but it's been the top accuracy performer for me in .45 Auto-Rim and .44 Special at the before-mentioned velocity levels.

Although now, in my senior years, I have no need for magnum revolvers, but when I did, my favorite was 2400. During one of my early "projects," I was able to get 50-yard five-shot machine rest groups reliably of 1.5" with an S&W Model 29 .44 Magnum using 2400. I've always considered handgun loads giving 850 to 1,000 fps as "service loads." For such, my top pick is Unique or Hodgdon's Universal.

Duke considers Bullseye and W231 (HP38) as his "accuracy" pistol powders.

COLT 7½" 1⅛"
SAA
.45
NEI
7.0-231

TEACH AN OLD DOG NEW TRICKS

Admittedly, I'm a dinosaur. However, I'm not averse to learning about new propellants. When Hodgdon/IMR introduced Trail Boss early in this century, I gave it a try because many of my favorite handguns are chambered for cartridges introduced in the black powder era. That means they have far more case volume than necessary for smokeless powders. And, for the most part, revolvers for which they are chambered are not known for their strength.

Trail Boss was designed to fill that volume yet not cause pressure to enter the danger zone. Mistakenly dump in a double charge and you will have spilled powder to clean up. Trail Boss is a fine smokeless powder for mild loads in revolver cartridges from .38 Special to .45 Colt. I even use it for .45 ACP to save wear on a couple of my collectible Colt 1911s. (Yes, Hodgdon does list it for .45 ACP on their Internet Load Data site.)

However, there are exceptions. Trail Boss doesn't give enough oomph in small-volume cartridges such as .44 Russian or .45 S&W Schofield. I tried it, but my chronograph said bullet speeds were in the 500 to 600 fps range. For those rounds, plan "B" is to fall back to Bullseye or W231/HP38. Those power the smaller cartridges' bullets into the 700 to 750 fps band.

SLAP FEST

Another old cartridge meant to give 750 fps with 195/200-grain bullets was the .41 Long Colt. However, those bullets were hollowbase and only 0.386" in diameter. They were then fired from Colt SAAs with barrel groove diameters nominally of 0.400". I have three .41 Long Colts and three HB bullet molds from which I'm trying to get adequate accuracy. Those bullets need a good slap in their HBs to expand 0.014" and grip rifling yet keep pressures safe. Bullseye hasn't worked. Unique works okay, but the best results so far have been with Hodgdon's Titegroup. Newer fast-burning propellants such as Hodgdon's Titewad or Vihtavouri N310 might be even better — if I can find some.

LIGHT LOADS FOR .45 AUTOS

We shooters and collectors of vintage American military .45s need to pause for a moment and consider something. All military .45 Auto handguns — semi-autos and revolvers — are old and now valuable. Model 1911s are from 112 to 97 years old, and 1911A1s can be 97 to 78. Colt and S&W Model 1917 revolvers (military-marked ones) were made at least 104 years ago. My .45 Auto M1 Thompson Submachine Gun is 81 years old, and my M3 "Grease Gun" is 79. Those two are worth as much as a bucket full of the above-mentioned handguns. Furthermore, no one knows what all these .45s went through in their pasts.

These are Duke's military .45 Auto firearms. At left is the M1 Thompson. Middle from top down: Colt Model 1911, Colt Model 1911A1, Colt Model 1917 and S&W Model 1917. At right is the M3 "Grease Gun."

TRAGEDY STRIKES

About five years ago, I was plinking at chunks of firewood in my yard with a recently acquired Model 1911A1 made by Remington Rand. With the first round from my second magazine, a case head blew out. The checkered plastic grips shattered, stinging my hand, and my face was scored by several bits of flying brass or plastic. And I had shooting glasses on! My thought after realizing I wasn't seriously injured was, "Oh, no! I've ruined this valuable piece of history."

Luckily, I had not. The pistol required a visit to a gunsmith friend to drive that stuck case from the chamber. The barrel appeared okay, but we decided to gunny-sack it for safety's sake. The gunsmith closely examined the rest of that 1911A1 with a magnifying glass and pronounced it safe. I searched for, bought and dropped in another World War II barrel. Then the same was done for a proper set of vintage checkered plastic grips. Some follow-up shooting revealed no problems.

Now here's an admission of guilt. I loaded that ammo, so I was responsible. The load was 5.4 grains of W231 under 225-grain commercially cast RN bullets. Depending on the exact handgun, velocity equated to factory FMJ ballistics, which was my intention. The miscreant load came from a batch of 200 freshly assembled rounds and I pulled the bullets from the other 192 rounds and noticed no problems. I will never know what went amiss.

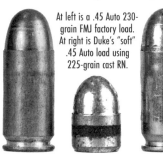

At left is a .45 Auto 230-grain FMJ factory load. At right is Duke's "soft" .45 Auto load using 225-grain cast RN.

TIME TO SLOW DOWN

On the good side, that mishap woke me up. I like shooting my military .45s. Who wouldn't get a kick out of letting loose a burst from a Tommy Gun? Plinking at firewood chunks with the 1911s and 1917s is fun: watching the big bullets slam them about. However, I wondered, "Do I actually need to fire factory duplication handloads with either lead alloy or jacketed bullets through my vintage military .45 Autos?" The answer to that is, as long as functioning is 100% and accuracy reasonable, I do not.

My goal for a light .45 Auto handload was that it uses lead alloy bullets to save wear on barrels. For velocity, I shot for (literally) about 750 fps from the handguns. For the Thompson and Grease Gun, chronographing wasn't important to me, but functioning was. Furthermore, I didn't want the powder charge to be a mere dollop in .45 Auto cases wherein a double charge might go unnoticed.

Here's where I got lucky. Hodgdon's Trail Boss powder was designed with cowboy action shooters in mind. Albeit on the fast-burning end of smokeless propellants, it's "fluffy." A smallish charge in grain weight still takes up plenty of case volume. Could it possibly work as a .45 Auto light powder? It certainly can. I perused Hodgdon's own Reloading Data website and found listed Trail Boss powder with 230-grain lead roundnose bullets. The starting load was 3.5 grains with a 4.5-grain maximum. The published velocities were 658 and 761 fps, respectively.

The first loads using Trail Boss in my .45 Auto handloads carried 4.0 grains under 225-grain lead RN bullets. Velocity was about 730 fps. I upped the charge to 4.2 grains, and the velocity was right at 750 fps. Handloads were assembled nor-

Duke's light .45 Auto handload is based on this propellant. It's typically associated with revolver handloading but works perfectly for Duke's "soft" .45 Autos.

mally and given a taper crimp. I chronographed those loads from the Remington Rand Model 1911A1 and they felt "soft." Perfect! Functioning from both submachine guns was 100%. Their RPM (rounds per minute) was down a bit to about 400 RPM for the Grease Gun and 700 RPM from the Thompson. I'd found my light .45 Auto load.

Now here's a final note. Recently I acquired a 3rd Generation Colt SAA from Colt's Custom Shop. It is actually caliber stamped ".45 ACP" and the first such I'd ever seen. From its 4¾" barrel, it chronographed 764 fps with the light .45 Auto handload.

ONE-HANDED SHOOTING

YOUR LIFE MAY DEPEND ON IT

There's really no debate anymore: Two hands on the gun is the best way to shoot a handgun. With two hands, the gun can be held more steadily. Recoil management and recovery are superior. I remember long ago, a two-hand hold was virtually unheard of.

Today the pendulum has swung so far that it's unusual not to see a two-hand hold. Don't get me wrong, I am as big a proponent of a two-hand hold as anyone, but I believe a competent handgunner should be able to shoot well one-handed and with either hand.

WHY

The practical reasons are obvious. It may be only one hand is available. The other hand may be needed to hold a steering wheel, ladder, door, phone, or safety rail. Or the hand may be in use to pull a bystander to safety, fend off an attacker, control a prisoner, or toss a grenade back at the thrower. Okay, the last is a stretch.

The other possibility is one arm may be disabled, for example, by a gunshot, knife attack, a bad fall, or a vehicle accident. In reading and hearing accounts of gun battles, it is surprising how often one or both arms are hit. I suppose because the arms and hands are in front of the chest area, plus the natural tendency to focus on what is most dangerous to you. It happens often enough that one would be foolish not to have the ability to stay in the fight even if one arm is rendered useless.

CHALLENGES

I'm an old-timer who started out shooting one-handed. From what I see today, most beginning handgunners start out with a two-hand hold and only learn one-hand shooting later, if at all. Compared to shooting with two hands, they find one-hand shooting has several challenges.

Accuracy is reduced, or perhaps a better way to say it is accurate shooting is more difficult because it's harder to hold the gun steadily. The splendid scores posted by bullseye shooters prove it can be done, but it does take more effort. Recoil management is more difficult and breaks between shots during fast strings of fire are generally longer.

The point of impact can change even with a good sight picture. Those who can shoot with reasonable accuracy using two hands often notice such a change. A right-hand shooter will often find their shots grouping to the left. How big a difference? It varies, but at 10 yards, I've seen shifts from only a couple to 6" to 8".

There are two reasons for this shift. One is the recoil action of the gun. When held in one hand, the gun tends to recoil away from the mass of the hand and toward the open side. The heavier the recoil, of course, the more this becomes apparent. The other reason is trigger pressure. Ideally, the trigger is pressed straight back along the axis of the barrel. It is very common to put some sideways pressure on the trigger during the press, typically to the left for a right-handed shooter. A solid two-hand hold can compensate for sideways pressure, but it becomes more evident when shooting with one hand.

WHAT YOU CAN DO

There are several things a shooter can do. One is to increase hand and arm strength. When I was doing a lot of competitive shooting, I used to keep

Shooting right hand only, from between 10 and 15 yards. The group is about the same size as with two hands but forms to the left as the gun recoils to the open side.

one of those grip squeezer things in my vehicle and use it on long drives. A rubber ball works as well if you can keep the dog from running off with it.

In training, focus on pressing the trigger straight back without adding sideways pressure. As a nice bonus, such skill will enhance your accuracy when shooting two-handed as well.

Another fix is to compensate for impact shift while aiming — for a right-hand shot, holding more to the right than you would shooting two-handed. I see this as a stopgap measure; impact shift should decrease as arm strength and technical skill improve. Personally, I am not very ambidextrous. I can barely wave hello or activate a turn indicator with my left hand. By dint of hard practice, I got to be reasonably competent shooting left-handed, but I confess to still holding a bit to the left.

The primary fix (you knew this was coming) is regular, focused, attentive practice. It may be boring, and the results may never be spectacular, but competent shooting with either hand can win you matches. It might even save your life.

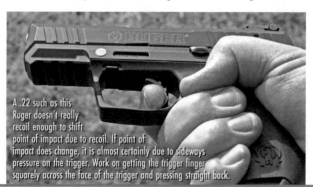

A .22 such as this Ruger doesn't really recoil enough to shift point of impact due to recoil. If point of impact does change, it is almost certainly due to sideways pressure on the trigger. Work on getting the trigger finger squarely across the face of the trigger and pressing straight back.

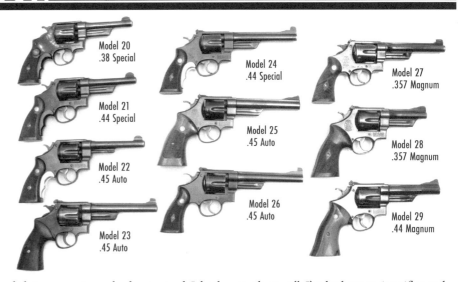

Model 20 .38 Special
Model 21 .44 Special
Model 22 .45 Auto
Model 23 .45 Auto
Model 24 .44 Special
Model 25 .45 Auto
Model 26 .45 Auto
Model 27 .357 Magnum
Model 28 .357 Magnum
Model 29 .44 Magnum

BEST OF THE BEST

As a firearms industry dinosaur, I'm sad to have seen the end of double-action revolvers' golden years. In my time, barrels were actually barrels, sometimes even forged with integral front sights, not tubes setting inside shrouds. Grip frames were steel and could be fitted with custom stocks crafted from wood, ivory or pearl. Quality when I entered the shooting fraternity in the 1960s was exquisite in regard to timing and smoothness, fit and finish. So much of this is gone now.

However, among all those revolvers was a genre of sixgun I considered the *Best of the Best* — N-Frame S&Ws. They ranged from fixed sight "military or army" versions to target models and from .38 Specials to .45 Colts. I owned them all at one time or the other. Never

did I encounter a bad one, and I had samples dating from as early as 1915 up to the 1990s.

In my horseback years traveling into the backcountry here in Montana, my "bear gun" was an S&W pre-Model 29 .44 Magnum with a 5" barrel. Luckily there was never an altercation with any bruins. Back in 1976, my sixth published magazine article focused on load testing a 6½" Model 29 from a machine rest. The target range was 50 yards, and after much fiddling with powders and cast bullets, I was able to achieve 1½" five-shot groups pretty

much on call. I've had expensive rifles and carbines that wouldn't shoot with such precision. (I must admit, however, the Model 57 .41 Magnums that came my way over the years would deliver tight groups with less load development than .44s.)

S&W Hand Ejector 4th Model with rare 4" barrel.

The small nubbin at the front of the cylinder's crane is the third lock that gave rise to the nickname "triplelock."

N-FRAME DOMINANCE

Perhaps my predilection for N-Frames started because I was born and raised in Mingo County, WV, the site of the 1920s Coal Mine Union Wars. By my understanding from talking to old timers in the 1960s, many men involved in the fracas went about armed. It seemed they wanted nothing to do with .38s and I judged they were telling the truth because early 1960s pawn shops in my hometown of Williamson had lots of large-frame revolvers. Most were S&Ws, but some Colt New Services were mixed in. My own grandfather was a coal miner in Kentucky, and in the 1950s, he let me play with his boxes of .44 Special factory ammo. I'd dump them out on the rug in front of the coal stove and place them back in their boxes one at a time.

Early in the 21st century, I got the idea of owning every one of the S&W Model 20-somethings. You couldn't just go out to a well-stocked store and buy such sixguns. For instance, Model 21 .44 Specials ceased production in 1966, with only 1,200 made. Model 26s were something I had to research because I had never encountered one; didn't even know what they were. They turned out to be lightweight barreled .45 Auto/.45 Auto-Rim with target sights. Luckily I stumbled upon one in a Montana gun shop, or I may never have completed my assortment of N-Frames. Complete it I did, but today I only have the Model 23 .38 and Model 27 .357 Magnum.

1st Model
2nd Model
3rd Model
4th Model

S&W's four versions of Hand Ejector .44 Specials all with 6½" barrels.

N-FRAME SPECIALS

Next, I focused on .44 Specials. There were four basic N-Frames made for the cartridge. They started in 1908 when S&W introduced both that frame size and that cartridge together as the Hand Ejector, First Model. They came to be known far and wide as "triplelocks" because they had an extra lock meshing the cylinder crane with the main frame. They were made with 4, 5 and 6½" barrel lengths, with target or fixed sights.

For various reasons, one being their price of $21 was considered high in 1915, a Hand Ejector, Second Model replaced triplelocks. By removing the third lock and eliminating the shroud for the ejector rod, the price was reduced to a more reasonable $19. In 1926 a request from a Texas-based firm spurred the S&W factory to reintroduce the ejector rod shroud. That became Hand Ejector, Third Model. Both Second and Third Models came with the same barrel length and sight options as the First Model. Second Model production ceased with the advent of World War II, and Third Model production had a hiatus for the war but resumed manufacture in 1946. And finally, a Hand Ejector, Fourth Model replaced it in 1950 that was renamed Model 24 in 1957.

I had them all at the same time in 6½" barrel lengths. They were shot plenty, but then my ardor cooled, and Third and Fourth Model .44 Specials were sold. Now of all the dozens of N-Frames I've owned, only six are in my vault. That's kind of sad.

Photos: Yvonne Venturino

COLT'S SAA 2ND GENERATION

A 2nd Generation Colt .45 Buntline with 12" barrel (top) and 4¾".

A .45 with custom-made fancy walnut grips (bottom).

Last issue (Nov/Dec 2023), we discussed the 1st Generation Colt SAAs. Now, let's move on to the 2nd Generation models.

Colt never envisioned bringing the SAA back post World War II, although some were assembled from parts and sold in the late 1940s. What resurrected the SAA was television. So many Western programs appeared that by the mid-1950s, Colt realized the big single action would be profitable once again. Consider this: In 1939, the suggested retail price of a stock SAA was $39.50. When the 2nd Generation ones appeared in 1956, the price was $125 and Colt was backordered by the huge demand.

WHAT'S NEW?

Not too much changed between the 1st and 2nd Generation. Barrel length and finish options remained basically the same as did interchangeability for most parts. Many early 2nd Generation SAAs were fitted with left-over 1st Generation hammers on which cone-shaped firing pins were solidly fixed. When those ran out, new hammers had bottle-shaped firing pins with some looseness. Except for special orders, grips were checkered hard rubber.

For the first time starting in 1957, a 12" barrel length was cataloged as the Buntline. Furthermore, a total of 503 Sheriff's Model .45s wore 3" barrels. In 1956, introductory calibers were .38 Special and .45 Colt. In 1958, the .44 Special was added, and in 1960 so was the .357 Magnum. By 1963, the .38 Special was dropped. The .44 Special got the ax in 1966. These are interesting facts; no .44 Specials came with 4¾" barrels, and all 12" Buntlines and Sheriff's Models were .45 Colt.

According to the book *Colt's SAA Post War Models* by George Garton, during 2nd Generation production, a total of 10,951 SAAs were chambered for .38 Special, 15,821 for .357 Magnum, only 2,073 for .44 Special and 38,794 .45 Colts were made.

Among 2nd Generation production, there were two genres of single actions made different from stock SAAs. One will be slightly touched upon here, and another not at all. The latter are target-sighted New Frontiers, which deserve a work devoted solely to them. The first genre is commemoratives. Colt put out a passel of those in the 1960s and early 1970s, and in general, they fell flat. Mostly, they were considered too gaudy by serious Colt fans.

The exceptions for me are the 1873-1973 PEACEMAKER CENTENNIALS, which actually didn't make it to dealers until about 1975. These SAAs were built precisely as the ones made in the 1870s. Those chambered as .45s duplicated

In Colt's 2nd Generation of production, serial numbers contained an SA suffix. (The SA suffix continued in the 3rd Generation starting at 80000SA and continuing to 99999SA.)

the military version, but .44-40s were fully nickel-plated. That was right down to very thin sights, fixed firing pins on hammers, one-piece wood grips on .45s and hard rubber eagle type on .44-40s. Their only commemorative feature was the 1873-1973 PEACEMAKER CENTENNIAL logo on the left sides of .45 barrels and right sides of .44 barrels. The .44s even had the acid-etched COLT FRONTIER SIX SHOOTER on the left side of the barrel and tiny ".44 C.F." on the rear of the trigger guard. Only 2,002 of each caliber were made. I have a pair of each, and for traditionalists, they are some of the finest SAAs.

END OF THE ERA

Production of 2nd Generation SAAs ceased in 1974, but this time, Colt meant to return the gun again after retooling and also making some engineering changes to lower manufacturing costs. So, let's settle some confusion about serial numbers. In the 1st Generation, only numbers were used starting with #1. To differentiate between 1st and 2nd Generation when the SAA returned in 1956, serial numbers started over but had four digits followed by an SA suffix. The 2nd Generation ended numbers at about 74000SA. (Exact numbers are hard to pin down, considering commemoratives had their own serial numbers.)

My first Colt of the 2nd Generation came in 1968. It was a .45. My second came in 1970 and was a .357 Magnum, and

Colt's 2nd Generation standard production was made in only four chamberings. From left, the .357 Magnum, .38 Special, .44 Special and .45 Colt.

my third was purchased in 1971. It was a .38 Special. Now get this: I didn't manage to land a 2nd Generation .44 Special until 2018. Of the several dozen Colts I've owned made between 1956 and 1974, there has not yet been one of questionable quality. Evidently, I'm not the only one who feels that way because today's prices for good quality 2nd Generation SAAs start at about 15 to 20 times their 1956 price. And they go up from there based on factors including the rarity of chambering or special lots like Buntlines and Sheriff's Models.

By 1860, someone at Colt realized their percussion-fired revolvers could be made graceful with round barrels and rounded barrel corners.

COLT'S
CAP & BALL
REVOLVERS

These are a 2nd Generation Colt Model 1860 .44 at right and Model 1861 .36 at left.

Some of Sam Colt's early efforts in creating workable revolvers seem like jokes today. Of course, they were loaded with either paper cartridges holding powder and bullets or loose powder and ball. Ignition was supplied by the relatively new percussion cap.

First was his semi-successful "Paterson," which had a hidden trigger that didn't "pop out" until the hammer was cocked. Most of those had to be disassembled for reloading, which was why big fighting knives were part of a ranger's accouterments. He started making them in 1836, but his company soon failed. Somehow, a quantity of Patersons made it to the Texas Rangers, where in 1842, they were used in an encounter with Comanche warriors. The Indians rarely came out second best, but they did in that encounter.

By 1847, Mr. Colt was back in business with a U.S. Government contract for 1,000 sixguns. These beasts became known as the Walker/Colt .44, weighing 4½ lbs. with 9" barrels. Thereafter followed a three-part sequence of Colt "Dragoons" where 7½" barrels and slightly shorter cylinders marginally made them smaller and lighter than Walkers. None of these first .44 revolvers could be passed off as "belt" carry. When issued to U.S. Army horse soldiers, they came with saddle-mounted holsters.

CARRY REVOLVERS

Aside from the big .44s, Mr. Colt quickly recognized a need for a concealable revolver. That little five shooter appeared about 1848, was .31 caliber, weighed only 22 oz. with a 4" barrel and came to be known as the "Baby Dragoon." This pip-squeak had to be disassembled into three pieces for reloading. It was soon followed by the Model 1849, also a .31, but at least with a loading rammer mounted beneath its barrel.

Finally came a true "belt" pistol, the legendary and universally beloved (in its day) Model 1851 .36, which somehow gained the nickname "Navy," with .36 becoming known as "Navy" caliber in regards to revolvers. Colt's '51 Navy quickly became the revolver by which all others were judged. It had a 7½" octagon barrel, a beautifully contoured grip frame still being copied today on single actions and weighed only 42 oz. Of course, Colt's .51 Navy sixguns have become identified as Wild Bill Hickok's favorites. He clung to them until his death in 1876, six years after metallic cartridge-firing revolvers hit the scene.

PRODUCTION... AND GRACE

Early on, Sam Colt realized that selling his revolvers in boxed sets was a good idea.

Now, let's consider some numbers. Taking into account Colt's Walkers, Dragoons, and Baby Dragoons, only about 36,300 were sold in all. That certainly wasn't going to make Mr. Colt the fabulously wealthy man he was upon passing in 1862. No, that came about because of the Models 1849 and 1851. His factory produced 325,000 of the '49s and 215,000 of the '51s, with another 42,000 '51s being produced in his short-lived London facility.

For almost a decade, the Colt Patent Firearms Company was at a plateau in revolver design because they were busy making those two prime money makers. However, someone at the Colt factory had a sense of aesthetics because in 1860 and 1861, Colt introduced two of the most graceful revolvers ever made. The '60 was a .44, and the '61 a .36. Both were based on the '51 Navy frame. It was adapted to handle .44-sized projectiles by having a rebated cylinder: small at the base but enlarged at the front. Also, its grip frame was made 1/4" longer. The timing of their introduction was also nigh on perfect as in 1861, the American Civil War broke out. The Federal Army was especially interested in the big .44, one reason Colt made 200,500 of them until production ceased in 1873. Only about 38,000 Model 1861s were made, but interestingly, the Model 1851 was so ensconced in America that Colt did not drop it upon unveiling the new Model 1861— both of those left Colt's lineup in 1873.

Worthy of mention were two five shooters. Someone figured out the .31 was too small for self-defense, so they converted the Model 1849's frame into Model 1862s. One version had the blocky design of the '51 and the other the rounded grace of the '61.

As for power, think of it this way in comparison to modern versus antique revolvers. The .31s were as .22 LRs are today. Stepping up .36s were as .38 Specials and .44s were as .44 Specials. By the way, except for the Model 1849 .31, I own Colt's 2nd Generation reproductions of all those mentioned here and have fired them. My favorite? The Model 1861 .36.

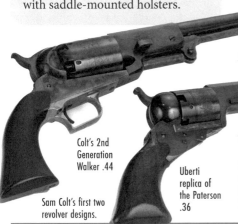

Colt's 2nd Generation Walker .44

Sam Colt's first two revolver designs.

Uberti replica of the Paterson .36

Photos: Yvonne Venturino

MAKING YOUR REVOLVER
PERSONAL

Duke insists that revolver grips must be right for you. The S&W 2"-barreled M&P .38 Special has factory grips. The 5" one has grips made especially for his hand.

In nearly 60 years of handgunning, during which I've owned hundreds of revolvers, I've learned much about making them suitable for me personally. That's more about making them as shootable as possible. In the beginning, when I bought a revolver, whether new or used, it came "as-is" regarding grips, trigger pull, or sight zero with fixed or adjustable sights. Being in my teens in the backcountry of West Virginia, there were just barely enough spare bucks to buy powder and primers and no one to do gunsmithing for me, even if I'd had solid notions as to what was needed.

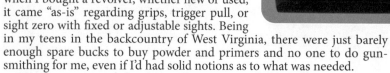

Here are some of the things I've come to feel important for good shooting revolvers.

Left: Duke's been called many names after admitting he put pliers' tracks on this front sight but you can bet its hits were aimed.

GRIPS

Top of my list is grips (or stocks, if you prefer). I'll use S&W K-Frames as an example. Almost all K-Frames came from the factory with their "Magna"-style grips. They were well made in-house and perfectly fit to frames. Their failing was they were "everyman" grips, suitable for all but specific to no one. Over the years, I've become acquainted with custom grip makers. One such knew exactly what I meant about K-Frame grips and crafted a set fitting my hand perfectly. They set on my late 1940s S&W Military & Police .38 Special, a revolver that has the smoothest double-action pull I've ever experienced. (I won't mention his name as he is long deceased.)

Contrary to S&W, grips have been those on Colt SAAs. For me, factory SAA grips are too bulbous. My desire for single action grips are ones more slender but yet still curvaceous. I've had Bill Fuchs of Spring Creek Armory in Ten Sleep, Wyo., craft several sets of one-piece grips for some SAAs and his feel perfect in my rather short-fingered chubby hands.

TRIGGER

Next in importance for me are trigger pulls. Nowadays, with the proliferation of lawyers, gun makers must err on the high side for trigger pull weights. For some new revolvers, I've put a trigger pull gauge to measure five, six, or even 7 lbs. for single-action pull. Way back in the 1970s, I acquired a used S&W Model 19 .357 Magnum with a 6" barrel. Its single-action trigger pull was right on at 2 lbs. I did

much "cow pasture" target shooting with it; one day bringing home four frozen turkeys. That's one of the very few handguns I regret selling or trading. My SAAs that have undergone custom action smoothing satisfy me with 3-lb. pull weights as I'm timid about asking gunsmiths to go lighter in this day and age.

Almost any Colt SAA revolver bought in the last 50 years likely needs an action smoothing right out of the box. Almost all of mine have been sent down that road. Collectively speaking, I've not been disappointed with the action jobs of several smiths. However, one well-known fellow made one of my Colt SAA's hammers fall so light it would not ignite primers when pointed uphill. By the way, anytime one of my revolvers goes out for work, I include in the order that their forcing cones smoothed with that 11-degree angle so popular now.

ZEROING

Some readers may feel zeroing should be placed at the top in importance — making it hit where it's pointed. Naturally, a great many revolvers wear fully adjustable sights, and that's a great thing when changing bullet weights, powder charges, etc. However, the sport of cowboy competition put literally thousands of single-action revolvers on shooting ranges. And I'd bet the vast majority of them did not shoot to their point of aim right out of their boxes.

Mine did not: usually hitting a bit left but on for elevation if bullets were close to factory weight for that cartridge. For example, 250/255-grain bullets for .45

Duke likes SAA grips to be slightly thinner than factory grips but still curvaceous.

These were crafted by Bill Fuchs, dba Spring Creek Armory.

Colt, 240/250-grain ones for .44 Special, and so forth. It became necessary to have their barrels turned just a bit to the left. That's a shoot-and-see situation but never has the amount of turn been radical, just barely noticeable if looking closely over the top strap. Twice in frustration, I grabbed a set of pliers from my pick-up's glove box and bent a Colt's front sight. I read about doing that in a long-ago article by the late Col. Charles Askins.

I've been called a nut-job and worse for admitting that, but those revolvers do hit the point of aim. The pliers' tracks on sights are visible. (I do not recommend this method of zeroing. Sight blades have been known to come unstuck!) You best have a competent gunsmith do the barrel twisting for you. Once sighted for a specific load, fixed-sight revolvers are thereafter always zeroed.

Not all of my revolvers are personally adapted to my preferences. Expensive collectible ones remain untouched. My ordinary shooters are set up as I like them.

THE BEST HANDGUNS I'VE KNOWN

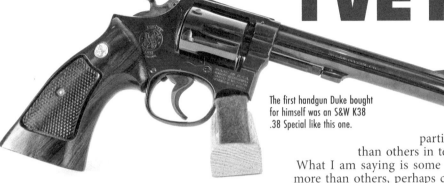

The first handgun Duke bought for himself was an S&W K38 .38 Special like this one.

Looking back on my long career of handgun shooting, I've come to realize some of the hundreds I've experienced stood head and shoulders over others in my estimation. Now understand this: I'm not saying some particular manufacturer made better handguns than others in terms of fit, finish or quality of production. What I am saying is some revolvers or autoloaders caught my fancy more than others, perhaps caused by me shooting them well, carrying them more comfortably, or as reminders of a grand time in my life.

REVOLVERS

My handgun buying started at age 17. I was newly enamored of bullseye target shooting and learned of a fellow who had a S&W K38 in a nearby town. (That happened to be Matewan, WV, the site of the famous coal mine union wars of the 1920s and memorialized by the 1987 movie of the same name.) I paid $55 for it, including a 50-round box of .38 Special target wadcutters. That .38 stands in my esteem not only because it was the first handgun I bought but also because it triggered me into becoming a reloader, which I remain avidly to this day.

However, another S&W K-Frame's pedestal stands just a mite higher than the K38's. That happened to be a Model 19 .357 Magnum with 6" barrel and 2-lb. trigger pull. In those days, I roamed around the western states quite a bit with the Model 19 accompanying me. At that time, it seemed perfect: Shooting .38 Specials for casual fun and far fewer full-power .357 Magnums when needed. By the time the Model 19 fell into my hands, I had acquired a Lachmiller triple-cavity bullet mold for a 150-grain SWC. Many thousands of bullets were dropped from that mold, with the majority going through the 19's 6" barrel.

Duke's all-time favorite pair of single-actions are these Colt Frontier Six Shooters (.44-40) with bison bone grips.

These two handguns were gifted to Duke. At left is the Colt SAA .45 with carved ivory grips and the Les Baer Thunder Ranch Special .45.

AUTO

An autoloader I hold in high esteem for two reasons. One is it was a gift from a good friend, and the other is it is just a great handgun. That is a .45 Auto Les Baer Thunder Ranch Special. Again, it's amazingly accurate, but more so, it's amazingly reliable. Once, at a Thunder Ranch five-day class, as a test, I shot it without cleaning. Anyone who has participated in one of those classes know that shots fired can reach nigh-on to 1,000 rounds. By the last day, I could feel the slide moving slowly to chamber the next round, but chamber it did and never failed to fire.

THE CLASSIC SAA

Another gift is on my list of best handguns. It's a full-blued Colt SAA .45 with a 4¾" barrel. What makes it dear to me is that it was ordered with my name engraved on its backstrap, and its factory letter of authentication says it was ordered that way by Hank Williams, Jr. After receiving it, I had an El Paso

craftsman (artist) named Paul Persinger fit it with ivory grips with my MLV initials relief carved. As we used to say in West Virginia, "It just don't get any better than that."

For a couple of decades, I shot the cowboy action game until a bum knee put me out. A usual event required a rifle, shotgun and two revolvers. The first two guns weren't important to me, but for revolvers, I always used Colt SAAs. Most calibers available in the SAA were tried at one time or the other, but one brace of Colts became my all-time favorites. Those were called Colt Frontier Six-Shooters, which always stands for .44-40. I fired those guns with both black powder and smokeless powder handloads. The former became my favorite due to their loud "blam" muzzle report and a long trail of fire and smoke.

My specific CFSS .44s were Colt's Peacemaker Centennial commemoratives for the 100th anniversary of SAAs. These were offered both as .45s and .44s, with the latter version being all nickel-plated with 7½" barrels, black hard rubber grips, and the old-fashioned tiny blade front sight with corresponding grove in the revolver's top strap. I managed to land two of the 2,002 made, then had their actions slicked up, and both fitted with custom-made bison bone grips. Neither of my pair ever let me down.

Those handguns have stood above others in my shooting history. In fits of extreme foolishness, I allowed others to buy my two favorite S&Ws. The others mentioned here are still with me. At my age, there may never be another favorite added to the best list — but then again, we never know.

This 25-yard group from sandbag rest shows how accurate a 0.357" diameter hollow-base bullet can be when fired from a 0.370+" barrel. The test gun was Duke's converted Colt Model 1861.

1861 .38 CONVERION RAPINE 150 HB 1¾ 3.0 BULLSEYE

HANDGUN CARTRIDGE NAMES

A logical question often asked by newcomers to the sport of handgun shooting is as follows. Why do .38s shoot .357-diameter bullets? Why the confusion?

We must go back in time to find some answers. When Colt brought out their first successful revolvers in the late 1840s, they were labeled .44s. Shortly thereafter, the extremely popular .36 caliber revolvers came about. In those days, a handgun barrel's caliber was set by its bore diameters instead of groove diameters. That's why so-called .44 cap & ball Colt revolvers fired balls/bullets of 0.451/0.454" in diameter. Continuing this thought, the proper ball/bullet size for .36 revolvers was 0.375".

So, how does this pertain to handgun cartridges being named improperly? That came about with the development of metallic cartridges. In the early 1870s, Colt had thousands of parts from their now obsolete cap & ball revolvers. Should they just junk them, or should they figure out a way to turn them into cash?

This photo shows several .38 Long Colt cartridges handloaded by Duke.

The far left one is loaded with a 130-grain heel-base bullet from a Rapine bullet mold. At left, is one loaded with a hollow-base 150-grain bullet also from a Rapine mold.

This is a .38 Long Colt loaded with a Speer 148-grain hollow-base wadcutter.

ORIGINS

And therein lies the origin of cartridge conversion revolvers. This wasn't just limited to Colt revolvers; some gunsmiths also got in on the act. Using barrels originally made for their cap & ball revolvers required the new metallic handgun cartridges to carry bullets similar in diameter to cap and ball projectiles.

So, some bright light decided revolver bullets should be made with two diameters. The main bullet segment would be full size in the same diameter as the outside cartridge walls. Then, the base part of the projectile was made small so as to fit inside the case walls. These bullets came to be unofficially named heel-base.

Lead alloy bullets need lubricant, so knurling or grooves were put around the outside portion of heel-base bullets, and bullets were dipped in melted lubricant. Sometimes, no knurling or grooves were applied. Instead, a card wad (thin wafer) went over the black powder, then a one-eighth disk of lubricant set atop the

card wad and finally, a heel-base bullet seated. I actually have some old factory .44 Colt loads assembled like that. I pulled some apart to examine them.

There were many of these early metallic handgun cartridges, but space won't allow all of them to be detailed. If the above paragraph has you confused, just look at a round of modern .22 Long Rifle. They are still made with heel-base bullets and dipped in lube.

.22 LONG RIFLE

So, let's use .38 Colt as our primary example. In the book *U.S. Cartridges and Their Handguns: 1795–1975*, the author, Charles R. Suydam measured outside bullet diameters of original .38 Colt rounds from various manufacturers. They ranged from 0.376" to 0.381" in diameter. Mr. Suydam didn't want to ruin valuable antique cartridges by pulling some apart, so he did not provide measurements for the heel-base portions. The ones I've measured have been in the 0.356/0.358" range. Also worthy of note is that .38 Colt, at this time, used a case length of 0.88", give or take a thousandth or two. Thus, .36 caliber revolvers came to be called .38s after the advent of metallic cartridges. Things were about to change.

In the early 1890s, the U.S. Army desired to move from its large .45 Colt

Colt 2nd Generation Model 1861s. Duke had the left one converted to .38 Long Colt.

cartridge to the smaller .38 Colt. But by that time, the era of heel-base bullets had passed in favor of bullets fitting inside cases. Some factory loads for obsolete cartridges still have heel-base outside bullets, but none were developed after the late 1800s. With the Civil War experience of shooting undersize hollow base Mini Balls in rifled muskets and counting on them to expand to grip rifling, the U.S. Army decided such a system should work for .38 Colt. It did.

Therefore, hollow-base bullets of (nominal) 0.357" were developed to set with their full diameter inside cartridge cases. In order to accommodate the same powder charge of 19 grains used in the .38 Colt heel base ammunition, case length was increased to 1.03" (again nominal), and we get the new name

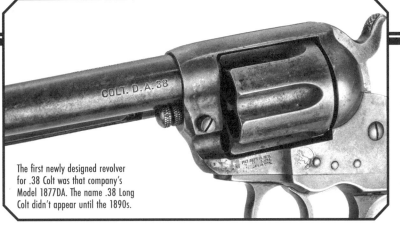

The first newly designed revolver for .38 Colt was that company's Model 1877DA. The name .38 Long Colt didn't appear until the 1890s.

of .38 Long Colt. However, I've never viewed any vintage revolver stamped ".38 Long Colt."

PERFORMANCE

Let's cogitate a moment. How accurate will a revolver be when a 0.357" bullet is shot down a barrel measuring somewhere between 0.370" to 0.375" across its rifling grooves? Well, let me tell you; they can be pretty darn accurate. I've owned Colt Model 1877DA .38 Colt revolvers and still have a Colt Model 1861 rep-

lica converted to .38 Colt using the original large-diameter barrel. They have been fine shooters with my own home case hollow-base bullets and even better with 148-grain Speer hollow-base wadcutters.

How does this discourse on .38 Long Colt explain why the .38 Special wasn't named .35 or .36 Special? It's because the .38 Special cartridge was simply the .38 Long Colt lengthened to 1.16". All other dimensions were the same. In the 1930s, someone at S&W based in reality named their new magnum cartridge .357 Magnum instead of .38 Magnum. So, if you wonder why cartridge names don't fit, it's because back in the early days of metallic cartridges, things were done and named differently from today.

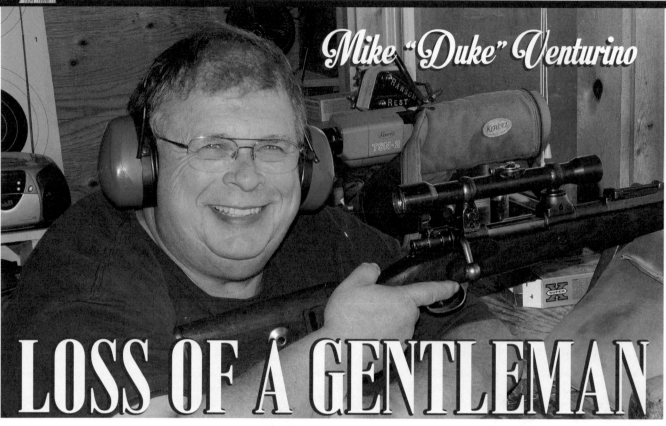

Mike "Duke" Venturino

LOSS OF A GENTLEMAN

Today's affirmation-driven world of "me, me, me!" does a lousy job of accurately portraying a man's impact on this earth. Thankfully, our late colleague and friend, Mike "Duke" Venturino, never placed much stock in such nonsense.

As one ages and acquires hard-earned wisdom, it becomes clearer that accomplishments are fine and expected from a lifetime of productive work, often leaving an indelible mark on this spinning ball we call home. But I think the real measure of a man's impact is the emotion that comes to mind when you think about him after his passing. What's your immediate visceral reaction before you start thinking about what he did on this earth as measured by the hamster wheel of humanity?

When I think of Mike "Duke" Venturino, a singular thought comes to mind — without fail or distraction.

"He's a real gentleman."

While seemingly simple and trite to those who don't yet appreciate the real value of a well-lived life, I think it's the epitome of a lifetime of wise investment in one's life priorities and fellow man. What could be more impactful on those whose paths you cross than to model by actions, day in and day out, the attributes of a true gentleman?

RIP Duke

Mike passed away on June 9, 2024, at his Montana home after a short illness. From some of his last conversations with folks in his circle, he was thankful to get home from the hospital to spend his remaining days with his wife, Yvonne (you've seen her wonderful photos here for years) and their dogs. Add in family and the kind of close friends they breed in Montana, and you know Duke was surrounded by those he cherished most.

When We Met ...

I first met Mike many years ago at the Shooting, Hunting and Outdoor Trade (SHOT) Show in Las Vegas. As I recall, he was in the Wolfe Publishing Group booth at the time, helping represent *Handloader Ammunition Reloading Journal*. He wrote quite a few stories for those folks over the years — and many other publications to boot. Anyway, this was long before I started to do any work with *American Handgunner* magazine or any of FMG's other publications. As a relatively new freelance gun 'riter, Mike wouldn't have known me from Adam.

Even back in that day, he'd racked up decades of peer-respected work as documented by thousands of articles and a generous helping of books.

To a gentleman like Mike, that didn't matter. We had a delightful conversation about, well, you guessed it, reloading and gun writing. By that time, he'd been in the writing business for 30 years or so and was an established rock star in the industry. No matter, Mike was as humble as they come while treating me as if I was the most important attendee to stop by the booth that day. I think describing someone as "humble" is just about the greatest compliment one can give, but that's just me.

Reminiscing ...

The folks here at FMG have been recalling a plethora of Duke stories, and as you might have guessed by now, just about all of them continue to add to his stature as one of the industry's true gentlemen.

Randy Molde, our company President, has known Duke for decades and chimed in with a happy memory.

"I'll always remember the time I got to shoot with Duke at Thunder Ranch in Oregon. He coached me through shooting his Sharps rifle with double-set triggers at a 1,000-yard target. He was knowledgeable, generous and a delight to be around. It was a true honor to have known him. He truly will be missed but his incredible wisdom captured in print and digital will live on."

Randy is kinda the company guru about remembering and putting to good use the vast library of stuff we've produced over the years, so you can count on Duke's articles popping up in plenty of future newsletters and special editions. He left us quite a library to share, so we'll do our part to keep his memory alive.

Roy Huntington, former *Handgunner* editor and publisher, had the pleasure of working with Mike for a couple of decades. In fact, it was Roy who lured Mike away from his previous columnist gig and brought him here. I'd say that worked out pretty well. Roy recalls that pivotal move.

"I recall reading Duke's stories from the very early 1980s, although he was busy writing before that. His first-person, down-home tone and the fact he actually did the things he wrote about always made him the first articles I'd read in a new magazine. How amazed was I when, in the late '90s,

I was attending a "Pre-1900" class at the old Thunder Ranch, and Duke was there? He knew me from my writing for *Handgunner* and *GUNS* and we just hit it off right away. He was kind enough to sell me a Shilo Sharps he had just gotten for what he paid for it (when they could be sold for handsome profits in those days!), then showed me everything I needed to know about it.

"After becoming editor at *Handgunner*, I twisted Duke's arm to leave *G&A* and *Shooting Times* and come to work with FMG. We never looked back."

Shooting Iron

Looking back, the "Iron" part of Duke's column's title wasn't much of a coincidence. He loved the metal stuff, primarily sixguns, but as many of you well know, he drifted into surplus handguns, rifles, and full-auto historical weapons in more recent years.

Roy recalls some discussions about those non-metal guns. "Duke was happy because we let him write what he wanted to write about and would never force him to cover some 'vile plastic gun,' as

he called them. I once asked him to do a shoot-off between a GLOCK (I heard the pause on the phone …) and a Colt Single Action Army. 'You had me at the Colt,' he laughed. 'But I'm not sure how I would have told you no if it was just the GLOCK!' The article was great fun, readers loved it and even Duke said, 'Roy, I think those GLOCKs aren't too bad after all.' Shhh…

"Over the years, we had countless pleasant phone calls talking about all things 'gun,' and I always left the chats in a better mood. I'd try to wind up the call, and he'd invariably say, 'Oh, wait a second, did I tell you what I found at the last gun show?' Then the call went on.

"Duke was one of the kindest, biggest-hearted, most patient gents I've ever met. To read his articles is to know the man. Duke was always a bit shy and humble when a reader wanted to meet him at a show and afterward would almost always tell me, 'You know, after all these years, I still can't believe I'm lucky enough to be doing this.' No, Duke, we were lucky enough to know you."

Farewell and happy trails, Duke …

Made in the USA
Columbia, SC
14 January 2025

51800819R00072